CARIBBEAN
Adventures in Nature

TEXT AND PHOTOGRAPHY BY
Michael DeFreitas

JOHN MUIR PUBLICATIONS
SANTA FE, NEW MEXICO

John Muir Publications, P.O. Box 613, Santa Fe, New Mexico 87504

Printed in Canada.
First edition. First printing April 1999.

Library of Congress Cataloging-in-Publication Data

DeFreitas, Michael.
      Caribbean: adventures in nature / Michael DeFreitas.
          p.   cm.
      Includes index.
      ISBN 1-56261-452-5
        1. West Indies—Guidebooks. 2. Natural history—West Indies—Guidebooks.
      3. Outdoor recreation—West Indies—Guidebooks. I. Title
      F1609.D44   1999
      917.2904'52—dc21   98-31655
                                              CIP

Editors: Dianna Delling, Elizabeth Wolf
Graphics Editor: Heather Pool
Production: Janine Lehmann
Design: Janine Lehmann
Typesetting: Marcie Pottern
Maps: Kathleen Sparkes, White Hart Design
Printer: Transcontinental, Inc.
Cover photos: © Michael DeFreitas
      Front cover, large: Britania Bay Beach near Mustique, The Grenadines
      Front cover, small: Tropical Butterfly
      Back cover, large: Snorkeling at The Baths off Virgin Gorda, British Virgin Islands
      Back cover, small: Rafting on the Río Grande in the Blue Mountains of Jamaica
Title page photo: © Michael DeFreitas (Wariruri Coastline and Blowhole, Aruba)

Distributed to the book trade by
Publishers Group West
Berkeley, California

CONTENTS

INTRODUCTION

CONTENTS

CONTENTS

ACKNOWLEDGMENTS

Putting together a book like this requires a tremendous amount of information, assistance, and the patience of dozens of people. Simply producing a list of individuals somehow seems inappropriate, like the litany of names read aloud at an Academy Awards presentation—they come so fast and in such quantity as to dilute the tribute. Those who helped with this book know how much I appreciated their assistance, and my tribute to them is a book that I hope best represents what they stand for.

With this in mind, I would like to thank the helpful staff at all the Caribbean tourism offices for their quick and efficient response to my requests for information. Without their help this book would never have been completed.

Thanks to John Muir Publications for giving me the opportunity to bring my love of the Caribbean to the public.

Last but not least, a special thanks to my mother for passing on her creativity and sense of adventure, and to my wife, Kathleen, and boys, Christopher and Philip, for their patience and understanding during the writing of this book.

To the Hesitating Purchaser

If sailor tales to sailor tunes,
Storm and adventure, heat and cold,
If schooners, islands, and maroons
And Buccaneers and buried Gold,
And all the old romance, retold
Exactly in ancient way,
Can please, as me they pleased of old,
The wiser youngsters of to-day:

—So be it, and fall on!

—Robert Louis Stevenson, *Treasure Island* (1883)

INTRODUCTION

The Caribbean has long been a destination for those trying to escape winter cold and the pressures of a fast-paced North American society. It's a place to kick back, relax, and soak up the healing and rejuvenating rays of the sun. But the tide of Caribbean tourism is changing; today, the islands appeal more and more to those seeking adventure, culture, and unique experiences. At the same time, a trip to the Caribbean is a journey back in time, for it was here that European expansion into the Western Hemisphere took root.

The following chapters are meant to help adventure-seeking visitors plan their next natural Caribbean experience. The first four chapters provide a general overview of the Caribbean, covering history, culture, the people, geography, flora, and fauna. Chapter 4, Special Interests and Activities, directs travelers to the best islands for certain activities.

Following these general chapters are chapters covering specific islands or a group of islands. Not every island in the Caribbean is covered—this book focuses on those islands and destinations that offer the best opportunities for the active, adventurous traveler. These chapters provide brief background information (history, flora and fauna, and so on), details on eco-adventures and things to see and do, and information on outfitters and guides, accommodations, restaurants, getting around, and sources of additional information.

At the back of the book is an appendix covering general tourist information on everything from safety and what to pack to festivals and holidays. Suggested readings and organizations where you can obtain additional information on the Caribbean are also included.

I hope that you will enjoy using this book to help plan your Caribbean experience and that you will take it with you for quick reference. I also hope it helps to promote a more responsible approach to tourism in one of earth's very special places.

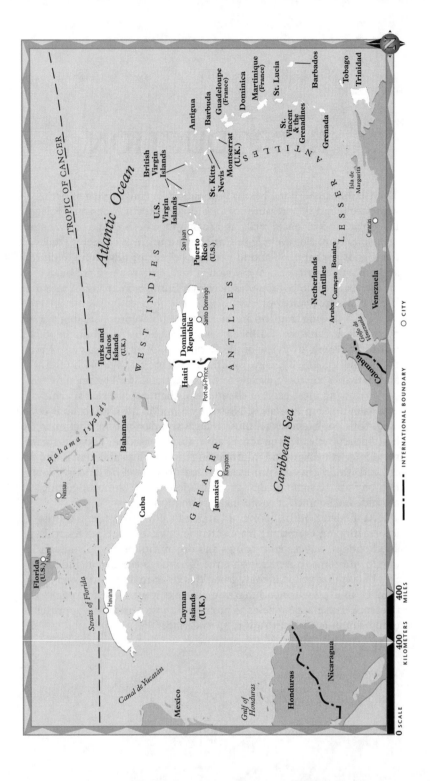

WHY VISIT THE CARIBBEAN?

Like emerald stepping stones spanning a turquoise pond, the Isles of the Caribbean form a seductive 2,500-kilometer arc, enticing travelers to step into a world where gentle trade winds and the Gulf Stream's warm caress combine to create a tropical paradise without rival. The Caribbean islands span the sparkling gap between the great western continents and protect the calm, clear waters of the Caribbean from the ravages of the mighty Atlantic.

Since the arrival of Europeans in 1492 the islands have been called the "Antilles" after "Antilia," the mythical group of islands thought to lie off the northwest coast of Africa, and the "West Indies" (or "Las Indies Occidentales"), a name Columbus gave them thinking they were islands off the coast of India. Today we refer to them collectively as "the Caribbean," a name that derives from the original inhabitants of the region, the Carib Indians. West Indians refer to their region as the "eighth continent of the world."

For years the islands have been a lodestone for people in search of warmth, relaxation, romance, and adventure. For as many years writers have tried with varying degrees of success to explain the Caribbean experience. Why is it difficult to describe the region? Because the Caribbean is not simply a destination, it's also a state of mind. What you find depends on what you are looking for.

The Caribbean appeals to so many because of its variety. Some islands, like the Tobago Cays, are no larger than a football field, while

Fast Facts About the Caribbean

The Caribbean Sea covers an area of about 2.72 million square kilometers, while the islands have a total land mass of 236,000 square kilometers. The Caribbean comprises 32 single- and multi-island nations, with a combined total population of about 34 million.

The region is dominated by mountainous volcanic islands with a few flat coral islands scattered in between. There are seven active volcanoes in the region. Elevations of over 2,100 meters are common in the greater Antilles while peaks over 1,200 meters typify the Lesser Antilles. Mount Pico Duarte (3,175 meters) in the Dominican Republic is the Caribbean's highest peak. Vegetation zones range from desert-like scrubland to lush tropical rain forests.

There are as many different forms of government as there are islands. Some, such as Trinidad and Tobago, Barbados, and Jamaica, have parliamentary-type independent governments; others, such as Anguilla and the Caymans, are still part of the British Commonwealth. Martinique and Guadaloupe are French territories while Aruba, Bonaire, and Curaçao are part of the Dutch Netherlands. Cuba is ruled by a communist dictatorship.

The four official languages in the Caribbean are Dutch, French, Spanish, and English, but an assortment of patois or creoles are spoken on each island. People of all races inhabit the islands; the majority are of African descent.

others, like Cuba, are among the largest in the world. There are beautiful white-sand beaches and even more beautiful black-sand strands; dry flat coral islands as well as lush mountainous volcanic ones. Some islands are densely populated while on others you will find only the occasional frigate bird and swaying palm to keep you company.

Every one of the islands is packed with natural beauty. *Caribbean Adventures in Nature* will focus on those islands and destinations that offer the best opportunities for exploring and experiencing the natural wonders of this extraordinary region.

THE GREATER ANTILLES AND THE LESSER ANTILLES

The West Indies, or Caribbean Islands, can be divided into two groups: The Greater Antilles and the Lesser Antilles. The Greater Antilles are situated in the northern half of the Caribbean Sea. They were probably so named due to their larger size as compared to the other islands in the Caribbean, but they are also older, higher, deeper, and more populated than all the others. The islands making up the Greater Antilles are Puerto Rico, Jamaica, the Cayman Islands, Hispaniola (the nations of the Dominican Republic and Haiti share the island), and Cuba. This diverse group of islands encompasses four official languages, four different types of governments (from dictatorship to American-style democracy), and a variety of religions and cultures found nowhere else in the Caribbean. The Greater Antilles have often been referred to as "the Cradle of the Caribbean" because most of the region's significant events over the last 500 years have taken place here.

Starting at St. Thomas, in the U.S. Virgin Islands, and extending almost 1,700 kilometers south to Aruba, off the coast of South America, are the islands that make up the Lesser Antilles. They are further divided into the Leeward and Windward Islands, the French and Dutch Antilles, the British and U.S. Virgin Islands, and off by themselves, Barbados and Trinidad and Tobago. In all, about 20 main islands and numerous uninhabited cays and islets make up the grouping. For the most part, these islands are smaller, less populated, and more difficult to get to than the Greater Antilles. Best of all, other than the occasional cruise ship, they are not heavily visited, with the exception of Barbados.

What makes these islands really special are their contrasts. Some are flat, arid, and busy while others are mountainous, lush, and untouched. Three different languages are spoken in the Lesser Antilles, and there is a diversity of cultures. But there is one thing all of the islands have in common: the friendliness of their people.

GEOGRAPHY

The Caribbean archipelago can be futher broken down into four main island chains that extend east from the Yucatán Peninsula towards Florida before curving south to South America. The Caribbean Sea covers about 2.72 million square kilometers, of which islands account for only 235,700 square kilometers. Cuba, at 114,000 square kilometers, is the largest island in the region and one of the largest in the world.

The first island chain, comprising Jamaica, the Cayman Islands,

Cuba, Puerto Rico, and Hispaniola (the Greater Antilles), is composed of outcroppings of three volcanic mountain ranges formed about 60 million years ago during the Cretaceous period. One range runs east through northern Cuba and Haiti. The Cayman Islands, Cuba's southern range (the Sierra Maestre), Hispaniola's Cordillera Central, and Puerto Rico's El Yunque range are part of the second range, while Jamaica's Blue Mountains and the southern coastal range of the Dominican Republic are part of the third.

The highest peaks in the Caribbean—Pico Duarte (3,175 meters) in the Dominican Republic, Blue Mountain Peak (2,256 meters) in Jamaica, Cuba's Pico Turquino (2,000 meters), and Punta Peak (1,338 meters) in Puerto Rico—are located along these mountains chains. So why is the highest elevation in the Cayman Islands a mere 43 meters? How did the Caymans escape the enormous forces that produced such high mountain ranges on neighboring islands? The answer lies just off shore in the Bartlett Deep and Cayman Trough, which reach depths of 6,400 meters. The Caymans are the coral-encrusted summits of one of the deepest submarine mountain ranges in the world.

Soon after the Greater Antilles were formed, two buckling plates extending from the Andes formed the second group of islands: Aruba,

Still-active La Soufrière volcano in St. Vincent

4

Bonaire, Curaçao (the ABCs), Trinidad and Tobago, and Barbados. These islands, except for Trinidad, are relatively flat and dry.

The third chain of islands, the Leewards and the Windwards, was formed during the late Miocene period. They appear along the fault line where the Atlantic Plate slides under the Caribbean Basin Plate. The plates' collision forced magma up through volcanic fissures along the fault line, forming most of the Lesser Antilles, which are characterized by rugged mountain ranges, with peaks over 1,200 meters. Because the plates are still sliding, many have active volcanoes.

The Bahamas and Turks and Caicos, a group of more than 700 small, low islands, make up the fourth chain of islands to be formed. They were created when millions of years' worth of sedimentary limestone deposits were left high and dry after the Caribbean waters receded.

Most Caribbean islands are the tops of mountains surrounded by narrow coastal plains, and they are true tropical paradises of lush rain forests, rivers, waterfalls, and a plethora of flora and fauna. The exceptions are the small, flat, dry limestone islands of the ABCs, Bahamas, Turks and Caicos, and Barbados, which do not receive enough rainfall to support lush vegetation.

CLIMATE

Early explorers called the Caribbean "the land of perpetual June" because the temperature varies only a few degrees over the year. In fact, in the southern Caribbean the temperature remains nearly constant year-round.

Kingston, Jamaica's winter temperature averages 25 degrees Celsius and 28 degrees Celsius in summer. For San Juan it's 26 degrees Celsius in winter, 28 degrees Celsius in summer. Curaçao averages 27 degrees and 26 degrees in winter and summer, respectively. There are only two seasons per year: the rainy season, May to October, and the dry season, November to April. These may vary by a week or two between Jamaica, in the north, and Trinidad, in the south. The climate is so consistent across the Caribbean in large part because of the trade winds and prevailing ocean currents.

Columbus had more going for him than he realized when he embarked on his first great voyage. Those early adventurers had the prevailing ocean currents and winds on their side. The Canary Current flows southwest from the Azores before becoming the North Equatorial Current, which flows through the Lesser Antilles into the Caribbean. From here it turns into the Gulf Stream, flowing northeast out of the Caribbean between Cuba and Florida and making its way all the way back to England and northern Spain. The Caribbean is also caressed by northeast trade winds, which blow year-round from the Azores to the islands at a steady 15 to 20 knots. North of Bermuda, these winds swing around and become the southwesterly trades. The ocean currents and trade winds combined to provide a convenient round-trip ticket for Columbus and his New World adventurers.

As the trades travel across the warm South Atlantic and eastern Caribbean waters they collect great quantities of moisture, which when cooled fall to earth as rain. These winds can be cooled either by orographic effects or convection. The orographic effect is produced when moisture-laden winds are forced to rise over high points of land, where they cool and their moisture condenses into rain. The higher the land, the higher the trades are forced to rise, resulting in heavier rain. Therefore, the rain falls mostly on the windward side of the mountains; the clouds continue to the lee of the mountains but don't have much moisture left to give up. The leeward side of the mountain in this case is called the "rain shadow." In the Greater Antilles, where typical elevations are over 1,500 meters, annual rains may exceed 750 centimeters.

Trades can also be coaxed to shed their moisture through convection, common on larger islands. During the first half of the day, the land heats up causing updrafts (convection) that in turn force trade winds to rise and cool, drenching the island with those brief late afternoon showers the region is famous for. Smaller islands, however, lack both the elevation to produce orographic effects and the land mass to produce convection; hence they tend to be dryer. Many of the smaller islands, like those of the Lesser Antilles, Bahamas, Turks and Caicos, and the ABCs, receive less than 50 centimeters of rain annually, only enough to support small shrubs and cacti. Relatively flat Barbados, on the other hand, has a large enough land mass to produce afternoon showers through convection.

During July and August, low-pressure troughs called "easterly waves" form in the eastern Caribbean and drift westward across the southern Caribbean, bringing calms and heavy rains. They form when the Intertropical Convergence Zone—where the Atlantic's southeast and northeast trades deflect each other—shifts north of the equator. It is here that tropical storms and hurricanes originate.

For reasons still unknown, powerful updrafts develop in these troughs and produce upward counterclockwise spirals. As these troughs drift west, updrafts increase in speed forming a vortex around an eye of calm air— otherwise known as a hurricane. By the time they reach the eastern Caribbean, some of these troughs have winds of up to 250 kilometers per hour. Because of the northwesterly track of these storms, the only hurricane-proof islands are those of the southern Caribbean, like Trinidad and Tobago and the ABCs. In the last 10 years, a number of killer storms have hit the islands, but only four or five of these cells turned into hurricanes.

If you wish to plan your trip to avoid hurricanes, simply remember the local rhyme: "June too soon, July stand by, September remember, October all over." Many hotels today have hurricane shelters, and new weather satellites give plenty of warning. Don't let the storms deter you from visiting the islands in the summer, when hotel rates are lowest.

HISTORY

When Columbus stumbled on the Caribbean, two indigenous peoples inhabited the islands, the Arawaks and Caribs. Scholars believe that both races originated in South America and used the islands as stepping stones on their migration north towards the Bahamas. The Arawaks started island hopping about 400 B.C., managing to reach the Bahamas by A.D. 100. By A.D. 500 there were three distinct Arawak groups living in the Caribbean: the Boringuens in Puerto Rico, the Tainos in the Greater and Lesser Antilles, and the Lucayans in the Bahamas.

Around A.D. 600 the peace of the Arawak nation was put to the test by the arrival of a new, more aggressive race of Indians from the Amazon jungles. The Carib (from the Spanish *caribal,* or "cannibal") commenced to overrun Arawak settlements as they island hopped north in massive 20-meter-long canoes called *piraguas.* These canoes could hold a hundred men and over short distances could outrun even European ships under sail.

Caribs practiced cannibalism, and by the time Columbus arrived, they had eaten their way through the Arawak nation as far north as the Virgin Islands. If not for the Spanish, the Caribs would have eventually taken over the entire Caribbean. Today the last Arawak is long gone, but Arawak features live on in the faces of native Cubans and Puerto Ricans.

The more dominant Caribs fared better than the Arawak; some of their descendants, the Black Caribs (African and Carib mixture), still live in isolated pockets on Dominica and St. Vincent.

Columbus

Born in Genoa, Italy, in 1451, Cristoforo Columbo worked by day in his father's weaving shop but spent most nights dreaming of the sea. Before his 20th birthday, he had already sailed around the Mediterranean and West Africa, eventually settling in Portugal to study under Prince Henry the Navigator. It was at this time that he became obsessed with the idea of finding a sea route to the Orient by sailing west.

In 1479 he married into a wealthy Portuguese family, gaining access to King John II and the Portuguese court. For the next eight years, he tried without success to convince King John II to finance an expedition west. Finally, in 1492, he got his break, but not from King John. Hearing of his ideas and eager to replenish the Spanish coffers after a long and arduous war with the Moors, King Ferdinand and Queen Isabel agreed to help Columbus. They gave him three *caravels* and sent him off to bring back riches for Spain.

On August 3, 1492, Columbus and 100 men on three ships (the *Nina, Pinta,* and *Santa Maria*) headed west. Seventy days later, on October 12, he sighted land, most likely one of the Bahamas, and stopped long enough to name it San Salvador. Sailing southwest to Cuba and Hispaniola (Little Spain), he found Arawaks wearing gold jewelry. Convinced he had found an island off the Indian coast, he set out to find the mainland but ended up running the *Santa Maria* aground in a shallow bay on the north coast of Hispaniola, present-day Haiti.

Early in 1493 he returned to Spain, leaving 39 men to search for gold and guard the settlement. He returned that year with 1,200 colonists and 17 ships only to find the fort destroyed and his men dead. After settling the colonists, he left them to fend for themselves and set out to explore the rest of the region.

Over the next nine years Columbus made two other voyages to the Caribbean, landing on and naming all the Lesser Antilles, including Trinidad in 1498. Even more important, for both Europeans and the indigenous peoples of the region, Columbus arrived on the Central American coast in 1502. Here he encountered new Indian cultures and gold in abundance, a factor that would lead to the rapid acceleration of European colonization of the region.

The Fight for Caribbean Dominance

Columbus paved the way for Spain to claim sovereignty over all lands 100 leagues west of the Azores. Rumors of Spanish galleons returning from the New World laden with gold spread far and wide. Fearing that Spain's new wealth would tip the balance of power in Europe, the Dutch, Danes, English, and French decided that it was time to take their share of the New World. However, rather than risk outright war with Spain, the other European powers engaged the help of "privateers," or pirates, to do their bidding. By the 1550s all the major European powers were locked in battle with Spain for the wealth of the Caribbean.

Spain found itself fighting on many fronts and attempted to counter intrusions into its territory by constructing massive fortifications on Cuba, Hispaniola, and Puerto Rico. In response, other European powers established permanent settlements and fortifications on the smaller, unprotected Leeward and Windward Islands. Because these islands were small and close together, it did not take long before French, Dutch, and British neighbors started fighting each other. As a result, many of these islands changed hands frequently, especially the more strategic islands like St. Croix, which changed hands nine times in less than 20 years.

The anarchy reigned for almost 300 years, until the 1815 Treaty of Vienna, at the end of the Napoleonic Wars, divided the region among the super-powers. Great Britain came out on top with Jamaica, the Caymans, the Bahamas, and most of the Lesser Antilles. France got Martinique, Guadaloupe, and a couple of smaller islands; the Dutch were left with the ABCs; and the Danes were granted the Virgin Islands. The Spanish kept Cuba, Puerto Rico, and half of Hispaniola. The French eventually gave their half of Hispaniola to the slaves, who eventually formed Haiti, the first black republic in the New World.

San Cristóbal Fortress in Puerto Rico

Colonization: A Time for Trade, Not War

During most of the war years, Spain concentrated more on draining the gold and silver out of Central America than they did on colonizing the Caribbean. The settlements they did establish were primarily used as staging areas for transporting gold and silver back to Spain. While Spain pillaged, the other European powers were busy fortifying their settlements and getting down to the business of commerce. By the time the gold and silver of Central America ran out, along with Spain's influence in the region, a new agricultural era—driven by Europe's new infatuation with cane sugar and tobacco—was already underway.

Some Spanish colonists, however, did pursue agriculture and realized early on that the Arawaks and Caribs would rather die than be slaves. By the time the other European powers discovered this, there were no Indians left to work the fields. To cultivate these labor-intensive crops the jails of Europe were emptied and prisoners sent to the New World to work. Unaccustomed to the heat and with no resistance to island diseases, most prisoners died within a year of reaching the sugar and tobacco estates. When the supply of prisoners ran out, the search for a new labor force began in earnest.

The Black Triangle

The Spanish were the first to introduce Africans into the Caribbean. Slaves from Spanish plantations in Africa were relocated to work the cane fields in Hispaniola. To their detriment, they proved to be good workers. News of Spain's success with Africans reached other islands and demand for African slaves quickly spread. The despicable Black Triangle was born.

On the first leg of the triangle, ships loaded with dry goods and trinkets left Europe bound for the Gold and Ivory Coasts of west Africa. Once there, dry goods were traded for slaves, and the empty ships were converted to haul human cargo to the West Indies, the second leg of the triangle. Once in the Caribbean, the slaves were auctioned off for gold, tobacco, or sugar, then the ships were converted back to cargo carriers to haul the sugar and tobacco back to Europe, the final leg of the trade triangle. In Europe, the goods were sold and the cycle repeated. This dark period in Caribbean history lasted until slavery was abolished in 1860.

By the 1730s black slaves outnumbered their white masters 50 to one, and slave insurrections started to spread through the islands. The first major insurrection started in St. John, then spread to Antigua, St. Croix, and Grenada before erupting in all-out rebellion on the French-controlled half of Hispaniola in 1793.

For 10 years an army of slaves held Napoleon's legions at bay until France finally relented, allowing the slaves to form the first black republic in the New World, on the western third of the island. This victory, and the resulting new republic of Haiti, paved the way for emancipation in the late 1800s.

Independent Identity and Freedom

Throwing off the yoke of slavery was an important first step in ending colonization. Many ex-slaves felt that true freedom was possible only with total independence from their old European masters. Led by a new generation of educated blacks, the people started to chip away at the cultural and racial prejudices of colonialism. One by one, each island gained its independence.

Spanish Colonies

As islands developed economically so did the people's political aspirations. Despite the abolition of slavery on most islands by 1860, the struggle for freedom continued until 1875 on islands including Puerto Rico, Cuba, and the Dominican Republic. For these islands, freeing themselves from colonialism would prove even more difficult than ending slavery had been.

With her empire in ruins and no more gold from Central America, Spain decided to hold onto her Caribbean possessions at all costs. Vast sugar and tobacco plantations on these islands provided Spain with much-needed cash, so the struggle to preserve slavery and colonization became one. Spain met each slave revolt with increasingly brutal suppression until the Spanish-American War broke out. The war was brief, and when the dust settled Spain surrendered and ceded Cuba, Puerto Rico, and the Dominican Republic to the United States. For the next 50 years, the governments on these islands would be no more than puppets of the United States. To the islanders, U.S. domination represented simply another form of colonialism.

Puerto Rico would eventually become a U.S. Commonwealth and the Dominican Republic an independent country. Cuba was ruled by one corrupt government after another until Fidel Castro defeated Batista in 1959 to establish a military dictatorship, still in place today.

Danish Colonies

After the Treaty of Vienna, the Danes were left with a group of about 70 islands in the western half of what was then the Virgin Islands. Only three of these islands were large enough for agriculture, but with poor soil and little rain the enterprise soon floundered. The Danes decided to make them free ports to capitalize on the trade that had developed in the

Kas di dal'i Maishi, *House of Corn Stalks Roof—slave hut in Curaçao*

region. Their strategic location, at the entrance to the Lesser Antilles, made them ideal locations for commerce. These free ports prospered until the sugar industry failed and piracy was outlawed. The islands then fell into ruin and the Danes actively sought a buyer. After declaring war on Germany during World War I, the United States, interested in protecting the eastern access to the Panama Canal, purchased the islands in 1917 from the Danes for $25 million. Between 1917 and 1934 the United States constructed a number of naval bases and allowed the Navy to govern. Since 1968 the U.S. Virgin Islands have elected their own governor, legislature, and non-voting House Representative every four years.

British Colonies

Colonialism was still the order of the day on Great Britain's 16 island colonies well into the twentieth century. Under colonialism, local governments were appointed by the queen and effectively excluded locals. When passive resistance to this political exclusion failed, post-emancipation blacks took more drastic measures, such as the 1880 Federation Riots in Barbados and the Water Riots in Trinidad in 1903. But these events only shook the walls of colonialism, they did not bring them down.

After World War I, Great Britain's need to rebuild itself left little capital for its Caribbean colonies. The islands found themselves in difficult times, with rampant unemployment, exploitive labor practices, and ruined local economies. The Great Depression created desperate situations in the islands. In 1935 tensions boiled over and bloodshed spread throughout the British islands.

The riots were so violent, they forced the British government to reexamine the plight of their Caribbean empire. A royal commission established to review the situation was headed by Sir Walter Citrine, who had strong connections to Britain's trade union movement. Appalled by the exploitation on the islands, Citrine helped to organize local groups into strong labor movements. These labor movements bred strong local, educated leaders who in turn put more pressure on Britain for reforms.

By the 1950s British colonialism was in retreat. First India gained its independence, then such larger islands as Trinidad and Tobago, Barbados, and Jamaica were given associated statehood. By 1966 most of the other smaller colonies were granted the same. Under associated statehood, islands were given the authority to elect independent governments based on the British Westminster model—a parliament and a prime minister. Today, only Montserrat, Anguilla, the British Virgin Islands, the Turks and Caicos, and the Cayman Islands remain part of the British empire. All the others are now independent nations.

Dutch Colonies

The Dutch colonies of Aruba, Curaçao, and Bonaire (the ABCs) and the smaller islands of Saba, Sint Eustatius, and Sint Maarten in the Leeward Islands relied heavily on sugar, so when the industry failed they were harder hit than most of their neighbors. The islands suffered through hard times until the construction of the Panama Canal began in the early 1900s. The ABCs' proximity to the canal brought steady work for many islanders for almost 30 years. The islands became a favorite stopover and port for goods heading to and from the canal.

The discovery of oil in Venezuela in the early 1900s, coupled with the deep water ports of the ABCs, propelled these islands into the lucrative oil business. Venezuela, faced with shallow coastal waters, had to find a deep-water port capable of handling large tankers. Their solution was to ship their crude to the ABCs in shallow barges, where it was transferred to larger carriers. In 1915 Shell and Exxon opened large refineries in the ABCs to process Venezuela crude. In 1954 all the islands in the Netherlands Antilles became regions of Holland, and islanders were granted the right to elect local politicians to represent their interests in the Dutch cabinet.

French Colonies

Besides slavery and colonialism, the French colonies—Guadeloupe, Martinique, St. Barthélemy, and St. Martin—had to contend with a revolution in France, which soon spread to the islands. Slaves on Guadeloupe erected a guillotine and lopped off the heads of more than 300 estate owners before order was finally restored. This era of "liberation" fostered distaste for slavery and prompted France to become the first nation to free its slaves. In 1946 France's National Assembly passed legislation making the islands overseas *departments*, and in 1974 they became regions of France. Today the "French Sisters" enjoy representation in France's National Assembly.

ECONOMY

From Columbus' first voyage to the New World to the early 1600s, the Caribbean was a place of plunder and anarchy. Although settlers flirted with the tobacco trade on Cuba, Hispaniola, the Dominican Republic, and Puerto Rico, many of the islands were no more than gateway ports between Europe and the New World. The turning point came in the mid-1600s when the Dutch, after being run out of Brazil, brought their mercantile doctrine to the region.

Lacking the fire power of other European nations, the Dutch decided to capitalize on the wealth of the Caribbean by establishing the West

India Company. Their aim was to divide the region into trading zones and control trade in the Caribbean. Within a century they singlehandedly transformed the region from anarchy to capitalism.

The Dutch realized early that the size of most of the islands prevented them from achieving the economies of scale necessary to compete with the vast tobacco and cotton plantations of the Americas, so they set out to find a niche cash crop. They had successfully experimented with sugar on a few island plots, so when Virginia put Barbados out of the tobacco business in the early 1640s, the Dutch were there with their sugar cane plants. By 1650 the entire island was planted in sugar cane.

Sugar produced the first West Indian socioeconomic revolution, and a period of great prosperity followed. By the early 1700s, sugar plantations dominated every island economy. But the once-fertile soils started to fail under the pressure of a single crop, and profits declined. The next-to-last fatal blow came when emancipation swept the islands in the mid-1800s. Freedom for the slaves meant higher wages, an almost crippling burden added to the already low yields per acre. The final blow to Caribbean plantations came when beet sugar saturated European markets forcing down sugar prices. The great plantations were abandoned and the vacated lands taken over by freed slaves and indentured servants.

So began a new socioeconomic stage in the Caribbean, with small subsistence plots of cacao, cassava, yams, ginger, arrowroot, and bananas. On every island farmers competed with each other and with those on neighboring islands for a few dollars. These economic conditions would last well into the mid-1900s, until some of the larger islands started to take advantage of their natural resources. Jamaica became one of the worlds largest exporters of bauxite and aluminum. Curaçao and Aruba prospered from oil reserves found in Venezuela, and Trinidad developed its petroleum resources.

By the mid-1960s, experienced Caribbean administrations realized that the only way to get economic clout was to create economies of scale that could compete with larger countries. To this end, they established a regional trade alliance called the Caribbean Free Trade Area (CARIFTA). During this period the Windward and French islands had reverted back to a single crop, bananas, and by 1970 the Caribbean Banana Association was formed to counter the bargaining strength of the European Common Market. Today bananas are a major source of foreign currency for many islands, but they are also a very fragile crop, not ideal for a region plagued by tropical storms and the occasional volcanic eruption.

The severe storms of the 1970s sent islands scrambling to diversify. Many turned to the only thing they had left: sun, sand, and sea. Tourism roared in like a lion; new airports and hotels, financed with foreign dollars, sprang up overnight. Relief from winter's bitter cold was but a few hours away for many temperate dwellers, and they headed to the Caribbean by the thousands.

Today tourism has replaced sugar as the economic mainstay of the Caribbean. Once again the islands find themselves dominated by single industry, but this time leaders are not standing idly by waiting for the next socioeconomic crisis. They are using tourism dollars to diversify their economy with such industries as fishing, agriculture, the garment industries, and more traditional cottage industries like knitting, basket weaving, and wood carving. Many are diversifying the tourism industry itself by developing environmentally friendly ecotourism. Although many of the jobs created by tourism are low-paying, it's a start.

Another new, important industry in the region originates from an unlikely but formidable group of people: West Indians living abroad. Today far more West Indians live abroad than in the Caribbean. They funnel huge sums of money back to the islands in the form of family financial support, gifts, and as returning visitors. They have also become a major export market for Caribbean agricultural goods, clothing, and, of course, hot pepper sauce and rum.

LIFESTYLE AND CULTURE

Like a Carnival mask hides the face of a reveler, modern tourism tends to disguise the enigmatic and diverse culture of the Caribbean people. Caribbean culture is an undefinable blend of countless peoples who have passed through the region over the last 500 years. Merchants, sailors, soldiers, slaves, pirates, and lords have all added brush strokes to the colorful Caribbean canvas. Most visitors, exposed only to the tourist mask of the islands, will never experience the rich melange of Caribbean culture.

It is difficult to define Caribbean culture (if there even is such a thing) in a single phrase because West Indians lack a regional identity per se. Each island is fiercely autonomous: a Jamaican is a Jamaican first, not a West Indian, for example. The same is true on other islands. In fact, the Caribbean is a "nation" of many nations each struggling with issues of identity. Should a black West Indian who has never set foot in Africa, speaks a European language, and calls home an island with a past steeped in slavery embrace an African heritage or a West Indian one?

Geography and history compound the dilemma. Because the islands' individual worlds are small, they lack the clout to deal with the mighty nations that influence their everyday lives. At the same time, historical differences in language, religion, and race complicate the regional approach. "Out of many, one people" seems far-fetched even for nationalistic Jamaicans, more so for other West Indians.

Yet despite their many differences, West Indians share at least one

15

historical commonality: they are all immigrants to the region. Of the 34-plus million West Indians, 40 percent are black (of African descent), 35 percent are white (mostly Spanish and English), 20 percent are a mixture of black and white ancestry, and 5 percent are Asian (Indian and Chinese). Except for the large mixed-race and white populations on Cuba, Puerto Rico, and the Dominican Republic, most islands are predominately black.

A great deal of racial intermixing has occurred over the years, but for demographic purposes mixed-race people are usually included in one of the four main ethnic categories. This racial blending has tempered prejudices but does not mean that all is peaceful and loving. Even so, disputes in these nations tend to revolve more around economic and political issues than racial ones.

One of the first things you'll notice when you arrive on any island is the lack of urgency. You seldom see anyone in a hurry. They even have a saying for it: "no hurry worry me," which means "don't worry about time." The sooner you adjust to "island time," the sooner you'll realize *they're* not moving too slow, *you're* moving too fast. But don't be fooled by the laid-back demeanor; the typical islander is anything but demure. West Indians are an expressive people. To find out just how expressive, point a camera their way without asking permission or linger at a boisterous game of dominoes.

And talk about talking! Talking is a national pastime in the islands. Once you get them started locals will talk about everything—sports, weather, politics, and especially each other. A good gossip, or *su-su*, as it is referred to locally, is an integral part of Caribbean life. Seldom will you take a bus or taxi ride without hearing about the government, sports team, or a relative someone has in your country.

Which leads us to another vibrant quality: pride. West Indians are a proud people. It shows on their faces when they talk about "their" island. You hear it in their music and see it in their art. They realize their role is small in the bigger scheme of things, but they are very aware of their uniqueness and determined to preserve it.

Each year more than 25 million visitors descend on the shores of these small, fragile islands. Despite the pressure tourism places on the islands' independent identities and natural resources, most islanders welcome visitors and their dollars. However, they strongly resist change just for the sake of change.

Islanders now understand that preserving their identities depends on developing an indigenous tourism industry that satisfies their needs without displacing their identity. They are slowly realizing that to preserve their independence, they must first maintain their Caribbean identity.

Mass tourism taxes the local resources.

For centuries before Columbus the islands evolved independently. They existed in isolation from each other, even though the distances separating them were small, and they developed independently from the rest of the world. But that all changed with Columbus. Since then, the Caribbean melting pot has been stirred by many hands, which has dramatically altered the land and the people. Today the Caribbean supports and residents from every corner of the globe. Movie stars and pop singers now reside on small islands like Mustique, which was once a small fishing community. Satellite dishes and Hindu prayer flags dominate the Trinidad skyline, once reserved for royal palms. The Caribbean is changing, but the recipe for the future lies in the hands that stir the melting pot today.

Language

Intertwined with the four official Caribbean languages of Spanish, English, French, and Dutch are a number of pidgin variants called "creoles," which many contemporary Caribbean scholars believe are the true languages of the region. With origins in slavery, these languages evolved over hundreds of years. Creoles are now an integral part of the culture of most islands, especially those that had large slave populations, such as the Windwards and Leewards.

17

English and French creoles are more typical, but Papiamento—a combination of Dutch, Spanish, Portuguese, and English—is widely spoken in the Netherlands Antilles. The predominately white islands of Cuba, Puerto Rico, and the Dominican Republic did not change hands like the others, and slavery was less established, so creoles did not evolve there. Most creoles contain African fragments blended with European phrases, but they differ from island to island depending on who ruled it and how many times it changed hands. The French and English both controlled Dominica at one time, so the creole there is a combination of French, English, and African phrases. Creoles are gaining popularity in the islands and are now being taught in the local schools. Since most visitors are from North America, the second language on most islands is English. Knowing a little French or Spanish is helpful, but not necessary.

RELIGION

Most of the Caribbean population is affiliated with at least one Judeo-Christian denomination, but many also practice other beliefs. Most religious beliefs are associated with the cultural and racial mix of the people. It is perfectly acceptable for someone who plants by the full moon on Thursday to put an *obeah* curse on his mother-in-law on Friday, participate in a spirit drum ceremony on Saturday, and attend Catholic Mass on Sunday.

Catholicism is the dominant religion among the Spanish- and French-speaking islands while Protestant denominations such as Methodist, Baptist, and Anglican are prevalent on the Dutch and English islands. Syncretic, or blended, religions that combine Christian and African elements are common on Haiti, Cuba, Puerto Rico, and Trinidad.

Over the years West Indians have chosen a particular religion not only for worship, but for social prestige, curative powers, entertainment value, and education. When East Indians arrived in Trinidad in the late 1800s, they were treated as outsiders and denied access into the better public schools, so many converted to Christianity in order to take advantage of that religion's educational system. Today, they make up 40 percent of Trinidad's population, and, with more political freedom, many are returning to their Hindu and Islamic roots.

Throughout the centuries, religion and the first missionaries became unwitting pawns in the drive for control and conquest in the New World. Early one-room missions were assumed to be more claims to ownership than missions, and as settlements grew and slavery increased the missions came under fire of the plantocracy, which treated any attempt to educate the slaves as dangerous and subversive. Because of this, many missionaries did little to halt the cruelty, electing instead to teach a social quietism in hopes of saving the slaves from excessive cruelty. In return for these gospels

Voodoo

In a small houmfort *(shed) in the Bel Air section of Port-au-Prince, Haiti, a Catholic-type liturgy unfolds. Men and women, white handkerchiefs adorning their heads, begin to sway and step slowly around a colorful pole in the center of the room. The drumbeat increases and soon the room is filled with flailing arms and thrashing bodies. Then the moaning starts, first as a murmur then building to a dull roar that echoes through the room. Suddenly a lone pulsating figure in a trance-like state utters words in a strange tongue, and the Voodoo ceremony goes into high gear.*

Although Haiti's official religion is Catholicism, Voodoo (also called vodun) is widespread. In fact, Haitians have a saying, "Haiti is 90 percent Catholic and 95 percent Voodoo."

A Voodoo-inspired black slave revolt in 1791 in Haiti paved the way for the leader of the slaves, Jean Jacques Dessalines, to declare Haitian independence in 1801.

In Voodoo rituals, there are loas—*spirits of love, fire, water, and so on—who may be angry or happy. Dumbly, the water loa, can send rain for crops or floods depending on what mood she is in. Other loas—such as Ogun, the war loa; Papa Legba, the guardian of doorways; and Erzulie Freda, the spirit of love—also have mood swings. Once a person is possessed by a loa at a Voodoo ceremony, the spirit's disposition depends on how it is treated.*

of obedience, the planters financed the missions and promoted the virtues of this brand of Christianity. Thus many missions became nothing more than purveyors of docility.

Catholicism was the first European religion in the region. A number of Catholic missionaries accompanied Columbus on his second voyage in 1493. They divided islands into parishes, each with its own priest who

*Santa Maria la Menor Cathedral
in the Dominican Republic*

was responsible for establishing a mission. Many islands are still divided along parish lines established hundreds of years ago. Catholicism was given a boost when the French established permanent settlements in the region. Today, the French Antilles are still mainly Catholic.

The British brought Episcopalianism and the Church of England to the islands. Barbados, the first major British settlement, became the Caribbean headquarters for the Anglican Church; St. John's Church, built in the early 1700s on the island, still stands. The Anglican Church, an upper-class white church with great political influence, forbade whites from marrying blacks. This decree was obeyed on the English-dominated islands, though the practice was common on other islands.

Alongside the Judeo-Christian religions, islanders observe a number of Afro-Christian religions such as Shango, which originated in Nigeria and combines Yoruba with Catholicism and Baptist practices. Historically popular in Trinidad and Cuba, this religion was banned in those islands in the early 1900s, then resurfaced in Trinidad in 1951 when the ban was repealed.

The most famous of the Afro-Christian religions is Voodoo, which takes its name from the African word *vodun*, meaning "spirit." Although prevalent throughout the Caribbean, it is strongest in Haiti. Voodoo is a formal religion incorporating symbols, dancing, singing, and chanting. Each ceremony is devoted to *Gran Met* (God) and overseen by an *ougan* (priest) or *mambo* (priestess). During the ceremony participants dance themselves into trance-like states until they are entered by *loas*, or spirits. Spirits carry messages from the spirit world to the participant.

During the Spanish Inquisition in the late 1400s, anything not Catholic was deemed heretical and eradicated. Among the first worshippers to be singled out were the Spanish Jews, who had been expelled from Spain. To escape persecution many fled to eastern Europe, but some headed for the Caribbean, settling as far as they could from Spain's reach on islands such as Curaçao and St. Thomas. The Mikve Israel–Emanuel synagogue, founded in Curaçao in 1732, remains the oldest functioning synagogue in the Western Hemisphere.

ARTS AND LITERATURE

The Caribbean people enjoy a strong traditional arts culture of crafts, paintings, carvings, embroidering, batik, music, and dance. Their literary tradition reflects the region's rich cultural diversity. Ingenuity and creativity abound in the Caribbean, but like the coconut, you must peal back the glitzy husk of tourism to find the meaty part.

Music

Without a doubt, music is the most important social glue in Caribbean culture. With rhythms that transcend political, racial, and ethnic boundaries, Caribbean music provides the frame that holds the Caribbean canvas. The pounding 2/4 or 4/4 beat is the heartbeat of the islands, a rhythmical expression of the emotions of the people. No matter which island you visit, you will hear music echoing from shops, minibuses, and homes.

Although the region's musical roots are African, they have been influenced by French and Spanish rhythms as well. Forbidden to talk to one another in the fields, slaves communicated with songs, and it did not take long for the music to develop a component of social commentary. Today Caribbean music is filled with political statements as well as sexual innuendo and ethnic allusions. Like the African drums, the music carries messages throughout the islands.

The instruments used to carry these messages vary, but drums are most important. The *ka*, a direct descendant of the African drum used by African tribes, was made by stretching cow or goat hide over barrels used to stored the salted meat and fish that fed the slaves. From this drum came the *conga, mambo,* and the more familiar steel drum of Trinidad. Guitars, marimbas, shack-shacks, and banjos were added along with a profusion of such ingenious percussion instruments as the Coke bottle, brake-drum, biscuit tin, garbage can, cowbell, and whistle. In the Caribbean anything that makes a sound qualifies as an instrument.

Some of the more popular rhythms are *soca* (soul-calypso) on the British islands, *zouk* on the French islands, *salsa* on the Spanish islands, and *reggae* in Jamaica. All have strong hypnotic beats and similarities are easy to spot. Caribbean music has always been used to express emotions associated with pain, poverty, political anguish, and, to some extent, racial sentiment. It is said that "when a West Indian is sad he sings, but when he is happy he sings and dances."

Dance

Like its music, Caribbean dance contains strong African influences and reflects many movements still seen today in Ghana and Nigeria. Slave

The Steel Drum

In the late 1700s elite Trinidadians (rich traders, estate owners, and their families) practiced masquerade or "Mas" each year between Christmas and Lent. Masked (masquerading) revelers formed groups and marched in disorderly processions all over town. Slaves were not allowed to participate in these masquerades, but after slavery was abolished they formed their own groups to party. They took to the streets with drums and percussion instruments of every kind in outward defiance of the Victorian government. Soon these celebrations turned violent and the government tried to stifle them by banning the use of drums. The ban lasted until the 1940s when once again revelers started using drums—except this time they used 55-gallon oil drums called pans.

Percussion musicians discovered that if they tempered and hammered one of the flat ends of the drum into various- sized raised sections, they could produce different sounds when a section was hit with a wooden stick. Over the years they perfected their trade and developed different drums (bass, tenor, etc.), each with its own range of notes. Today there are 120-drum steel orchestras capable of playing not only calypso but some of the most difficult classical music ever written. The bands practice in pan-yards all over Port of Spain, Trinidad, and compete for "Band of the Year" each year at Carnival.

dances like the *calenda, haute taille,* and *bel air* were banned by the French, who considered them obscene and pagan, but they still survive in Martinique's interior. *Calenda* moves are also entrenched in the popular *béquine* dance of Martinique and Guadeloupe and in the Afro-Spanish dances like the *plena, merengue, rumba,* and *samba* popular in Cuba, Puerto Rico, and the Dominican Republic.

Legends, Lore, and Literature

In the cool shade of an old mango tree a teacher sits with her pupils. "Crick crack," says the teacher. The children answer, "Break your back," and so starts another West Indian story-time tale. When the teacher says, "Wire bend," the children respond, "Story end," and so it does. West Indian literature has strong African influences. Many favorite American oldies like "Br'er Rabbit" started as "Buh Rabby." "Br'er Annancy," the plump, four-armed, four-legged half-man-half-spider character originated with the African word *anase*, meaning "spider." Because the stories derive from African folklore, and animals are important metaphors of African life, animals such as Dog, Tiger, Rabbit, Snake, and Owl play an important role in conveying messages in West Indian folk tales. Some are smart (like Owl), others are fierce (Tiger), and some, like Annancy, are lazy. Metaphors have long been used to express messages or ideas when peoples of different cultures interact.

West Indian metaphors also surface in sayings or proverbs; a good number of these have European origins. The popular West Indian proverb "Not everything whit sugar is sweet" comes from the European saying "All that glitters is not gold." In Dominican patois *"Si ou plante cassave, m'pas kefe fig"* roughly translates as "If you plant cassava, you cannot get bananas." It probably takes it origins from the Biblical verse "So he sows, so shall he reap." Most Caribbean metaphors evolved from the more recognizable regional commodities.

On a more serious note, most West Indian writers are enthralled by historical and identity issues. The African dilemma is front and center in Caribbean writing; the region's segmented geography only magnifies its relentless search for identity and belonging, undertaken by not just black West Indians but white and mixed-race people as well. For example, Jean Rhys' powerful novel *Wide Sargasso Sea* tells the tale of a West Indian white girl growing up on Dominica; it shocked many readers with its description of island life. The distinguished writer V. S. Naipaul, a Trinidadian and East Indian, was knighted by Queen Elizabeth II in 1989 for his contribution to West Indian literature with his powerful works *The Mystic Masseur* and *The Loss of El Dorado*.

A peaceful island beach on St. Croix

2
CONSERVATION
AND RESPONSIBLE
TOURISM

Island economies are too small to compete with the economies of larger nations. Try as they might to maintain their independence, they can't avoid their obvious dependence on the outside world. Most have tried agriculture, at least once, to raise needed foreign capital. But they soon realized that to achieve any economy of scale, they must plant nearly every available square centimeter of arable land in a single crop. Many times the plan has worked only to be ruined by a hurricane or volcanic eruption.

In 1970 a number of islands joined together to form the Caribbean Community and Common Market (CARICOM), a customs union developed to foster free trade between members. Although this and other organizations like it improved the situation, the islands were still trapped in a position of dependency, exporting cheaper agricultural goods and mineral ores in exchange for more expensive value-added manufactured goods such as farm equipment, cars, and home appliances. Either alone or in their collectives, they could not produce enough of any one commodity to impact the international market. The resulting trade deficits, negative balance of payments, and reliance on foreign investment amounted to a kind of neocolonialism—a bitter pill to swallow for people who over the last 20 years had fought hard for their independence.

To free themselves from this dependency many islands began marketing their remaining resources: sun, sand, sea, and warmth. With the advent of rapid transit, tourism literally took off. Airports and hotels, most foreign owned, sprang up overnight. Tourism made the strongest impact on the region since the sugar revolution. On many islands today it accounts for a major portion of total gross national product.

As more tourist dollars came in, more arable land (mostly coastal plains) gave way to development. Critics warned that tourism amounted to putting the same eggs in a different basket. But the lure was irresistible: "If you build it, they will come," said the politicians in support of mega-resorts or deep-water piers. Off to the International Monetary Fund they ran to get loans to build airports and piers needed to attract the big money, not truly realizing that they would be dealing with large offshore multinationals interested in only one thing: profit.

By the time these multinationals get their tax incentives, or "tax holidays," not much is left for the local economy or loan repayment. The jobs created tend to be minimum-wage positions such as maid, bartender, and laborer. While some income does come in from foreign sources, a large percentage of hotel infrastructure (furniture, air conditioners, etc.) comes from offshore—exit the cash. The small percentage of cash left behind undoubtedly helps island economies in the short run, but at what long-term cost?

THE WINDS OF CHANGE

Today few island administrators woo multinational enterprises as they did in the past and instead promote tourism that has less negative impact on natural resources and cultural diversity. They now realize that mass tourism will destroy the very thing that attracts millions of visitors to these shores. For example, visitors lured by fantasies of beautiful, secluded beaches come only to discover that many of the best beaches in the region are overdeveloped and crowded.

The big eye-opener for tourism proponents was the realization that mass tourism was not the non-polluting, low-impact industry they thought it would be. For example, cruise ships have had a major impact on the region. Over the years laws governing the disposal of garbage at sea were lax and seldom monitored, but when cruise ship passengers started videotaping the dumping, the situation suddenly improved. Stiff fines were handed out to a number of cruise lines, and monitoring has been stepped up. How much dumping has occurred or continues today is anyone's guess, but with almost 9 million cruise passengers and thousands of registered sailings each year, one can only imagine. The real kicker is that most of what was dumped originated outside the Caribbean.

Land-based tourism also has serious adverse effects on the islands. Retaining walls and breakwaters have been erected on many Caribbean beaches to keep them from washing away. This practice interferes with water movement and the natural aeration process along these beaches, resulting in excessive silt buildup and exploding weed and algae growth. This in turn has led to the suffocation of entire reef animal colonies. Add to this the unintentional damage caused by inexperienced snorkelers and swimmers, and pollution run-off from overdeveloped beach properties, and it is no wonder that shore reefs are disappearing at an alarming rate. The walls and beach overdevelopment have also interrupted the nesting habits of the region's three main sea turtle species, which are already on the endangered list.

Local infrastructure services like fresh water, waste water and sewage treatment, and solid waste disposal are also reeling under the pressure of tourism. There are only a couple recycling plants in the region, and the problem of collection is compounded by the distances between islands. As a result, solid waste is burned either in open pits or incinerators, which in turn leads to other environmental problems. Solid waste has reached such mountainous proportions on some smaller islands that they have resorted to dumping at sea. Plastic, the scourge of the industrial era, now litters every beach and roadway in the Caribbean.

The damage tourism causes goes beyond environmental issues. Numerous social and cultural issues are now major concerns on most islands. Large resorts with their security gates and walled compounds have all but blocked local access to beaches. Most Caribbean beaches are still considered public, but on many islands the best beaches have almost no access points except by boat, so locals are left with the least desirable beaches for their traditional weekend outings. This has caused acute resentment among local inhabitants. Also, on islands with high concentrations of wealthy tourists, crime has raised its ugly head, and many hotels have countered by introducing safes in rooms and armed security patrols within their compounds.

Traffic congestion also causes problems. Take a small island with a population of 40,000, of which 20,000 live in the port city. Now throw in a cruise ship terminal capable of handling three cruise ships at a time, each carrying 1,800 passengers. Imagine how frustrating this must be for the locals, who have to deal with this scenario every week during the high tourist season. Indeed, the Caribbean now averages about 26 million visitors a year compared with a total resident population of 34 million.

Most importantly, tourism officials realize that the Caribbean does not have a monopoly on scenic beauty or the natural experience, and they are all eager to protect the "golden tourism goose." They know that if the problems of mass tourism are left unchecked, visitors will eventually head elsewhere. In their search for answers they have discovered "sustainable tourism." This form of tourism promotes a more positive interaction between visitors and island resources. The islands are now embracing responsible tourism in an effort to save what little they have left.

Responsible tourism, also called "ecotourism," is a promising alternative to mass tourism because it aims to preserve, rather than consume, the islands' fragile ecosystems and cultural identities. But every new concept is subject to interpretation. Especially noticeable are the contrasting philosophies of the larger and smaller islands, where the understanding of responsible tourism can be vastly different.

Larger islands, with their huge investments in resorts and cruise terminals, tend to limit their ecotourism efforts to offering four- or five-hour ecotours. In a way, they take a mass tourism approach to ecotourism by finding something else for the visitor to do besides spend his or her day on a crowded beach. It does not appear that they have made the true connection between responsible tourism, local culture, and the environment, but maybe these limited efforts are necessary steps toward developing a more diverse local ecotourism industry.

In general, on the smaller, less developed islands, the transition to responsible tourism appears to be working quite well, probably because most don't have large mass tourism investments to deal with. Islands such as the Windwards learned from the mistakes made by their more developed neighbors, who were entrenched in mass tourism programs while the smaller islands were just beginning to attract tourism. Now, these smaller islands have become models of ecotourism for the more developed islands to follow.

A nature trail in Puerto Rico gives visitors a chance to see beyond tourist traps.

HABITAT LOSS PREVENTION

One of the first steps taken by island administrators, especially on the smaller islands, was to secure the remaining indigenous habitat by establishing wildlife refuges, national parks, forest reserves, and marine parks. These first steps curtailed slash and burn agriculture, poaching, indiscriminate logging, and the felling of trees for charcoal production. Larger islands soon followed suit and have collectively established more protected areas during the last 10 years than in the previous 50.

In 1993 Jamaica, for example, an island considered primarily to be a mass tourist destination of all-inclusive resorts, established its first protected area when it designated almost 81,000 hectares of the Blue and John Crow Mountains as a national park. The park is now one of the largest tracks of protected land in the Caribbean.

The region's conservation efforts have caught the attention and financing of international governments and wildlife and conservationist groups. Some of these programs started as early as 1975. For example, that year the World Wildlife Fund and RARE (a Chicago-based tropical bird conservation group) organized local and international fundraising programs to purchase large tracts of tropical marine forests on three Windward Islands to save endangered parrot species. These programs aimed to educate the people about their environment and why it was important to protect it. They also led to the creation of more than a hundred permanent guide and park ranger positions in the Windwards alone. Not only have the parrots been brought back from the brink of extinction, these islands now take a completely different approach to tourism.

Today local governments, industry, and international groups fund ecotourism infrastructure to promote lower-impact tourism. The success of these conservation programs has contributed to higher awareness of environmental issues throughout the region. As a result, many island administrators solicit international assistance to improve the situations on their islands. Over the last 10 years the U.S. Agency for International Development, the World Wildlife Fund, and the Nature Conservancy have all been active in the region.

Due to the fragmentation of the Caribbean into many small nations, the level of awareness and advancement in matters concerning the environment varies greatly from island to island. Islands with few natural land-based resources left, such as Barbados and Antiqua, are trying to protect their surrounding seas while others, such as Bonaire and St. John, have designated almost their entire land mass and surrounding reefs as protected areas. Cuba has established dozens of protected areas in the last 20 years and has also embarked on an extensive reforestation program. Other countries, such as Guyana and Jamaica, have not yet taken great steps to protect their huge tracks of threatened virgin tropical forest.

HOW YOU CAN HELP

Some of the islands have turned to ecotourism simply to capitalize on the trend, but many environmentalists agree that the region as a whole has turned the corner. More and more governments are actively promoting some form of responsible tourism, and more international help is flowing into the islands. Heightened global interest in the environment coupled with the trend toward active, "go local" travel suggests that future visitors to the Caribbean will more likely want to learn about and engage with their host island and its people rather than lie on a beach all day.

There are a number of local and North American organizations doing conservation work in the Caribbean. Earthwatch, World Wildlife Fund, and RARE are but a few. These groups welcome donations as well as volunteers to help with research and field projects. Contact information on conservation organizations is included in the following destination chapters and the Appendices at the back of the book.

All of the islands, signatories to CITIES (Convention on International Trade in Endangered Species), are working to protect indigenous endangered species. Never buy souvenirs made from any part of an endangered species. Do not purchase sea turtle products or patronize places that peddle them (sea turtle shell jewelry is common and sea turtle meat and eggs are featured on many restaurant menus throughout the Caribbean). The same is true for parrot or parrot products such as feathers. It is best to inform the owners or sellers of such products why you will not do business in their establishment. You can be prosecuted if you are caught with endangered species products when reentering the country.

When you travel the region, try to help out. Tip everyone who made your stay enjoyable, not just your waiter. Pack small items like pencils, pens, note paper, and the like to give to schools you come across. Ten or twenty dollars' worth of pencils or pens goes a long way to help kids at a small rural school, and it will make you feel good about yourself. Sometimes it doesn't take much to make a big difference.

Above all, prepare for your trip by finding out about all the things you should and should not do. Go to the library, surf the Net, and contact organizations active in the region for information. Among the do's and don'ts: Do not feed the wildlife or touch the coral reef. Do stay and eat at locally owned establishments. Don't dwell on the poverty you will surely see; West Indians are a proud people and don't need to be reminded. Do read the Responsible Traveler's Code of Ethics, below.

THE RESPONSIBLE TRAVELER'S CODE OF ETHICS

Most travelers don't give much thought to the impact they will have on the people and places they visit. They consider only whether they will enjoy their trip, not whether the country will enjoy having them. Responsible travelers consider their impact and strive to make it as positive as possible. The following will help you to be a more responsible traveler.

1. Study your destination in advance. Learn as much as you can about the people and place, tour operators, local hotels, and so on. Contact organizations active in the region.

A sign in Dominica urges locals and visitors to help save the Sisserou parrot.

2. Patronize tour operators, hotels, restaurants, and so on that are smaller, locally owned, and environmentally responsible. Check these closely; many "greenwash" their actions and policies.

3. Respect local customs, religions, culture, and lifestyles no matter how strange they may seem to you. Accept the fact that people are different. Don't take a missionary approach and try to change the people or places you've come to visit.

4. Consider the impact you will have simply by being there. Remember how much you are spending on your visit compared with how much your host or guide makes in a year.

5. Present yourself honestly. Don't play the big shot or great adventurer—the media already glamorize Western culture and wealth. Instead, when asked, share information about the social, economic, and environmental issues facing you at home. This will establish common ground with the local people.

6. Remember that the adventure doesn't have to end when you return home. Find a way to help the islanders from back home. Join an environmental group or donate to local conservation projects.

7. Keep in touch with the people you meet. It's easy to say "This place was great! I'll drop you a line," then never do it. By keeping in touch you sustain the positive impact you made.

The extravagant-looking flamingo

FLORA AND FAUNA OF THE CARIBBEAN

3

Because of the islands' topography and geology, the Caribbean is one of the most biologically diverse regions on the planet. Despite the fact that most of the islands are separated by only a few kilometers of water, each has evolved independently. Darwin could have saved himself considerable travel time if he had realized just how diverse these independent habitats were. Perhaps he should have taken note of what Columbus wrote on his first visit to the Caribbean: ". . . all is most beautiful, and filled with trees of a thousand kinds, some so tall they seem to touch the sky. And I am told they never lose their foliage, as I can understand, for I saw them as green and as lovely as they are in Spain in May. Some were flowering, some bearing fruit, and some in another stage, according to their nature. And the nightingale was singing, and there were other birds of a thousand kinds."

To the untrained eye, most of the islands look very similar from a distance. And because they share a tropical climate, it's easy to assume that the plants and animals found on each island are also similar. But the differences far outweigh the similarities. The types of Amazon parrots found in the Windwards, for example, can differ from island to island— even when less than 40 kilometers of water separates the two.

The watery gaps between the islands have almost assured the separate evolution of most animals and birds, but since many plants propagate by wind and water it is not unusual to see similar varieties of flora on each island. Additionally, early indigenous people and European colonists had a hand in spreading plant varieties throughout the islands as well as introducing new animal species. In fact, non-indigenous flora and fauna from all over the world now populate the Caribbean. The breadfruit, a tree originally from Tahiti and today a mainstay in the Caribbean diet, was introduced by Captain Bligh as an inexpensive food supplement for the slaves. The same holds true for the fig and banana trees from the Indian Ocean region. The ferocious mongoose, a civet-like animal native to India, was introduced into the islands to control snake and rodent populations in the sugar cane fields, but has proven deleterious to many endemic bird and animal species.

Entire books have been written about Caribbean flora and fauna (see "Suggested Reading," in Appendix B) and these exhaustive efforts will not be duplicated here. Instead what follows is a general discussion of a few of the species you are most likely to encounter during your adventures into the natural world. Island-specific flora and fauna are covered in the island chapters.

FLORA

As discussed in Chapter 1, there are two main types of Caribbean islands: volcanic and coral. Volcanic islands tend to be mountainous and green. Ideal temperatures, volcanic soils, and regular rain make these islands immensely fertile—so fertile, in fact, that locals must be careful which kind of wood they use for fence posts. More often than not, wooden posts cut from the branches of some trees start growing after being put into the ground!

There is, however, one large misconception regarding the fertility of these volcanic islands: technically, the soils are not fertile. In a tropical ecosystem most nutrients are not in the soil but in a thin layer of vegetation covering the soil. In a rain forest it is the rotting vegetation that sustains growth, not the soil itself. Once plant growth is stripped away, the soil quickly erodes and becomes sterile. Early settlers had to burn discarded crop material and utilize animal manure to keep their crops growing. This soil factor and the lack of a steady supply of fertilizer contributed to the demise of the sugar industry in the Caribbean.

The heavy rainfall characteristic of mountainous volcanic islands forces nutrients down deep into the soil where they benefit mainly the deep, extended root systems of larger trees. This explains why the first explorers found most of the islands covered in rain forests instead of grasslands. Many tree species, along with other indigenous plant and animal species, were nearly eradicated in colonists' efforts to clear the land to plant crops like tobacco and sugar. In some areas of Puerto Rico and Haiti, where slash and burn or clearcutting were implemented, the delicate soils have been forever destroyed. In these areas the soil is so badly eroded it can no longer support plant growth. However, despite this early devastation, visitors will still be dazzled by the endless variety and color of plants found on most areas of the islands.

In contrast to volcanic islands, coral islands are low, flat, brown, and less fertile. Their low hills are not high enough to trap the moist trade winds, and their soils tend to be sandier, poor conditions for rain forests but perfect for scrub and desert flora and fauna.

In addition to timber trees, a wide variety of fruit trees abound on the islands. Red and yellow plums, cherries, and six varieties of citrus were all introduced as supplementary food sources for the slaves. Early settlers, weary of incessantly green forests, imported hundreds of species of flowering trees such as the flamboyant or royal poinciana and the scarlet African tulip, which blossom at different times insuring year-round color on the slopes.

Most islands boast botanical gardens—among the oldest in the Western Hemisphere—where visitors can see these exotic plants, trees, flowers, and spices up close. The oldest, founded in 1765, is on the tiny island of St. Vincent.

The best way to approach a discussion on Caribbean flora is to divide it into its six distinct habitats: coastal beaches, thorny woodlands or dry scrublands, dry grasslands or savannahs, tropical deciduous forest, semi-deciduous forest, and tropical rain forest. The type of island, amount of rainfall and when it falls, and the impact of people determine the type and amount of flora an island can support.

COASTAL BEACHES

The beach habitat is a very specialized and inhospitable piece of real estate. Nutrient-deficient sand or soil, relentless wind, and a steady dose of salt make existence in coastal habitats difficult. But the sea is a great purveyor of seeds and the hardier ones, like coconut, seagrape, and mangrove, thrive in an environment of bountiful sunlight and little competition. As a result, these species can be found on all beaches and coastal areas of the region.

Most of the plants typical to this habitat have broad, thick, fleshy leaves and produce toxins to discourage plant eaters. The palms and seaside almond hold their leaves well above the reaches of foraging animals. Some of the plants found along coastal reaches follow.

Beach morning glory—This creeping vine has erect leaf stalks capped with fleshy leaves and bright pink flowers. Some vines reach

9 meters long and can extend down almost to the water's edge. Sap from this plant may burn skin.

Seagrape—This plant has broad, fleshy fan-like leaves (some 20 centimeters in diameter) and sports clusters of green grape-like fruit. Purple when ripe, the fruit is sour but edible. Plants can grow up to 9 meters high.

Manchineel—Resembling a crab-apple tree with green apple-sized fruit, this plant is highly toxic and should be avoided at all costs. Don't touch, eat, or even shelter under this tree or you run the risk of being badly blistered.

Mangrove—Although all beach plants are an integral part of the beach community, no other plant is as important to this habitat as the mangrove. Its thick cluster of stilt-like roots, capped with tufts of small fleshy leaves, is responsible for trapping much of the tideborne sediment that formed many of the islands, especially the coral ones. The mangrove swamp is the nursery of the sea: its tangled root system provides ideal cover for small marine organisms and fry. There are three common varieties of mangrove in the Caribbean: the red, black, and white Mangrove.

Red mangrove—The most tolerant of salt water, this species can be seen growing well away from the beach or coast. It has red stilt-like roots and drops roots from its branches.

Many Caribbean islands were "built" by red mangroves.

Black mangrove—Usually found behind the reds closer to shore, it has smaller leaves with clusters of small pale green fruit at the end of each branch.

White mangrove—The least tolerant of salt water, it is usually found close to shore behind the red and black varieties. Long oval leaves pointed at both ends surround clusters of small gray-green fruit.

The best place to explore mangroves in depth is in the Bahamas and Turks and Caicos. Most of the islands that make up these groups were formed by mangroves.

Swamp bloodwood—Also found in the mangrove swamp slightly upriver is this magnificent tree. It is characterized by tall, enormous buttressed roots up to 2.4 meters high and 3.6 meters long. The best place to view these giants is along the lower reaches of the Indian River on Dominica.

THORNY WOODLANDS/DRY SCRUBLANDS

The driest habitat found in the Caribbean, it is common on islands that receive less than 76 centimeters of rain annually and are punctuated by long droughts. Cacti and short torn bushes dominate the vegetation. Huge tracts of this type of vegetation can be found in Puerto Rico's dry forest and on the western slopes of the central range in Haiti, but nowhere is it as noticeable as on the Dutch islands of Aruba, Bonaire, and Curaçao. It can also be found on Barbados, in the Bahamas, Virgin Islands, Turks and Caicos Islands, and, to a lesser extent, on the dry leeward coasts of the smaller volcanic islands. Probably the most common form of flora in this habitat is cacti.

Century plant—Similar to a yucca, this plant can grow to a height of 6 meters. It has thick sword-like leaves with serrated edges and a large thorn at its tip. Every 20 years or so it sprouts a gigantic flower stalk with deep yellow flowers. The plant dies after the flower fades.

Aloe—Originating in the Mediterranean, the aloe now flourishes on all dry islands. It looks something like an upside-down octopus. Its medicinal property for treating burns (including sunburn) is legendary.

Cacti—There are many varieties in the islands, including the prickly pear, Turk's cap, and the organ pipe (called *kadushi* in the ABCs).

Acacia—This is the most common of the larger trees in the dry woodland. There are more than 600 species worldwide and many in the Caribbean. In season they sprout a mass of yellow flower balls. At the base of each leaf node with the branch are two long, deadly spines.

Frangipani—This small, sparsely-leaved tree has beautiful, white five-petal flowers that are very fragrant. The large colorful frangipani caterpillar is a resident of these trees.

DRY GRASSLANDS/SAVANNAHS

This type of habitat occurs naturally in areas of hard soils that receive about 76 centimeters of annual rainfall. They are frequently found on the leeward, or rain shadow, side of coastal mountains. Prior to Columbus' arrival, there were naturally occurring grasslands on only a few of the larger islands, such as Trinidad and Cuba, and in Guyana. Today, largely due to deforestation, they are found on many islands. Grasslands contain a variety of seasonal drought-resistant grasses and low-lying shrubs or trees.

Razor grass—Aptly named, this species sports tufts of tall bright-green grass with serrated leaf edges that can cut careless hands or unprotected legs.

Sugar cane—Introduced from eastern Asia, sugar cane now grows throughout the islands. The long, sectioned woody stem contains sweet sap. Most of the wild clumps seen growing are not as sweet as those of the cultivated type.

Wild cane—This looks like sugar cane and reaches a height of 3 meters. It's definitely not sweet so don't try to eat it.

Calabash—This species has long, straight wand-like branches with clusters of small leaves. Along these branches grow gourd-like fruit that can reach about 30 centimeters in diameter. The skin of the fruits has been used for centuries to make bowls and containers.

Tamarind—Introduced from India, this tree now grows everywhere. It's a bushy tree with branches that contain very small oblong leaves. Quite noticeable on the tree are brown lumpy fruit pods from 10 centimeters long. The pulp around the seeds inside these pods is tart but enjoyable. It is used to flavor many local dishes.

Screw pine—Not actually a pine and closer to a palm, this species grows in clumps of long, ribbed stems with tufts of grass-like leaves. The leaves have barbed edges and can deliver a nasty cut. The plant originated in the Mediterranean but is now widespread throughout the islands. The leaves when dried are used by locals to make straw hats and bags.

TROPICAL DECIDUOUS FOREST

Habitats that receive between 101 and 127 centimeters of rain a year are able to support larger trees in "dry," or deciduous, forests. These forests are sparse and punctuated by dense thorny clearings amid small groups of 60-meter-high trees that drop their leaves every dry season. They are especially common on the leeward coasts of the smaller volcanic islands. Many of the trees found in the dry scrublands also fair well in this environment, and even some of the trees found mainly in the semi-deciduous habitats can be found here. It is the transitional zone between the wet and dry forests.

Mango—Most likely originated in India, this tree is now widespread throughout the islands. There are hundreds of varieties of this densely foliaged tree, and the pear-sized fruit is a delight at any time.

Guava—This is a short, crooked-branched shrub with small, round green fruit that turns yellowish when ripe. The fruit is a favorite of locals, who turn it into guava cheese and jam.

Logwood—This small shrublike tree was imported into the Caribbean as a source of black dye, which is derived from its heartwood. Originally from Mexico, it blooms large clusters of yellow flowers from December to May.

Tropical deciduous forest of pine trees and logwood

SEMI-DECIDUOUS FOREST

Semi-deciduous forests require between 127 and 177 centimeters of rain a year and deep soils. These forests typify the lowland areas and border the rain forests. Not found above 900 meters, they usually occupy the leeward slopes of the big islands. This type of forest is representative of the forests on most of the volcanic islands.

Within this type of forest are two leaf canopies: one at about 18 meters and the other at about 6 meters. Some of the trees that form the higher canopy are mahogany, banyan (from Ceylon), bamboo, and some of the larger palms including the "mountain cabbage" and "royal palm," which can attain heights of more than 30 meters. Making up the lower canopy are small tropical pines, cedars, guava, and naseberry (the basis of chewing gum). About half the species in this forest shed their leaves during the dry season.

Bamboo—Resembling giant reeds, bamboo can reach a height of 12 meters. It was introduced to the islands about two centuries ago from many origins. It is used widely for building material, and the smaller stems are used for fishing poles.

Cecropia—This is a large tree with immense seven-leaflet leaves. The leaves have silver undersides that stand out against the dark green background when blowing in the wind.

Mountain cabbage—Found at the higher levels, this palm grows up to 15 meters.

Swiss cheese plant—There are more than 30 species throughout the Caribbean of this most recognizable of the aroids. It is a tree climber with huge elephant-ear-like leaves riddled with holes.

Philodendron—Like the Swiss cheese plant, this too is a tree climber with large heart-shaped leaves.

TROPICAL RAIN FOREST

The tropical rain forest is found primarily on lower windward slopes below 900 meters where rainfall can exceed 380 centimeters annually. These forests support three distinct tree canopy levels, with the top level at about 36.5 meters. They contain an abundance of hardwood trees including the chataigner, gommier, and the tallest tree in the islands: the West Indian mahogany. The size and quality of these hardwoods are the very things that threaten their survival. Most of the islands and Guyana permit logging. On the slopes above 900 meters, rain forests give way to mountain or mist forests with prehistoric-looking tree ferns, bromeliads, and trumpet trees. Above 1,215 meters, the mist forest gives way to elfin woodland and alpine grass (a tundra-like vegetation).

Gommier—This tree has a deep root system and a small buttressed base. The thick gray bark yields an aromatic gum when damaged or cut. The gum is used as incense and the fruit it bears is eaten by parrots. Because of its length and straightness it was the tree the Caribs most often used for making canoes.

Tree fern—Like giant umbrellas these magnificent ferns can grow to be 6 meters high or more. A straight thick stem is topped with delicate fronds, most of which are uncoiled but some are coiled like those New Year's Eve party favors you blow through to extend.

Heliconia—Known locally as "crab claws," these come in many varieties. Related to the banana, they have large paddle-shaped leaves and bright yellow or red flowers.

FAUNA

Although the trade winds and Gulf Stream played a major role in spawning the diversity of flora on the islands, it is unlikely they assisted much with the fauna. The islands are habitat to hundreds of species of reptiles and birds—Cuba alone has over 300 species—but there are few mammals. Except for a few varieties found on Trinidad, such as the squirrel, brocket

The Oldest Gardens in the Western Hemisphere

Just north of St. Vincent's capital, Kingstown, lie the St. Vincent Botanical Gardens. Founded by Dr. George Young in 1765, they are the oldest botanical gardens in the Western Hemisphere.

In the early 1700s England's Royal Agricultural Society, anxious to acquire new species from the Caribbean, offered cash prizes and awards to anyone finding and growing important varieties of tropical plants. Newly discovered varieties were sent to the Royal Botanic Gardens at Kew, England, for study and display. In an effort to attract the prize money and Royal Society recognition, Dr. Young established the gardens.

Soon Dr. Young and the gardens gained great acclaim, and the gardens became the main quarantine staging area for Caribbean endemic plant species before being sent to Kew gardens. When his grant money ran out, Dr. Young started cultivating exotic flowers as well as a variety of valuable commercial plants like herbs and spices, which he exported to England. Some of the plants first propagated in the gardens were medicinal plants such as aloe and cinchona and spices including allspice, nutmeg, ginger, and cinnamon.

In 1773 Dr. Young returned to England and the gardens fell into ruin—Governor William Leyborne even grazed his livestock in them. Things started to improve for the St. Vincent Gardens when Alex Anderson volunteered to take Dr. Young's place. He was still curator when Captain William Bligh sailed into Kingstown harbor on January 23, 1793, on board the HMS *Providence* with its cargo of 530 breadfruit trees destined for the colonists. Bligh was so impressed with Anderson's work that he donated 50 plants. A third-generation tree from one of the original plants still grows in the gardens.

Today the gardens cater mostly to local needs for decorative flowers and ornamental and fruit trees, but they are also still home to a few exotic trees like the famous breadfruit tree and spachea perforata, *found only on St. Vincent.*

deer, armadillo, and bats and rodents, which are numerous throughout the islands, few other mammal species survived the crossing from South America. Fauna in the islands are adapted to the various habitats found on the islands.

BIRDS

Along the coast you will find a wide variety of shore birds and soaring birds. Most are large and, without the dense vegetation, easy to see.

Magnificent frigate bird—This large black bird has a formidable hooked bill and a wingspan of 2.5 meters. The short forked tail opens and closes during flight like a pair of scissors. Males have a strip of pink skin on the throat that they blow up like a balloon during mating season to attract females. Females have white breasts and sides. They nest in colonies, the largest of which can be found in Barbuda's Cordrington Lagoon.

Scarlet ibis—A wading bird found primarily in coastal swamps of Trinidad and Guyana, as the name implies it is deep red in color and stands about 60 centimeters. Each evening, in Trinidad's Caroni swamp, the ibis return by the hundreds from their daily foraging to roost. It is one of the more spectacular bird sights in the Caribbean.

Further inland, between the coast and the rain forest, the birds are smaller and adapted to the drier habitat.

Tropical mockingbird—This shy, medium-sized bird is about 25 centimeters long with a gray head and white-edged wings and tail. The underparts are white with white around the eyes. Ranging from Hispaniola to Grenada, it's probably the "nightingale" that Columbus wrote about on his first voyage.

 Flamingo—This large, graceful pink wading bird uses its oddly hooked bill to strain brine shrimp from the water. It is found primarily in drier swamp areas and near salt ponds on Great Inagua in the Bahamas, Anegada in the British Virgin Islands, swamps along Cuba's southern coast, and on Curaçao and Bonaire in the Dutch Antilles.

As you move inland where the habitat supports larger trees and a larger variety of flowering plants, the birdlife explodes. This habitat is packed with hummingbirds, warblers, bananaquits, doves, and bullfinches.

Green-throated Carib—This 10-centimeter-long hummingbird is most common. It's all green except for the dark tail and breast, which is violet. Its color, as that of most hummingbirds, changes depending on the angle at which sunlight hits it. The resulting rainbow of color is similar to the effect of oil on water. These birds feed mainly on nectar.

Bananaquit—Ten centimeters long and very active, this bird is abundant in the islands. It communicates in wheezy squeaks and feeds on nectar and insects. Dark in color with bright yellow bellies and backs with slender curved bills, it is also a favorite pet bird in the islands and seems to do well in captivity.

Deeper in the rain forest the birds get larger again. Here you will find the rare parrots and macaws, toucans, and the magnificent Guianan cock-of-the-rock.

Amazon parrot—There are six species of Amazon parrots remaining in the islands and all are on the CITIES endangered list. Fewer than 500 St. Lucian, St. Vincent, Puerto Rican, and Bahamian Amazons remain and fewer than 100 of Dominica's two species. The largest and most endangered Amazon in the world is the imperial parrot, in Dominica; only about 30 breeding pairs remain. Needless to say, wild sightings of these birds are rare but most of the islands have captive breeding programs and aviaries where you can see them. Two of the best places to see wild parrots is the Buccament Valley in St. Vincent and the Soufrière Valley in St. Lucia.

Red-necked pigeon—This is the largest dove in the Caribbean, measuring some 38 centimeters in length. It is dark gray with a purple head and red throat patch. Found on most islands with rain forest habitat, it has a different local name on every island. It is a prized eating bird and threatened on many islands. On some islands it is now protected.

REPTILES AND AMPHIBIANS

Reptiles are one of the animals that have successfully colonized the islands over the years. Some probably drifted in on vegetation rafts (a clump of vegetation, a log, or a downed-tree) from other areas and some may date back to a time when land bridges connected some of the islands. The wide variety of reptiles, found in all habitats and on all islands, includes snakes, iguanas, tree and ground lizards, toads and frogs, skinks, turtles and sea turtles, and caiman crocodiles.

Sea turtle—Some six species live in the Caribbean, the most common being the hawksbill, green, loggerhead, and the largest of all species, the leatherback. All are endangered in the Caribbean. Although efforts are underway to protect them, sea turtles are still slaughtered for their flesh, shell, and eggs. You will see the odd hawksbill and green turtle while diving the shallow reefs, but all species can be observed May and October when the females come ashore on soft sand beaches to lay eggs. Some of the best places to see hawksbills and greens is on Long Island off Antigua, the Turks and Caicos, the smaller Bahamian out islands, and in the Grenadines of St. Vincent. Matura beach in Trinidad is the spot for loggerheads and leatherbacks.

A meter-long iguana on Bonaire

Iguana—Of the several varieties that make their home in the Caribbean, the largest iguana is the green, which can reach almost 2 meters in length. This throwback to the dinosaur age is still widely hunted for food, and though its numbers may appear abundant they are actually slowly reaching endangered levels on many of the islands.

Giant toad—Introduced from South America to rid the sugar cane fields of insects, these large dark brown toads have reached the status of pest in most of the islands. When attacked, this hardy toad secretes poison from glands behind the eyes that can cause blindness and even kill a large dog. The toad forages at night and hides during the day. The animal is known by many names in the islands.

Coquí, or **piping frog**—Less than 2.5 centimeters, this light brown frog is one of the smallest animals in the Caribbean, yet it packs a loud call. Its high-pitched two-note call can be heard over most other forest calls and is often mistaken for a bird call. It has webbed feet with suction discs used for climbing trees. It is found only on Cuba, Puerto Rico, Jamaica, and a few islands in the Lesser Antilles.

Fer-de-lance—This highly poisonous pit viper is the most deadly of the region's snakes. With a diamond-shaped head and dark body that can reach a length of about 2.5 meters, it is a formidable predator in the rain forest. Its venom can kill an adult within hours, so avoid it at all costs. It hunts at night in the Windward and the larger French islands.

MAMMALS

Mammals are not good colonizers and the watery channels between islands were serious obstacles to migration. Many of the mammals on the islands today were introduced by human immigrants. Endemic species include the manatee, agouti, armadillo, opossum, and some bats.

Agouti—This dark brown oversized rodent looks like a cross between a guinea pig and a rabbit. It lives in burrows or hollow logs and forages along the forest floor. It is shy and has been hunted to near extinction on many islands. The best places to see agoutis are on the larger mountainous Windward Islands. The agouti is also known as coney or *hutia*.

Manatee—Weighing up to 1,300 pounds and reaching about 3.6 meters in length, these large sea mammals are closely related to the elephant. These pudgy creatures have grayish-brown skin and blunt, wrinkled faces. They are usually found eating marine vegetation close to shore in quiet lagoons and brackish backwaters. Their numbers have been drastically reduced in the region because of hunting and pollution, but you can still see them lumbering about along Puerto Rico's southeast coast and in Cuba and Hispaniola.

Mongoose—This brown mammal resembling the ferret is the most commonly seen wild animal in the islands. It was originally introduced from India to control the rodent population in cane fields. Today it is the scourge of endemic bird and reptile species and is a major carrier of rabies. Since sugar was planted on most islands, mongoose inhabit most forests. Only on Dominica, where no sugar was planted, are there no mongoose.

MARINE LIFE

There are thousands of miles of pristine coral reefs in the Caribbean. Great reefs surround all the islands, but those of the Bahamas, Turks and Caicos, Virgin Islands, Caymans, Grenadines, and the ABCs are renowned worldwide for their variety and beauty. These islands are a diver's or snorkeler's paradise but can also be explored by glass-bottom boat and submarine. Coral reefs are marine forests offering even more diversity than their land-based cousins the rain forests. Thousands of varieties of coral, fish, mollusks, sponges, and anemones make their home in the reefs.

Snorkeling at Big Knip Beach in Curaçao

SPECIAL INTERESTS AND ACTIVITIES

4

One of the things that makes adventuring in the Caribbean so worthwhile is the diversity of adventures and activities available to the nature enthusiasts. Some of the best diving, snorkeling, hiking, spelunking, sea kayaking, birding, and natural history in the world can be found in the islands. Sure, there are nightclubs, big tourism resorts, and cruise ships disgorging hundreds of people at a time, but there are also hundreds of uninhabited islands, mountains where it snows in winter, some of the largest cavern systems in the world, spectacular secluded beaches, and rain forests that have never felt a human footstep.

The purpose of this chapter is to help you narrow your selection of an island or group of islands for your next Caribbean trip. Following are some of the most popular activities and adventures the Caribbean has to offer. Each activity section lists the islands recommended for that specific activity. For reliable operators, outfitters, and guides providing these activities, see the "Outfitters and Guides" section within each island chapter.

MARINE ADVENTURES

DIVING, SNORKELING, AND SNUBA
All the superlatives you can think of would fall short of describing the diving and snorkeling possibilities in the Caribbean. Three of the top five diving destinations in the Western Hemisphere—if not the world—are

located in the eastern Caribbean, according to recent ratings published in several diving magazines.

While most major international diving destinations specialize in one or two types of diving, such as ledges or deep drop-offs, shallow reef, warm water, night diving, or wreck diving, few offer the concentration of multiple specialties that the Caribbean does. The region's geological formation and history is the reason for its wide variety of diving sites. As discussed in Chapter 1, some islands are but the tops of submerged mountains (great ledges or drop-offs) while others are exposed sea beds (shallow reef diving). And given all the shipping activity during the colonization period, it's no surprise that many ships ended up on the bottom. In fact, storms, reefs, and pirates have given the region the highest concentration of ship wrecks in the world, except possibly the Mediterranean.

With water temperatures averaging 25 degrees Celsius in the winter and 30 degrees Celsius in the summer, only the lightest bodysuit is necessary. Add to this excellent visibility (25 to 40 meters near shore and 50 meters further out) and marine life second to none, and it's hard to find a bad diving or snorkeling spot in the islands. As diving is the most popular adventure sport in the Caribbean, visitors needn't worry about finding the right island or dive operator to satisfy their needs.

A popular alternative for those not yet certified is to take the time to get certified while on your Caribbean adventure. On every island you will find licensed operators offering NAUI or PADI certification in less than a week. Most operators are flexible, and certification can be arranged around your other nature activities.

Shallow Reef Diving and Snorkeling

Shallow reef diving and snorkeling are usually done in waters between 5 and 20 meters deep. The waters around the Dutch Antilles of Aruba, Curaçao, and Bonaire (the ABCs) fit this category to a tee. Bonaire coastal waters have all been designated a marine sanctuary and offer especially great beach dive sites and miles of shallow reefs teeming with protected marine life. Another top spot is along the long strands of barrier reefs that surround the Grenadines of St. Vincent.

Wreck Diving

Conservative estimates put the number of Caribbean wrecks at around 700, excluding those that occurred during the last 50 years. Given that the islands form a natural barrier to ships entering or leaving the Caribbean and that treacherous reef formations surround all the islands, it's a wonder more ships didn't go down. Throw in a few tropical storms each year and dozens of pirates and buccaneers and maybe the estimate

The Best Islands For . . .

Most of the islands covered in this book offer similar opportunities for nature lovers, but certain islands stand out when it comes to specific outdoor activities. (All activities are discussed in more detail in this chapter and in the destination chapters that follow.)

Diving - Shallow reef diving: Bonaire; Wreck diving: British Virgin Islands; Big drop-offs and ledge diving: Windwards; Night diving: Grenadines

Snorkeling - Aruba, Bonaire, Curaçao, Grenadines

Snuba - U.S. Virgin Islands

Sport Fishing - Big game (marlin, sailfish, etc.): Cuba, Puerto Rico, U.S. Virgin Islands; Shallow water and reef fishing: British Virgin Islands, Grenadines, Aruba, Bonaire, Curaçao

Sailing - U.S. Virgin Islands, British Virgin Islands, Antigua

Sea Kayaking - Trinidad, U.S. Virgin Islands, British Virgin Islands, Dominica

Whale Watching - Dominican Republic, U.S. Virgin Islands, Puerto Rico, British Virgin Islands

Hiking - Mountainous hikes: French Antilles, Dominica, St. Vincent, Dominican Republic; Volcano Hikes: St. Vincent, Martinique, Guadeloupe; Tropical rain forest hikes: Trinidad, St. Vincent, Dominica, Guadeloupe; Dry woodland walks: Bonaire, Dominican Republic, Cuba

Birding - General birding: Cuba, Jamaica, Trinidad, Puerto Rico; Rare birds: Windward Islands, French Antilles

Wildlife Viewing - Jamaica, Cuba, Puerto Rico, Trinidad

Mountain Biking - U.S. Virgin Islands, St. Vincent, French Antilles

River Rafting - Dominican Republic, Puerto Rico, Jamaica

Cave Exploring - Cuba, Puerto Rico, Jamaica

falls short of the true number. The British Virgin Islands (BVIs) have probably the highest concentration of ship wrecks in the world (over 250 around Anegada alone). The U.S. Virgins (USVIs) and St. Vincent and the Grenadines also have their share of old wrecks. Within the last 20 years various island governments have sunk old boats and ships in an effort to create artificial reefs and diving spots.

Big Drop-Offs and Ledges

Drop-offs occur where the seabed plunges to the depths forming walls of marine life instead of reefs. Typically islands with rugged topography usually have deep-water drop-offs fairly close to shore. The Windward Islands, USVIs, and the French Antilles (Martinique and Guadeloupe) head the list for this type of diving.

Night Diving and Snorkeling

Night diving is usually done in depths of 25 meters or less in water with plenty of reefs or abundant marine life. Though typically good all over the Caribbean, Bonaire, all the Virgin Islands, and the barrier reefs in the Grenadines offer spectacular night diving and snorkeling.

Snuba

A cross between scuba and snorkeling, "snuba" is catching on fast. Similar to old-style diving sans the big, heavy helmet, it involves wearing a mask that fits over your entire face and a long breathing hose connected to the surface, down which air is forced enabling you to visit the reefs close up for an hour instead of for one- or two-minute snorkeling forays. Although the underwater range is limited to about 15 meters, it gets snorkelers off the surface and closer to the marine life, with only an hour of instruction. St. John in the USVIs is the number one snuba destination.

SPORT FISHING

The deep trenches surrounding many of the Greater Antilles offer some of the best deep-sea fishing in the world. The currents through these deep marine trenches stir up nutrient-rich waters from the deep that attract clouds of phytoplankton and bait fish, which in turn are hotly pursued by such big-game fish as tuna, marlin, kingfish, and sailfish. Big-game hot spots are Cuba, Puerto Rico, Jamaica, the USVIs, and the BVIs. Each year these and other islands hold sport-fishing tournaments with prizes in the tens of thousands of dollars.

The broad, flat, shallow coastal waters surrounding most coral or limestone islands are ideal for shallow-water and reef fishing. Anegada, in the BVIs, is great for flats fishing for tarpon, bonefish, and permit while the Grenadines, ABCs, and the Leewards are hot spots for bonita, barracuda, and crevalle.

Freshwater fishing is confined to the larger islands with freshwater lakes and larger rivers, such as Cuba, Puerto Rico, the Dominican Republic, and Trinidad. Most of these islands have implemented fish restocking programs, and the lakes and rivers on some islands are catch and release only. Most fishing operators supply equipment, but it is best to check before leaving.

SAILING

The calm waters of the Caribbean, along with the endless supply of 20-knot trade winds, translates into great sailing. Each year there are no less than 40 international sailing regattas attracting hundreds of entries from all around the world. If you have sailed before or carry a sailing certification, you can bareboat it (rent a boat and sail it yourself). Those without sailing experience can charter (rent a boat with a captain). The captains usually cook and pilot the boat while you crew. A third option is to take a cruise on a fully staffed boat; all you do is sit back and enjoy. Many charter boats and cruises offer fishing, diving, snorkeling, and sailing certification as part of the sailing package. The last option allows you to learn sailing while enjoying a sailing vacation. Sailboats can range in size from 8 to 15 meters with the typical cruiser averaging 12 meters and sleeping six. When expenses are shared among six people, the weekly rate is usually less expensive than hotel rates.

The largest bareboat and charter fleet in the Caribbean, and probably the world, is based in the BVIs. With more than 60 different islands and cays to explore, it's no wonder the fleet is so large—more than 400 boats. Other good bets are Antigua, the USVIs, and the Grenadines.

SEA KAYAKING

Sea kayaking is becoming very popular in the Caribbean. The combination of warm water, narrow channels between islands, calm leeward coasts, and mangrove-lined estuaries makes for ideal paddling. Exploring coastal mangrove

Sea kayaks at Pomato Point Beach in the British Virgin Islands

51

swamps, especially those on larger islands, is really only possible by boat or kayak and is popular with birders. Although most islands offer kayak rentals as part of their water-sport offerings, the premier sea-kayaking destinations are the BVIs, the USVIs, and Dominica. Operators on these islands offer multiday trips through or around the islands. Trinidad is tops for kayaking trips through coastal mangrove swamps, backwaters, and estuaries.

WHALE WATCHING

Between 2,000 and 3,000 humpbacks winter in the Caribbean each year, preferring the narrow deep water channels of the Greater Antilles and the quiet bays of larger islands. The best spot to view them is on the Dominican Republic's northeast coast, along the Samaná Peninsula. Whale-watching tours are also available from Puerto Rico, the USVIs, and BVIs.

LAND ADVENTURES

Land adventures in the Caribbean include hiking, birding, camping, mountain biking, river rafting, spelunking, cascading, and canyoning. All the islands offer at least one good land-based activity to match your level of fitness and sense of adventure. They range from easy to moderate on the difficulty scale and from one hour to one week in duration.

The larger islands of the Greater Antilles tend to offer a greater diversity of land-based activities, due in large part to the diversity of their topography and geology. Smaller islands tend to have specialties in certain activities.

HIKING

The various types of terrain and vegetation zones in the Caribbean offer a great choice of hiking options. Islands with higher elevations are characterized by more strenuous mountain trekking through lush tropical rain and elfin forests while the flatter islands tend to favor less strenuous hikes through dry woodlands and deciduous forests. Longer, more difficult mountain hikes are characteristic of such larger islands as Cuba, Jamaica, and the Dominican Republic.

A few of the small and mountainous islands such as Guadeloupe and Martinique, in the French Antilles, and Dominica and St. Vincent, in the Windwards, also offer outstanding mountain hiking. These islands have large tracts of primary tropical rain forests along with other vegetation zones. The USVIs, St. Kitts and Nevis, and Puerto Rico offer less strenuous rain forest and mountain hikes, but most of the vegetation is second-growth deciduous not primary rain forest. Grenada, St. Lucia, and Trinidad offer moderately difficult hikes with some primary rain forests.

Hiking at Boca Prins sand dunes, Aruba

Dry woodland walks, which tend to be found near the coasts and on smaller flatter islands, are popular with birders because of the variety of forest dwellers and shore birds found in fairly close proximity. Many of these areas include coastal mangrove swamps, which also contain some of the last American crocodiles and manatees remaining in the Caribbean. The southwest coasts of Puerto Rico, the Dominican Republic, and Cuba have large tracts of dry woodlands bordering coastal mangrove swamps. The Dutch Antilles are flat, dry islands with large tracts of dry woodland and cacti forests and abundant desert-type wildlife.

BIRDING

Since most of the islands have various vegetation zones and topography, and are situated along the Atlantic flyway, the region is rich in birdlife. Top this off with each island's unique set of evolutionary conditions and you get hundreds of different bird species, found nowhere else in the world.

The larger islands support a larger variety of species, but the smaller islands tend to have rarer, more exotic species. For example, Cuba, Jamaica, the Dominican Republic, and Trinidad support large numbers of species while the smaller islands of the Lesser Antilles such as Martinique, Dominica, Guadeloupe, St. Lucia, and St. Vincent offer glimpses of such rare

birds as the endangered Windward Island parrot. The Caribbean flamingo can be seen in the ABCs, BVIs, Cuba, and the Dominican Republic.

CAMPING

Environmental concerns and scarcity of undeveloped land mean there are few camping facilities in the islands. Although many islands allow independent camping on beaches or in some parks, most sites are very basic, with little or no security, no water or toilet facilities, and no cooking areas (open fires are not permitted on most islands). What good sites there are seem to be always full, with tents pitched so close together that tent lines overlap. Many outfitters provide camping as part of their overnight trips and take care of all the basics.

Permanent sites that offer more security, have fully equipped canvas tents on permanent wooden platforms, and are more environmentally friendly are becoming quite popular. Puerto Rico, the USVIs, BVIs, Martinique, Guadeloupe, and St. Vincent offer good camping.

MOUNTAIN BIKING

The rugged terrain on most islands puts mountain biking out of reach for all but the very fit. Nevertheless, it is popular on the smaller islands such as Martinique, Guadeloupe, St. Vincent, the BVIs, and the USVIs, where terrain is less steep. The Dominican Republic, Jamaica, and Puerto Rico offer more strenuous trails. It is not advisable to bring your own bike unless you are visiting the larger islands via a direct international flight. Some of the smaller regional airlines servicing the smaller islands don't allow bikes on board, or if they do, charge an arm and a leg for transporting it—more than the cost of renting a bike once you get there. Most islands have cycling clubs that offer weekly biking tours, so it is always best to check with them first before booking with a tour operator.

RIVER RAFTING

Only a few islands have rivers large and long enough to offer good white-water rafting. Jamaica, Puerto Rico, and the Dominican Republic are the only islands offering white-water rafting, but Cuba will soon have runs on three southern rivers. Jamaica offers a type of activity called "river rafting" that is actually done on bamboo rafts on flat meandering rivers. Each raft is made of several lengths of bamboo (about five meters long) lashed together, propelled downstream by a guide using a long bamboo pole.

SPELUNKING, CANYONING, AND CASCADING

Some of the longest cave systems in the world are found in the Greater Antilles. Cuba, Puerto Rico, the Dominican Republic, and Jamaica have vast tracts of raised limestone deposits that have eroded to form a karst topography. Over the years, rainwater and underground rivers have carved out large underground caverns through much of these karst regions, making them ideal for spelunking. Sinkholes (the collapsed ceilings of some caverns) have provided access to these extensive underground systems where visitors rappel down to explore the caverns and sometimes "tube" or float underground rivers through cavern systems.

Cascading, which is no more than rappelling down a waterfall, and canyoning, rappelling down canyon walls to reach caves or swimming holes, is usually done in tandem with spelunking. Cuba, Puerto Rico, the Dominican Republic, and Jamaica are best for all three activities while canyoning and cascading are popular on Guadeloupe and Martinique.

Canyoning in the Dominican Republic

© Rancho Baiguate

OTHER ACTIVITIES

Horseback riding is popular on every island with some, such as the USVIs and Jamaica, offering rain forest trips by horseback. Windsurfing is also commonplace on most islands, but Aruba, with its constant and dependable trade winds, is the windsurfing capital of the Caribbean and a popular international windsurfing competition spot.

Volunteer conservation programs are still new to the Caribbean, but some, such as the turtle watch program in Trinidad and the parrot programs in the Windwards, are becoming more popular. Earthwatch, the Peace Corps, the World Wildlife Fund, and a number of religious organizations also offer limited volunteer programs in the islands. Check the Appendix at the back of the book for information on conservation groups.

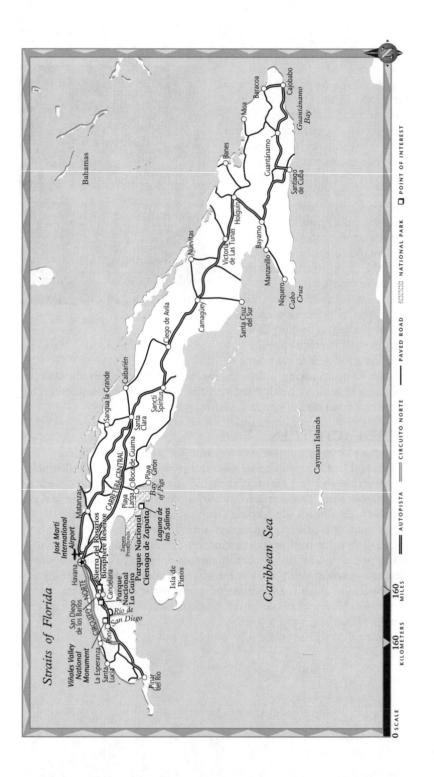

5

CUBA

Cuba, 1,250 kilometers long and 191 kilometers wide, is one of the largest islands in the world (about the size of England) and dominates the Caribbean landscape. At more than 114,478 square kilometers and with a population of almost 11 million, it accounts for almost half of the Caribbean's total land mass and population. Lying only 145 kilometers south of Key West, Florida, Cuba is the only remaining communist country in the Western Hemisphere.

Almost a third of the island is mountainous and the land rises gradually along a west-to-east axis. Along the north coast, from the western tip of the island to the capital city, Havana, run the Sierra de los Organos and Sierra del Rosarios. Reaching elevations of 700 meters, they form the Cordillera de Guaniguanico range. The fertile plains to the south of this mountain range are Cuba's premier tobacco-growing areas. Stretching along the central region of the island (from Matanzas east to Sancti Spíritus) are the Sierra Escambray, rising to 1,100 meters. Finally, in the south, stretching between Cabo Cruz and Guantánamo Bay are the rugged Sierra Maestra, where the island's highest peak, Pico Turquino, tops 1,870 meters.

Since the fall of eastern block communism Cuban politics has mellowed, but the failure of the sugar industry (the eastern block imported most of Cuba's sugar) coupled with the U.S. economic embargo has brought considerable hardship to the island. In an attempt to offset these hardships and acquire much needed foreign currency, Cuba embarked on an optimistic tourism program. Although this has led mainly to mass tourism and large resorts, steady progress has been made in the ecotourism sector. Luckily, mass tourism is confined to two or three main resort areas.

Environmental problems have added to Cuba's hardships; pollution and deforestation are the main culprits. When Columbus first set foot on the island, more than 90 percent was forested. By 1960 less than 15 percent of the forests remained, and only about half of that comprised endemic species, mostly semi-deciduous with a smattering of rain forest. In 1970 the government took steps to slow the rate of deforestation in an effort to save the remaining endemic forests and satisfy the people's need for timber. This conservation effort, along with other environmental education programs, increased woodlands to about 20 percent by 1980. But as most of Cuba's timber was supplied by the former Soviet Union, the collapse of that country all but cut off Cuba's supply of imported timber and the rate of deforestation skyrocketed. With the forests again under threat, the Cuban government initiated an aggressive reforestation program called the Manati Plan. Since then more than 700,000 hectares have been replanted and today Cuba is one of the few countries that has actually increased their forested areas in the last 10 years.

Because of its large size, Cuba supports thousands of varieties of flora and fauna. There are almost 400 bird species ranging in size and type from the 1.25-meter-high flamingo to the smallest bird in the world, the endangered hummingbird, *Mellisuga helenae*. This active four-centimeter-long bird is affectionately called *zunzuncito*, for the sound it makes when in flight, or *pájaro mosca*, "fly bird," for its size. Besides unique bird species Cuba boasts the world's smallest frog (*Sminthillus limbatus)* and bat (the moth or butterfly bat) as well as a few of the world's largest reptiles, including the crocodile. The forests also support small deer, *jutías*, and the endangered *solenodon*, an indigenous insectivorous rat-like mammal with large padded feet and a long snout.

Although the island's ecotourism programs are still in their infancy, there is plenty to please those seeking adventures in nature without the masses. There are still large tracts of undisturbed coastline, offshore cays, coral reefs, caves, forests, and mangrove swamps virtually untouched by *yanquis* (visitors), and, despite what you have heard or read, most are accessible to visitors. Just don't expect to find amenities like interpretive or visitors centers, park maps, organized campsites, marked trails, and the like, which one may find in parks on some of the other islands, such as Puerto Rico and Dominica. However, the recent creation of a new government organization, The National Ecotourism Group, should help address these problems. The group's mandate is to promote and develop Cuba's parks and reserves for eco-enthusiasts.

Camping in Cuba

What the Cubans call "camping" is very different from North Americans' idea of it. For Cubans camping is going to a cabaña in the mountains or the beach. We call that going to the cottage for the weekend. As a result there are few official campsites (a few are listed in this chapter). But don't be discouraged. If done with subtlety you will not be bothered. Some campismos, Cuban summer camps, will allow you to pitch a tent among their cabañas for a small fee. Unless you are a camping fanatic, leave your tent at home; rooms are inexpensive.

In short, Cuba's natural areas are largely unexplored, the island is ruggedly beautiful, inexpensive, and safe, and the people are among the friendliest in the Caribbean. If you want a friendly, uncomplicated nature experience without the masses, put Cuba near the top of your list.

The sights recommended in this chapter are located in two of Cuba's most beautiful provinces: **Pinar del Río** and **Matanzas**. Pinar del Río is Cuba's westernmost and third largest province (11,000 square kilometers). The landscape is dominated by the 175-kilometer-long **Cordillera de Guaniguanico** mountain chain. This is Cuba's primary tobacco-growing region, producing some of the finest tobacco in the world.

Matanzas, Cuba's second largest province, lies east of Havana. It encompasses an area from Matanzas east to Corralillo (about 115 kilometers) and stretches from the main tourist area of Varadero, on the northern coast, to the Zapata Peninsula, on the southern coast.

Cuba History

Cuba's history, like much of the Caribbean's, has been splattered with violence. Within a few decades of Columbus' landing on the island in October of 1492, the Spanish had systematically wiped out the indigenous native population of Taino and Ciboney. As Spain's major New World base for forays into gold-rich Central and South America, Cuba was frequently attacked by other European powers (or pirates acting for European powers). The last major invasion was undertaken by the

British in 1762. Throughout the 1800s there were numerous civil wars and slave rebellions against the Spanish, culminating in an intervention by the United States in 1899. After a brief war the Spanish surrendered, paving the way for Cuban independence in 1902. Over the next 50 years the island was rocked by riots, rebellions, and coups until Fidel Castro took power in 1959.

HAVANA
The island's capital city, Havana, is the oldest city in the Caribbean and one of the oldest in the Western Hemisphere (one or two cities in Brazil are thought to be slightly older). Founded in July of 1515 as **San Cristobal de la Havana**, it quickly became Spain's main port in the New World and today is the largest city in the eastern Caribbean (population 2.2 million). Havana's metropolitan area is divided into five sections, the most famous of which is **La Habana Vieja**, or Old Havana. It is without a doubt the most beautiful city in the Caribbean and probably the best remaining example of Spanish architecture in all the Americas. Old Havana is so unique that in 1982 it was declared a UNESCO World Heritage Site, and each year millions of dollars of international aid flows into the city to restore some of the older buildings, baroque cathedrals, and colonial palaces. As you stroll the tree-lined cobblestone streets, you can't help but feel that this is the most peaceful, clean (street sweepers clean the streets each day), and friendly city you will find anywhere in Latin America.

Things to See and Do in Havana
There are no significant natural sites in or around Havana, but since most flights arrive and depart Cuba in Havana, it would be a shame not to spend one or two days exploring this great old city. Many of the older buildings in Old Havana have been converted into historical sites or museums and dozens more are under restoration by international historical organizations. The **Plaza de Armas** is the oldest part of the city where, in the northeast corner of the square under the boughs of a large ceiba tree, you will find a small stone column believed to mark the spot of the city's first Mass in 1519. Visible across the square is the tower of **Castillo de la Real Fuerza**, Cuba's oldest building and the second oldest fort in the Caribbean, completed in 1542. A spiral staircase leads to the top and a spectacular view over the old city. Atop the fort's lookout tower is the city's symbol, **Giraldilla**, a statue of a woman bearing a cross and palm tree.

No stay in Havana would be complete without a trip to one of the cigar factories. The most famous is **El Laguito**, where Cuba's premier cigars, Montecristos and Cohibas, are hand-rolled. You will find the factory in an upscale neighborhood on Calle 146 #2302, Marianao.

NOT TO SCALE   ━━━ PAVED ROAD   ❑ POINT OF INTEREST

About 10 kilometers southeast of Havana is the picturesque town of **San Francisco de Paula** and Ernest Hemingway's former home, **Finca Vigia**, where he lived from 1939 to 1960. Here he wrote many of his books including *Islands in the Stream*, *A Movable Feast*, and *The Old Man and the Sea*. The quaint old house, now a museum, remains as he left it almost 40 years ago, with his books and furniture still visible through the windows (you cannot enter, only look in).

Where to Stay in Havana

Hostal Valencia, Old Havana, Calle Oficios #53, esq Obrapía y Lamparilla, tel 62-3801, fax 33-8697. Operated as a joint venture between Spain and the Cuban government, this restored eighteenth-century mansion is modeled on a Spanish *paradores*. Instead of room numbers, each of the 12 spacious rooms is named after a famous Spanish town. Although situated on a narrow street that tends to be noisy at times, this charming hotel is a favorite with many independent travelers. Its inner courtyard encircled by a lofty balcony is a great place to

Castillo de la Real Fuerza in Old Havana

experience lively local music and to share a one-dollar beer with *habaneros* (Havana locals). This is a heavily booked hotel, so make reservations well in advance. Rates $44 and up.

Hotel Ambos Mundos, Old Havana, Calle Obispo #153, esq Mercaderes, tel 66-9530, fax 66-9532. This 52-room hotel occupies a five-story historic building dating back to 1887. The building was totally restored in 1996. One of the attractions of this hotel is room 511, where Hemingway lived for five years. The room remains as he left it in 1941. Rates $60 and up.

Hotel Inglaterra, Havana Central, Paseo del Prado #416, tel 62-7071, fax 33-8254. Immortalized in Graham Greene's novel *Our Man in Havana*, this is probably one of Havana's most charming hotels. Built in 1875, it was a favorite haunt of visiting dignitaries and correspondents. Today it is the favorite unofficial meeting place for independent travelers. Many of the 83 rooms have balconies offering panoramic views of the city. Rates $70 and up.

Where to Eat in Havana

The hotels listed above all have excellent restaurants, and your hotel will likely be the only place to have an early breakfast since most restaurants don't open until 10:00 a.m. For visitors speaking Spanish there are numerous *paladares*, restaurants operated out of private homes. They are not that easy to find, but most are located in the Vedado area of Havana. Three are listed below. Many also serve breakfast.

El Balcón del Edén, Vedado, Calle K #19/21, tel 32-9113. One of a few *paladares* open 24 hours a day. Be prepared for large helpings of Cuban delicacies.

La Bodeguita del Medio, Old Havana, Calle Empedrado #207, tel 61-8442. Once a favorite haunt of "Ernesto" Hemingway, this is also a great place to experience Cuban dishes like roast pork, black beans, sausage and bean soup, and fried bananas. Do try one of "Papa's" (Hemingway's nickname) favorite rum drinks, the *mojitos*. Lunch and dinner.

La Mina, Old Havana, Calle Obispo #109, tel 62-0216. A great place to mingle with *habaneros* and Latin American tourists. Its menu is limited to a few local dishes but its location, across from the Palcio de los Capitanos, its music, and two-dollar *mojitos* make it a must stop for anyone visiting the city. Lunch and dinner.

La Rejita Mayéa, Old Havana, Calle Habana #405, tel 62-6704. This small *paladare* has a limited selection of tasty meals for lunch and dinner.

Paladar El Amor, Vedado, Calle #23 at B & C, tel 32-8150. This *paladare* is owned by a young local singer and her family. Local cuisine. Lunch and dinner.

SIERRA DEL ROSARIOS BIOSPHERE RESERVE

The 25,000-hectare Sierra del Rosarios Biosphere Reserve is located on the eastern edge of the Sierra del Rosarios range, about 70 kilometers southwest of Havana. Established in 1985 this was the first UNESCO-sanctioned reserve of its kind in Cuba and now encompasses two main areas: Soroa and Las Terrazas. For the past 20 years the Cuban government has conducted an aggressive reforestation program throughout the reserve. The endemic forest disappeared decades ago, but the reserve is now covered by thick semi-deciduous forests where you can find almost 800 endemic plant species, including the rare cork palm found only in this province. In the spring the hills are ablaze with red *flamboyant* and the roadsides lined with *poma rosa* and *yagruma*.

The forests teem with wildlife including 90 species of birds such as the Cuban trogon, parrot, and *tocororo*, Cuba's national bird. Here you will find the smallest frog in the world, small timorous deer, turtles, and five varieties of bats, including the infamous vampire bat and the large Jamaican fruit bat with its 50-centimeter wingspan.

The 1959 Revolution

In March 1952, with the backing of the Cuban military and the American Mafia, Fulgencio Batista y Zaldivar seized the presidency of Cuba. Many people were angry, especially 26-year-old Fidel Castro Ruz, a young lawyer from the southeast. On July 26, 1953, Castro led 130 brave men and women on an attack of a garrison at Santiago de Cuba. It was a dismal failure, and those not killed were put on trail for treason. Castro was sentenced to 15 years in prison.

Although many protested that the election was fixed, Batista was elected president of Cuba in November 1954. He restored the constitution and, in a gesture of goodwill, freed a number of political prisoners. One of those was Fidel Castro, who fled to Mexico to continue the fight against the Batista regime.

In October 1956, Castro and 80 armed men set sail for Cuba in a small boat. They lost much of their equipment in the crossing, and within a month of landing in Cuba, most were killed by Batista's troops. Castro and a few followers managed to escape into the Sierra Maestra mountains.

From his mountain bases, Castro orchestrated large general strikes and attacks on military bases. When about 10,000 of Batista's troops poured into the mountains in May 1958, they suffered a humiliating defeat at the hands of a few hundred rebels. Castro headed west toward Havana, picking up even more supporters along the way.

On January 1, 1959, Batista fled the country and the military surrendered. Castro and his revolutionary army marched triumphantly into Havana on January 8, 1959. Castro has held power ever since.

The reserve's two biggest attractions are the eco-retreats at Soroa in the west and Las Terrazas in the east. Around these retreats is an assortment of interesting nature sites.

Nature Trails of Las Terrazas

In 1971 the government started a reforestation program with the aims of replenishing the dwindling forest and providing employment for some of the region's poor farmers, or *campesinos*. The trees were planted on terraced slopes, hence the name of the area. The workers were housed in a resort-like setting tucked away within the scenic hillside. Today it is a small ecological community surrounded by some of the best nature trails in the country. Although many of the residents work directly for the reserve, some have started to revive Cuba's traditional arts and crafts, and a number of workshops and studios are scattered about the village. This area is ideal for hikers and bird lovers as well as those wanting a real taste of *campesino* hospitality.

There are six main trails all leading from the valley into the surrounding hills. The trails range from 3 to 16 kilometers and vary in degree of difficulty from easy to moderate. Four of them, **Cañada del Infierno, San Juan River, Las Delicias**, and **La Sefina Trails** are especially rewarding and ascend the surrounding hills along thickly forested ancient river valleys. Along the trails, hikers will pass ruins of old plantations, thermal bathing pools, and waterfalls. Most of the trails in this area are generally easy to moderate in difficulty with a few strenuous spots.

While the trails may be hiked independently, it is not recommended. The best way to explore these trails is with a guide from one of the resorts, La Moka, Villas Turística, or at the Centro Ecológico in Las Terrazas. They can provide maps of the region and English-speaking guides. There is no water or food and no place to camp while on the trails, but the nature lodges have restaurants and will be happy to provide both food and water for your hikes. There are also a few small markets where you can buy food, and bottled water is sold at lodges, restaurants, bars, and small shops.

El Salto Cascades

Within the Soroa eco-retreat near the **Bar Eden**, which serves lunch and refreshments, is a pathway that descends about 400 meters to the bottom of these waterfalls. The falls are 35 meters high and the water plunges down a rock face into a set of pools called **Baños Romanos**. The baths have sulfurous water, which the locals believe has therapeutic powers to cure an assortment of ailments. Early in the morning the rising sun hits the mist from the falls at just the right angle creating a beautiful rainbow. Admission to the falls and baths is two dollars, but it is free if you are staying at the Villas Turística Soroa.

Orquideario Soroa

The Orquideario Soroa Gardens has a magnificent collection of orchids. Founded in 1934, the gardens cover three hectares of limestone hillside, and the combination of weathered limestone and bright orchids beneath the shade of tall epiphyte-covered cork palms and pine trees is quite beautiful. A meandering pathway up the hillside takes visitors through the various displays nestled in lush green pockets between the limestone outcroppings. The house at the top of the slope belonged to the gardens' founder, Tomas Felipe Camacho, who called it his "castle in the clouds," or Castillo de las Nubes.

Orchids are found all over the Caribbean, but each island has its own unique species. Cuba has about 250 indigenous varieties, most of which are found here at Orquideario Soroa. The gardens are maintained by the University of Pinar del Río. Guided tours are offered daily between 10 a.m. and 6 p.m.; admission is three dollars.

Outfitters and Guides near
Sierra del Rosarios Biosphere Reserve

The eco-sector is still largely unorganized, so the best way to explore this region is to stay at a local eco-resort and use their excellent guide network.

For less independent travelers there are two national tour operators that can also arrange a variety of nature excursions to any destination on the island. **Villas Turística Soroa**, tel 82-2122 or 82-2041, and **La Moka**, tel 85-2996 or 85-2921, fax 33-5516. They can arrange a variety of excursions—with English-speaking guides—for horseback treks, hiking, bird watching, and mountain biking.

For an even more organized approach **Havanatur's Tour & Travel**, Calle 23 y M, Havana, tel 33-0166 or 33-1549, fax 33-1547, offers a selection of overnight and day excursions to this region. They can also provide accommodations as well as information on booking local guides through their own network.

A smaller operator, **Fantàstico**, Avenida 146 at Avenida 11 and 13, Havana, tel 33-1700, fax 33-1656, offers personalized excursions to any corner of the island. They will also assist with booking accommodations.

Where to Stay near Sierra del Rosarios Biosphere Reserve

Campismo el Taburete, one kilometer east of La Moka, caters mainly to Cubans but also accepts tourists. There are 54 tiny, very basic concrete *cabañas*, a small grocery store, bar, and restaurant; camping is permitted. Set up your own tent or rent one. Rates five dollars and up. **La Moka**, Candelaria, tel 85-2921 or 85-2996, fax 33-5516. This is one of Cuba's newest showcase eco-resorts, established in 1994. The complex, surrounded by lush landscaped grounds, is situated on forested slopes overlooking a small lake. Red-barked trees shoot up from the ground, passing straight through the front lobby and the balconies of La Moka's 26 rooms, giving the resort a unique treehouse-like atmosphere. Amenities include a modest-sized swimming pool, tennis court, café, and bar. The resort's head guide is fluent in English and can arrange a variety of excursions. Rates $80 and up.

Villas Turística Soroa, Carretera de Soroa, Kilometer 8, Candelaria, tel 85-2122 or 85-2041. This is a modest eco-resort complex with 49 small *cabañas* (cabins) tucked into forested slopes, each with fridge, air conditioning, and hot shower. Villas also has 10 *casas* (houses), each with kitchenette, air conditioning, and hot shower; some have private dip pools. The complex has a large pool, three restaurants, and a nightclub offering local music and refreshments. The front desk can arrange a variety of mountain-biking, hiking, bird-watching, and horseback-riding excursions. Rates cabins $30 and up, houses $90 and up.

Where to Eat near Sierra del Rosarios Biosphere Reserve
Other than the hotels listed above, there are few places to eat. Two kilometers above the Orquideario Gardens, at Castillo de las Nubes, is a small restaurant serving sandwiches and refreshments. Near La Moka resort is the **Terraza de la Fonditab**, a small restaurant serving splendid Cuban delicacies. Ask for directions at La Moka.

Getting to Sierra del Rosarios Biosphere Reserve
You can take the Havana-to-Pinar del Río train that leaves Havana's Tulipan station daily at eight in the morning and get off at Candelaria (about a five-hour trip). From there you can take a taxi or hike the nine kilometers north to Soroa. You can also try one of the tour operators mentioned above.

The best way to get there is by car. Three highways lead to the reserve, though most visitors tend to take the six-lane Autopista from Havana. The other two routes, the Circuito Norte, along the coast, and the Carretera Central, through the mountains, offer much better views of the Cuban countryside. They are both well marked on maps but take about twice as long as the Autopista.

From the 51 kilometers sign on the Autopista follow the winding road that runs north through the hills to Las Terrazas, about 5 kilometers north of the Autopista. You will pass a guidepost or toll gate along the way. Soroa is about 17 kilometers west along the Carretera Central. Ask for directions at the gas station just outside Las Terrazas. If you are heading directly to Soroa from Havana, take the Autopista west to the 80 kilometers sign and head north about 8 kilometers through the village of Candelaria.

Although there is a toll gate at the east and west entrances to the reserve, entry is free. No official tourist information is available, but you can get answers at the Villas Turística Soroa, 82-2041, La Moka Hotel, 85-2996, and the Centro Ecológico in Las Terrazas.

PARQUE NACIONAL LA GUÍRA

Established about the time of the neighboring biosphere reserve, this 21,850-hectare park protects a large tract of pine forests on the higher slopes of the Sierra de los Organos, 130 kilometers southwest of Havana. Sandwiched between the small villages of La Guíra and San Diego de los Baños, the park occupies the former estate of wealthy landowner Manuel Cortina, who cut down most of the old growth for profit.

After the revolution the land was expropriated and converted into a preserve for Cubans. Some of the old ruins remain, but many are recent structures that resemble old ruins. Cortina's former estate house is now a museum containing all his possessions (he must have left in a hurry), including large antique tapestries, antique porcelains, a few pieces of furniture, and a variety of statues. Some of the original ornamental gardens that encircled the old house are still there, but others have been added. These themed gardens include a Japanese garden, a Chinese pavilion, an old English garden, and a newer Cuban garden with plenty of flame trees and butterfly jasmine. You actually enter the park through the estate's old fortress-like gates, complete with gun turrets.

Do not expect to find well-developed trails, but what little there is, is quite rewarding for those who don't mind a bit of trail blazing. (You'll have to force your way through dry, scratchy underbrush about one meter high that has grown over the trails.) Trails tend to be moderate to strenuous in difficulty. The area teems with wildlife and is especially worthwhile for bird lovers. The lack of traffic through the park improves the chances of seeing not only many shy bird species like the parrot and *pedorreras* but also some of the country's more timid animals, such as the timorous deer *jutías*, and anacondas.

There is no park entry fee, but expect to pay a few dollars at caves and sulfurous baths. While there is no official tourist information, you can get answers at the Hotel Liebertad and El Mirador in nearby San Diego de los Baños.

Cuevas las Portales in Parque Nacional la Guíra

Cuevas de las Portales

Within the park on its western edge, four kilometers from the turnoff for Cabañas Los Pinos resort, is the Cuevas de las Portales, a dramatic cave formation that should not be missed. The caves were formed by the passage of the Río Caiguanabo cutting through a large *mogote*, or freestanding limestone hummock. In fact, the river still flows through the *mogote* under a spectacular natural arch that marks the entrance to the cave system. Within one wall of this gigantic arch is the 30-meter-high cave complex first discovered in the mid-1800s by the Spaniards. It was here, in 1962, that Che Guevara, commander of Cuba's western army, established his military headquarters during the Cuban Missile Crisis. Old relics (most covered in bat guano) like tables, chairs, and even Che's iron bed are still scattered throughout the cave system.

Balneario San Diego

Built on the site of a series of thermal springs discovered in the seventeenth century, this thermal bath complex located in San Diego de los Baños is one of the finest on the island and well worth the $5 to $10 (depending on services provided) entry fee. The 40 degree Celsius water is loaded with sulfur, magnesium, and carbonates believed to relieve the aches of rheumatism and cure skin disorders. Along with the thermal baths the spa offers massage and mud therapies great for aching muscles and especially soothing after a hard day of trekking through the park. The spa is open daily eight to five.

Outfitters and Guides for Parque Nacional La Guíra

As in other areas in Cuba, there is no real organization handling arrangements for guides. A few young guides often hang out around the restaurant/bar just inside the park gates and will offer their services. For about five dollars these guides can take you to some of the area's best birding spots.

You can also inquire at your hotel (local bilingual guide Gilberto Cruz is well known at the resorts listed below) or contact tour operator **Havanatur's Tour & Travel**, tel 33-0166 or 33-1549, fax 33-1547, or the smaller **Fantástico**, tel 33-0166 or 33-1549, fax 33-1547.

Where to Stay near Parque Nacional La Guíra

Most people visiting the area stay in nearby San Diego de los Baños. There are a few basic resorts that cater to Cubans but will accommodate other visitors.

Cabañas de los Pinos, seven kilometers uphill from the park gates. This small complex of 23 wooden *cabañas* built on stilts is tucked into a heavily forested slope and resembles a complex of treehouses. There are communal cold showers, and some cabins have only a bed. Electricity comes and goes, but there are lamps for those who need them. Rates here are $4.

Cajalbana, at the entrance to the Las Portales caves, has a few concrete bungalows and campsites with BBQ pits. Most of the time there is no one here, so just pitch your tent. Bring your own food and water. Rates $1.

Hotel El Mirador, San Diego de los Baños, tel 33-5410. Located in the center of town adjacent to the hot springs and bathhouse, this is the place most foreigners stay. This attractive colonial-style property has a good-sized swimming pool, great restaurant, and cheerful staff. The 30 large rooms have hot water baths, air conditioning, and telephones. Rates $34.

Hotel Liebertad, San Diego de los Baños, tel. 83-7820. Close to the Mirador, this smaller property is officially reserved for Cubans only, but nevertheless rents rooms to foreigners. The 20 rooms are clean, small, and have ceiling fans but no hot water. Rates $15.

Hotel Saratoga, tel 83-7821. Close to the others, this hotel is another "officially reserved for Cubans" property. It is simple but adequate with 39 rooms and no hot water. Check here if the others are full. Rates $5.

Guajiro (farmer) and his oxen near Viñales

Where to Eat near Parque Nacional La Guíra

Besides the hotel restaurants (the best of the bunch is El Mirador's), you can try the **Paladar La Sorpresa**, opposite the Hotel Liebertad. Like most restaurants outside the big resort areas or Havana, this one serves Cuban food and is very casual—shorts will do.

Getting to Parque Nacional La Guíra

Take the Autopista freeway southwest from Havana. After you pass the signs for Los Palacios, start looking for the signs for San Diego de los Baños, about 120 kilometers from Havana. Turn north and follow the winding road for about 10 kilometers. You should see signs for the thermal springs; follow them.

Continuing west about seven kilometers from San Diego de los Baños on the road to La Guíra, you will find the sign for the park entrance. Further west along the road, about 11 kilometers, are the caves.

VIÑALES VALLEY NATIONAL MONUMENT

Situated about 210 kilometers west of Havana, this 70-square-kilometer region is to Cuba what Yosemite is to California. Tucked into the Sierra de los Organos range are a series of fertile valleys that make up the area called Viñales. Dividing the valleys are great free-standing rock outcroppings called *mogotes* that resemble the limestone hills of Quilin in southern China. These rounded, sheer-sided mounds were once part of a great limestone plateau thrust up from the Caribbean almost 160 million years ago. Over time water and wind eroded the plateau leaving these immense 300-meter-high hummocks. Some of the rivers that dissected the plateau now run through many of these *mogotes* forming interesting cave networks. Over the centuries these caves were used by indigenous peoples and more recently by runaway slaves.

Because the *mogotes* formed natural barriers to plants and animals, much of the flora and fauna found in the region is endemic. There are some species of snails that are found only on one or two *mogotes*. You will also find in abundance the rare cork palm; the royal palm, Cuba's national tree; and the mariposa, the national flower. The large birds riding the evening thermals around the *mogotes* are buzzards.

The sediment washed down by the water formed the flat-bottomed canyons, *hoyos*, between the *mogotes*, creating some of the most fertile soils in Cuba. It is here that the prized tobacco is grown, and in the spring the sweet smell of blooming tobacco plants fills the valleys. Throughout the area you will find *guajiros*, tobacco farmers, in their fields, or *vegas*, riding logs pulled behind pairs of oxen (used to level the ground). They will be only too happy to show off their drying sheds and some of their prized plants growing under cheesecloth canopies. You will be immediately struck by the pride they have in their crops, but once you get them talking prepare yourself for the narrative on what the revolution has done for them. Nowhere else in Cuba will you feel so welcomed. Be sure to bring lots of film to Viñales.

Fees at the caves vary between one and three dollars. No official visitor information is available, but you can get answers at the Hotels Las Ermitas and Las Jasmines.

Cave Exploration

As mentioned above, there are a number of cave sites scattered throughout the valley around the tiny village of Viñales. Some are worthwhile while others are to be avoided—at least two local caves have been turned into restaurant/bars with noisy disco music scaring away both fauna and visitors. The following caves offer the best opportunities for a natural experience.

Cuevas del Indio, about six kilometers north of Viñales, was named because of the Indian artifacts found inside. Enter the main grotto through a narrow crack in the face of the *mogotes* and follow the well-lit path for a kilometer or so before coming to a small jetty. You heard right, a jetty, where you will find a boatman who will row you through the rest of the cave. Along the watery trail you will be treated to bats swishing past your head and a number of magnificent stalactites and stalagmites, all with names. The boat ride ends at a wonderful little waterfall and quiet pool. Please tip the boatman. Open daily until noon; three dollar admission.

Caverna de Santo Tomás, about 20 kilometers west of Viñales and just north of the village of Pons, is the largest subterranean system in Latin America, with more than 45 kilometers of caverns. It is not yet known how many caves there are, but 37 have been mapped. These caves are more extensive than the others in the region and are best explored with a guide. Visitors will see enormous chambers containing huge stalagmites and stalactites. Several bat species live in the system, so those who can tolerate the strong smell of bat guano will enjoy visiting their colonies.

Outfitters and Guides for the Viñales Valley Region

As in other areas there is no real organization handling arrangements for guides. Your best bet is to inquire at your hotel or utilize **Havanatur's Tour & Travel**, tel 33-0166 or 33-1549, fax 33-1547. Local guides can be hired near the entrances to most of the caves. Don't haggle too much about the price. A couple of dollars goes a long way in Cuba and this region is poor.

Where to Stay near Viñales Valley National Monument

Hotel Horizontes Las Ermitas, Carretera de La Ermita Kilometer 2, Viñales, tel 82-9-3204, fax 82-9-4974. Nestled atop a tall *mogote* two kilometers south of Viñales, it has 62 air-conditioned rooms with balconies and hot showers. Other amenities include a small grocery store, poolside bar, large pool, and decent restaurant. Rooms facing the valley are best. Rates $30 and up.

Hotel Horizontes Las Jasmines, Carretera de Viñales Km 25, tel 82-9-3265. An older twin of Las Ermitas is also located high atop a *mogote* overlooking the valley 25 kilometers southwest of Viñales. It has 62 rooms and 16 private *cabañas*, all with air conditioning and hot showers. They are never fully booked so hold out for a room overlooking the valley. You'll find a large pool, small grocery store, restaurants, and well-stocked bars serving *guayabita*, a lethal local liqueur. Rates $30 and up.

Where to Eat near Viñales Valley National Monument

The restaurants in both hotels are good, and the four small eateries at the entrance to Cuevas del Indio are not bad for a quick lunch or late afternoon snack.

La Casa de Don Tomás, at the south entrance to Viñales, 141 Calle Salvador Cisnero, tel 89-3114. This is your best bet for such Cuban delicacies as the house special, *las delicias de Don Tomás,* a rice and fish platter, or tasty beef dishes such as *tasajo a lo campesino.* Lunch and dinner.

Getting to Viñales Valley National Monument

Buses (bus #124) departs Havana's Terminal Omnibus for Viñales daily at 9:20 a.m. and 1:00 p.m. If you rent a car head west on the Autopista, which ends in Pinar del Río, about 180 kilometers away. From there take the Carretera Viñales highway north to Viñales, about 27 kilometers. You will pass the Hotel Las Jasmines on the left before heading down the hill to Viñales.

PARQUE NACIONAL CIENAGA DE ZAPATA

The Zapata Peninsula in the Mantanzas province takes it name from the Spanish for shoe (*zapato*). This immense shoe-shaped peninsula, nearly all of which is part of this 4,000-square-kilometer national park, is Cuba's largest peninsula and most important wetland habitat. Similar to the Florida Everglades, this diverse ecosystem supports more than 900 species of flora, including marsh grass, mangroves, and woody swamp. It supports 171 species of birds, including 18 of Cuba's 22 endemic species, such as the bee hummingbird, Zapata wren, Zapata sparrow, Zapata rail, Cuban parrot, and the national bird, the *tocororo.* It has more than 16 species of reptiles, including the two crocodile species (*rhombifer* and *caimán*) that have been reintroduced into the wild from nearby breeding farms. There are also 12 varieties of mammals, including the tiny pygmy *jutía* and the four-meter-long manatee (*manati*). In the fall and winter the area, an important stopover along the Atlantic flyway, becomes temporary home to thousands of water fowl and other migratory birds.

The peninsula is also an important archaeological area. It is believed that the area's original inhabitants, a meso-culture called *guayabo Bianco,* threw their valuable possessions into Laguna del Tesoro rather than let them fall into Spanish hands. They were renowned for making household utensils and religious objects from shells. Many artifacts recovered from the lagoon are on display at **Museo Guamá**, a museum on an island in the center of the lagoon.

Over the years the local swamp people, *cenagueros,* have been called *carboneros,* because they eke out a living felling trees and making charcoal. Although many still make charcoal, ecotourism is quickly becoming a major employer in the region. Many *cenagueros* now work as guides or hotel staff for the major eco-resorts on the peninsula.

The peninsula also has significant political importance, for it was here on April 17, 1961, that a CIA-backed invasion force of exiled Cubans was defeated by Castro's revolutionary army. The **Bahia de Cochinos**, or Bay of Pigs, a small inlet on the western edge of the Zapata swamp, was selected as the invasion site because of its remoteness, but the Cuban revolutionaries were waiting and the invasion force was easily defeated.

Parque Nacional Cienaga de Zapata

Much of the peninsula is now considered sensitive for political and ecological reasons, and most areas are off-limits even to the *cenagueros*. There is a guard post at the entrance to the park, and you must be chaperoned by a licensed guide to enter. A word of warning: Don't try to enter the park or surrounding swamp without a guide, and be aware that the mosquitoes are as big as small birds—bring plenty of repellent and a long-sleeved shirt.

A host of activities awaits the visitor to the Zapata. Coastal waters and freshwater lagoons teem with fish and are ideal for snorkeling, scuba diving, and fishing. The swamp contains a large network of narrow channels built by *cenagueros* to transport their charcoal; you can explore these by kayak or small boat. For fisherfolk, the shallows off Laguna de las Salinas are packed with bonefish, tarpon, and permit, and the many freshwater lagoons are famous for their lunker bass. Besides the numerous nature trails that crisscross the swamp, the world-renowned International Bird-Watching Center lies just west of Playa Larga.

Playa Larga

On the northeastern edge of the park, this is not a pretty town. Be prepared for the throngs of young men wanting to sell you everything from stuffed crocs (from the game farm, not wild) to cigars. It's best just to say *no gracias* and walk on. Still, there are some good nature opportunities nearby.

West of the town is the **International Bird-Watching Center** and

Cigars

What do Cuba and capitalism have in common? Believe it or not, the cigar. It's a bit ironic that the last communist country in the Western Hemisphere supplies most of the capitalistic world with undoubtedly the most ostentatious symbol of capitalism. But you can't expect to politicize a good cigar.

A good cigar starts in the tobacco fields, or vegas, *of the Vuelta Abajo region of Pinar del Río province, where the plants are grown under canopies of muslin or cheesecloth by tobacco growers, or* vegueros. *When the plants mature, the leaves are picked and sorted into bundles, or* plunks, *which are placed in drying sheds and cured, sometimes for years. From the drying sheds the cured leaves go to the cigar factories, where they are sorted by a blender according to color and strength.*

Cigar makers, called tabaqueros *(male) or* tabaqueras *(female), take great pride in rolling the cigars, but the job is boring so each factory employs a* lector, *or reader, who reads aloud everything from government propaganda circulars to Ernest Hemingway novels. Workers make a modest $10 to $15 per week and, of course, all the cigars they can smoke on the job.*

There are a number of factories around the island, each producing a certain brand or brands. Each type or brand is usually a different size, color, and flavor. Two of the top brands in the world are Montecristos and Cohibas, which can be purchased anywhere outside the United States. The best brand in the world is the Trinidad, made especially for Castro himself, who distributes them as gifts to foreign dignitaries. Only some 20,000 are made a year; they were Castro's favorites before he stopped smoking.

There are many cigar factories, most of which are in Havana. El Laguito, H. Upmann, Partages, and La Corona are among the better ones. Wings of the World Travel, 1636 3rd Ave., Suite 232, New York, NY 10128, 800/465-8687, can arrange cigar tours that include factories, museums, plantations, and growing areas along with general sightseeing excursions.

Tobacco farm near Viñales

a number of nature trails through the swamp. And about 25 kilometers southwest along the west side of the bay is **Laguna de las Salinas Wildlife Refuge**, where huge flocks of migratory birds gather from November to May. A guide is needed for both.

On the western side of town is a chained road with guard post. It marks the entrance to **Corral de Santo Tomás Wildlife Reserve**, another great place for wildlife viewing—manatees and birds such as *tocororo*, wood ibis, sandhill crane, and a few flamingos. You must have a guide to enter, so inquire first at the Hotel Horizontes Playa Larga. They will be more than happy to help you with all of your nature excursions.

The area has great diving, and the local resort dive shops offer lessons and dive packages and rent snorkeling equipment. They also offer guided diving and snorkeling trips. Again, the Villa Playa Larga can make arrangements. The trails in Corral de Santo Tomás are easy to moderate in difficulty, but be prepared for the heat.

There are no park fees. No official tourist information is available, but you can get answers at Hotels Horizontes Playa Larga, Playa Girón, and Guamá (see "Where to Stay," below).

Playa Girón

If you like diving or snorkeling, this is the place for you, but be warned this is the spot where socialism and communism came to blows that April day: everywhere you turn there are reminders of that glorious event. The most blatant revolutionary propaganda is the message on the huge billboard in the main square, which reads, "Playa Girón—The First Rout of Imperialism in Latin America."

Once you have digested all the revolutionary hype, take a break and head to **Cueva de los Pesces**, about 15 kilometers north of town, and experience diving or snorkeling in a huge 70-meter-deep freshwater sinkhole, or *cenote*. The hole is honeycombed with channels teeming with fish. Columbus wrote of these *cenotes*, ". . . with their subterranean streams of waters so cold, and of such goodness and so sweet that no better could be found in the world." Offshore are a number of great dive sites at **Punta Perdiz, Jaruco, Las Canas, Los Cocos**, and **El Brinco**. The dive shop at Villa Playa Girón will see to all your needs.

Around Playa Girón are a few land-filled trails so visitors can go deeper into the swamp and get better views of the wildlife. The straight, level trails are from three to four kilometers long and are not difficult, but you must have a guide. Flamingos, ibis, and spoonbills are common along these trails.

Outfitters and Guides near
Parque Nacional Cienaga de Zapata

Bohio del Don Pedro, in Playa Larga. You can hire a guide through Don Pedro (get in touch with him through the Hotel Horizontes Playa Larga or by simply asking any resident in this small town). Expect to pay $50 per person per day, but you can negotiate a lower price for groups of three or more.

Hotels Horizontes Playa Girón, **Playa Larga**, and **Guamá** all have nature excursion desks where you can book guides, fishing trips, and dive tours (see "Where to Stay," below). The Playa Larga offers bird-watching tours for $20 each.

Puertosol, Calle Cobre #34404, e/2da y 4ta, Villa Marina, Tarará, Havana, tel 33-3510, fax 33-5501, offers sport fishing from 18 marinas around the island.

Rumbos, office at Fiesta Finca Campesina, Playa Larga, can supply you with a licensed guide and information on the area. Guides usually offer general tours of the region, but visitors can request a naturalist-type guide who knows the wildlife and vegetation. The naturalist-guides are a bit more expensive but worth every penny because they can identify the rich biodiversity of the area.. Rumbos can also arrange boat tours through the swamp and up the Río Hatiguanico, where you will encounter crocodile, manatee, and the extraordinary alligator gar or *manjuari* (*Atractosteus tristoechus*), a prehistoric-looking fish. Trips average $54 per person, lower for groups. **Tour & Travel**, tel 33-0166 or 33-1549, fax 33-1547, can make arrangements for you to see the area.

Where to Stay near Parque Nacional Cienaga de Zapata

Hotel Horizontes Guamá, Laguna del Tesoro, Peninsula de Zapata, Mantanzas, tel 59-2979. Located 8 kilometers east of Boca de Guamá and 16 kilometers south of the Autopista, this unique nature resort was built to resemble an Arawak village. The resort is actually built on several small islands (connected by narrow foot bridges) in the middle of Laguna del Tesoro. The 59 primitive-looking thatch-roofed huts, most of which are on stilts above the water, are actually far from primitive: they have air conditioning, private baths, and phones. Castro frequently stays in unit 33 when he comes here to fish. There is a bar and fine restaurant that serves barbecued crocodile (from the farm, not wild), and the only drawback is the loud music emanating from the bar, which doubles as a disco at night. You get to the hotel via a five-dollar boat ride from the pier in La Boca. Rates $35 to $45.

Hotel Horizontes Playa Girón, Playa Girón, tel 59-4118. There is a summer camp atmosphere about this place that is favored by Cubans. It is a much larger resort than its sister properties, with 292 rooms. There is a pool, bar, restaurant, and tourist information desk. It is quite the festive place, maybe a bit too festive for those looking for peace and quiet, but at least you won't be pestered. Rates $30 to $35.

Hotel Horizontes Playa Larga, Playa Larga, tel 59-7219. Typical resort feel with 57 well-spaced but small *cabañas*, each with air conditioning, small beds, and kitchenette. It's on a small beach where you will be pestered by young men trying to sell you everything from stuffed crocs to cigars. There is a bar, restaurant, nightclub, and international dive center. Rates $25 to $35.

Where to Eat near Parque Nacional Cienaga de Zapata

The hotels above have good restaurants, and there are a few good *paladares* in all three towns. These places are well known so just ask a local for directions.

Getting to Parque Nacional Cienaga de Zapata

Although there are three buses per week from Havana to Playa Girón, don't count on them. Better to rent a car or call **Tour & Travel**, tel

33-0166 or 33-1549, fax 33-1547, which arranges group tours. If you are driving take the Autopista southeast from Havana to Kilometer 142 at the small town of Australia. Head south on highway 3-1-16 to La Boca (16 kilometers) and Playa Larga (32 kilometers). To get to Playa Girón, head east from Playa Larga along the eastern side of the Bay of Pigs (about 30 kilometers). The more reliable local bus (#818) runs each day between Playas Larga and Girón.

CUBA SPECIFICS

Getting There

There are no direct flights between Cuba and the United States, but there are daily flights between Cuba and Canada, Mexico, Jamaica and the Bahamas. Plan on traveling to one of these countries to get to Cuba or plan on waiting months for a visa. Most flights from outside Cuba land at José Martí International Airport. Many major Canadian and Mexican charter carriers have direct flights to Cuba daily; check with one of the tour companies listed above.

Entry/Exit Requirements

U.S. citizens heading to Cuba from the United States require a valid passport and visa, which can be obtained from the **Cuban Interest Section**, 2369 16th St. NW, Washington, DC 20009, 202/797-8515. Another, less complicated approach is to obtain a "tourist card" from a Cuban consulate or through an approved tour agency or airline. **Marazul Tours**, 250 W. 57th St., Suite 1311, New York, NY 10107, 800/223-5334 or 212/582-9570, can help with a tourist card for about $15. U.S. citizens can also book a flight out of the country to, say, Canada, Jamaica, or Mexico, then fly to Cuba and return from there. The foreign tour company or airline you purchase your return ticket from usually issues a tourist card as part of the package. Canadians require a valid passport and tourist card, obtained from the airline or tour operator.

All visitors must have a return ticket and may also be asked to show they have adequate funds to cover their expenses while in Cuba.

Three helpful tour companies are **Cubanacán Canada International**, 372 Bat St., Suite 406, Toronto, Ont., Canada, tel. 416/601-0343, fax 416/601-0346; **Cubanatours**, Baja California 255, Edif. B, Despacho 103 Colonia, Hipodromo Condesa, Mexico DF, tel 574-4921; and **Havanatur Nassau**, W. Hill St., P.O. Box 10246, Nassau, tel 322-2796, fax 238-7980.

Getting Around

Don't be fooled by its size on the map of the Caribbean: Cuba is decep-
tively large. Since the collapse of the Soviet Union, gas shortages, though
better today, still occur. The cheapest, least reliable, and most uncomfortable way to travel is by bus. At the best of times they are late or filled,
so your best bet is to rent a car, take a plane, or use local tour companies.

By far the best way to see the island is to rent a car. With more than
16,000 kilometers of paved roads, there are few places you cannot get to.
Do not believe what you have heard or read about many places being off-
limits; it is simply not true. There are actually very few places off-limits
and you wouldn't be interested in them anyway. The roads are good and
the high gas prices guarantee you will encounter little traffic on most
highways. Cubans are very safe drivers and with a minimum of road sense
you will avoid trouble, except for getting lost.

Expect to pay $50 to $60 per day including insurance and a deposit
(better rates for weekly rentals). Gasoline is about $3.40 per gallon.
Havanautos, with booths at most airports, is the largest agency with
island-wide coverage, so they can quickly deal with any situation that may
crop up regardless of where you are. All car rental companies have representatives at the major airports, so shop around for the best rate/car combination. You can rent bicycles and scooters at many hotels.

Hitching is a very popular and accepted way to get around.
Everybody stops to pick up foreigners, but your Spanish must be good or
you might end up miles away from your destination.

Air travel within Cuba may be a viable and affordable option. **Aero
Caribbean**, Calle 23 3113, Vedado, Havana, tel 79-7524, flies to most
destinations within Cuba for $18 to $75 one way.

Package Tour Organizers

Hoteles Horizontes, Calle 23 #156, Vedado, Havana, tel 33-4142, fax
33-3161. This company has hotels all over Cuba and can offer one- to
ten-day tours to every part of the island. It also offers one-week ecotour
packages to some of the locations discussed (Viñales, Soroa, and Zapata).
Packages include transportation, hotel, and excursions.

Tour & Travel, Calle 23 y M, Havana, tel 33-0166 or 33-1549, fax
33-1547, can arrange transportation, guides, and accommodations. They
are a good operator but not cheap.

Tourist Information

Information is hard to come by outside Havana, so it is a good idea to
get what you need before heading off into the countryside. **Infotur**, tel
23-3376 or 63-6960, operates a number of kiosks around the island that

dispense information and brochures. Call to find out which one is nearest and stock up. Other private agencies, such as **Cubatur**, Calle F #157, Vedado, Havana, tel 23-6733 or 30-1512; and, your best bet, **Cubanacán**, 372 Bay St., Suite 406, Toronto, Ont., Canada M5H 2W9, tel 416/601-0343, fax 416/601-0346, are also very helpful.

You will find some public phones (which take 20-centavo coins), but do not be surprised if many don't work. Your best bet is to make calls from your hotel or use the international phone centers in the main cities. Another good idea is to purchase phone cards at the airport. These cards come in various denominations and can be used for international and domestic calls. The catch is, there are few public phone boxes (mostly at hotels and airports) that accept the card.

Many U.S. and Canadian travel bookstores carry maps and it's best to take one with you. **Infotur** and **Rumbos** (at the airport) have maps for sale, or try **Tienda de las Navegantes**, Mercadares 115, Habana Vieja, tel 61-3625.

Health and Safety Issues
No vaccinations are required for North Americans. However, Cuba is a tropical country and some illnesses, such as hepatitis A, have been reported. Cuba's tap water is safe to drink and so is the milk, which is pasteurized, but to be safe drink bottled water in rural areas. Use your judgment when purchasing food from roadside vendors—the ones that BBQ on the spot are best.

Most of Cuba is quite safe. Watch out for petty theft such as pick-pockets and purse snatchers in the larger centers, but don't be too worried; most of Cuba's larger cities are much safer than their counterparts in Canada and the United States.

Carry with you only as much money as you'll need for the day and a photocopy of your tourist card and passport. Leave originals and valuables in the hotel safe. Unlike other countries that pay lip service to drug and alcohol abuse prevention, Cuba is as tough as they come. Don't take any chances. Drink in moderation, and don't ever attempt to buy, transport, or use illegal drugs while in Cuba.

Cuban men treat women with great respect and assaults on women are extremely rare. Men, on the other hand, will be frequently approached by *jiniteras* (prostitutes). Try to ignore them, but if they persist seek out one of the many uniformed police officers.

What to Bring
Pack light and forget about flashy clothing that will only attract hustlers like "flies to a mango." Think simple and practical (hotel laundry services

are cheap), which means at least one long-sleeved top, a pullover for the mountains, hat, good walking shoes, and some bacterial soap.

It is becoming fashionable to bring only the bare necessities and buy a few local things here. Cuban clothing is inexpensive and tasteful, and you won't stick out like a mango. Forget the suit and evening dress!

North American medications are scarce, so bring enough to last your whole trip plus a couple of extra days just in case of emergency.

Carry a bunch of U.S. one-dollar bills and tip where you feel you received good service. This will be greatly appreciated. Also, tip your guides and hotel staff and make sure you press the money into their hands. Don't add it to your bill because they may never see it.

It is becoming more common among responsible visitors to carry a small quantity of things like pens or pencils (50 or so) and donate them to a school in one of the towns you visit. Always give them to the head teacher to hand out to the class; otherwise, you run the risk of an enter-prising Cuban selling what you donated.

Money

The official Cuban currency is the *peso*, but the currency Cubans love is the U.S. dollar, so take plenty. Traveler's checks and credit cards issued by a U.S. bank are useless. If you are uncomfortable taking large sums of cash, purchase U.S. dollar traveler's checks (Thomas Cook are the best) in your stopover country (Canada, Mexico, Bahamas, Jamaica). Still take U.S. dollars and have a good assortment of smaller bills because a U.S. dollar goes a long way in Cuba, especially outside the main tourist areas.

Check exchange rates at such big banks as **Banco Financiero International S.A.**, but don't be too quick to convert your dollars into pesos at these banks. The money exchanges called **Cadeca** (at key points throughout the main cities) will give you the street rate, which was 30 pesos to one U.S. dollar at time of publication. The official government exchange rate is one peso to one dollar, but nobody uses it, not even the banks.

In any case most places don't want pesos from a foreigner and are willing to bargain for U.S. dollars. Keep a small number of pesos (100 pesos, about four U.S. dollars, will last a long time) to use in the rural communities, where vendors usually don't have many U.S. dollars for change. Remember, pesos are worthless outside Cuba so make sure you spend all of them before leaving.

Two words of warning. First, before making a purchase make sure you understand what the exact price and currency is before you buy. The peso has the same designation (the $ sign) as the U.S. dollar. Second, stay away from the black market or street "money changers." Their rate is comparable to the Cadeca but it is illegal.

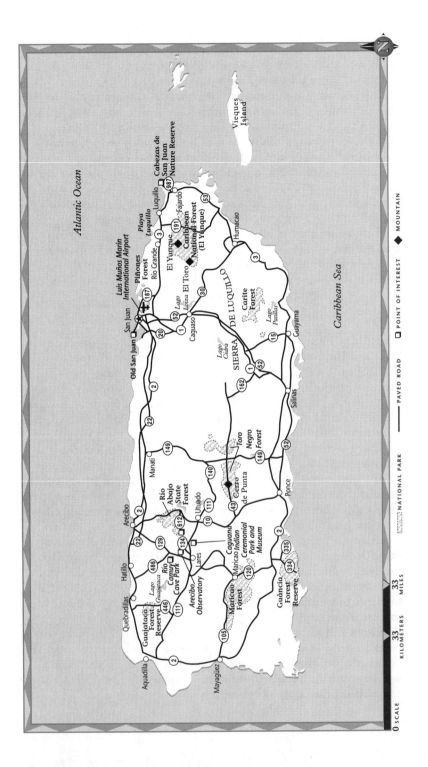

PUERTO RICO

6

Puerto Rico, the Island of Enchantment, is the smallest of the four main islands that make up the Greater Antilles. At 179 kilometers long by 58 kilometers wide, Puerto Rico has more than 480 kilometers of coastline and two rugged volcanic mountain ranges. The Sierra de Luquillo range covers most of the eastern corner of the island, rising to about 1,770 meters at the top of El Yungue (The Anvil). The Cordillera Central range runs east to west for almost the entire length of the island and is home to Puerto Rico's highest peak, the 1,335-meter Cerro de Punta. The coastal waters surrounding the island are dotted with numerous small islands and cays. And just 75 kilometers off Puerto Rico's north coast is one of the world's deepest marine trenches, the Milwaukee Deep, which descends to a depth of 8,540 meters.

Puerto Rico is an island of contrasts that is best described in two parts: Greater San Juan and everywhere else ("everywhere else" is known locally as *en la isla*, or "out on the island"). These two "sides" of Puerto Rico offer glaring cultural and natural contrasts that enhance the overall ambience of the island. Busy Greater San Juan is flat and American in appearance and style, with casinos, luxury hotels, nightclubs, imposing billboards, and tall glass-sided skyscrapers. The rest of the island is mountainous and undeveloped, radiating the more laid-back attitude characteristic of other Caribbean islands, but with a definite Latin flavor.

Because of its location and status as a self-governing commonwealth of the United States, Puerto Rico attracts more than one million visitors annually. But tourism is not the island's major industry. The manufacturing sector is strong and will get stronger with the introduction of new tax incentives. This fact, coupled with a population density of almost 1,200 per square kilometer (total island population: 3.5 million) and large tracts of land given over to agriculture, has resulted in tremendous habitat loss over the years. When Columbus arrived, about 75 percent of the island was covered by lush rain and deciduous forests. Today less than 25 percent of the island is forested; only 10 percent of the forests are original.

The Puerto Rican government has undertaken a number of environmental and conservation programs over the last 30 years to preserve what's left of the forests. It has established more than 14 forest reserves and a system of national parks and wildlife sanctuaries. Today most of the remaining forests are protected. The Caribbean National Forest, Puerto Rico's largest, contains almost 75 percent of the island's remaining forested land within its 11,300-hectare boundaries.

The island supports more than 3,300 plant species (mostly indigenous) and more than 270 bird species. It is home to 547 native tree species, including the enormous *ceiba*, or silk cotton tree, some of which are 300 years old, and the *guayacán*, one of the densest woods in the world—it actually sinks in water. Trunks of these trees were in such demand for ship masts that they were actually used as currency by the Dutch and Spanish throughout the sixteenth and seventeenth centuries. Twenty-four species of cacti can also be found on the drier south coast.

Because of loss of habitat, many of the island's indigenous birds, such as the Puerto Rican nightjar and the Puerto Rican parrot, are now teetering on the brink of extinction. Reptiles and amphibians are numerous and range from the diminutive *coquí*, a tiny, 36-millimeter-long tree frog also known as the piping frog, to the two-meter-long, 700-kilogram leatherback turtle. Except for a few bat species and the few remaining manatees, the island has no indigenous mammals. Migrating humpback whales can be seen off the southeast coast around Humacao.

The U.S. National Park Service and the U.S. Forest Service have established hundreds of miles of hiking trails through most of the forest reserves. The trails (excellent for bird watching) range from easy walks to more difficult overnight treks to the highest peaks. The northwest karst country is honeycombed with an extensive cave system while offshore cays and coastal reefs offer excellent diving, kayaking, and snorkeling. The deep ocean trenches teem with big-game fish.

Puerto Rico History

Archaeological records indicate that the island was settled by a variety of indigenous peoples from as early as 3000 B.C.; the more recent arrivals, the Taínos, arrived around A.D. 1000. The Taínos inhabited the island when Columbus arrived in 1493 and christened it San Juan Bautista (St. John the Baptist). Juan Ponce de León, who accompanied Columbus on his second voyage, returned in 1508 to establish the island's first settlement at Caparra, south of the present San Juan. In 1521 Ponce de León relocated the settlement to the breezy islet at the mouth of San Juan Bay and renamed the town Puerto Rico ("rich port") in hopes of attracting more colonists. Due to an early cartographer's mistake, the name of the island and town were somehow switched, and the mistake was never corrected.

Spain ruled the island for almost 400 years before ceding it to the Americans in the 1898 Treaty of Paris settlement, which ended the Spanish-American War. In 1947 the U.S. government granted Puerto Rico commonwealth status (self-rule), and Puerto Ricans now elect their own representatives in Congress.

OLD SAN JUAN

Most visitors to Puerto Rico will fly into San Juan—the island's capital city, and not a "nature destination" by any stretch. But there are a few

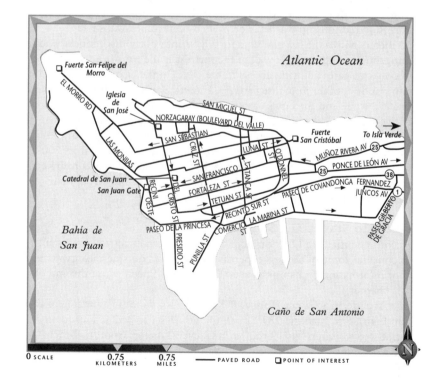

things worth seeing if you spend a day or two here en route to or from the airport.

While the Greater San Juan area captures the unique blend of American and Spanish cultures, colonial Spain is well preserved within the original eight-square-block area of Old San Juan. The original settlement was housed within a gigantic fortress with massive walls almost 10 meters thick. Since being declared a historical zone in 1949, the Institute of Puerto Rican Culture has been busy restoring many of the old Spanish colonial homes and buildings to their eighteenth-century grandeur. In 1965 the original eight-square-block area was designated a United Nations World Heritage Site, and additional funding was set aside to complete the restoration. Walking along the narrow cobblestone streets and alleyways transports visitors back to a time when gas street lanterns, busy rum shops, lively Spanish music, and pastel-painted buildings added color to an otherwise commercial city.

In all, nearly 400 buildings have been restored in Old San Juan. The **Cathedral de San Juan** (circa 1550) and **Iglesia de San José** (circa 1560), where Ponce de León's body is enshrined, are two of the oldest. On the west tip of the Old San Juan peninsula is the towering fortress of **San Felipe del Morro**, completed in 1783 to defend the city and harbor. Referred to simply as El Morro, its 6-meter-thick walls rise 50 meters above the sea and contain a labyrinth of rooms, tunnels, and dungeons. Along the west wall of the fortress is the **San Juan Gate**, one of only two gates allowing access to the city. On the east side of the old city stands another immense fortress, **Fuerte San Cristóbal**, completed in 1772 to defend the city's eastern approach. The fortification consists of five separate forts linked by a system of tunnels and dry moats.

Outside the city in the suburb of Río Piedras is the delightful, 57-hectare **Botanical Gardens**, where visitors can see more than 200 species of the island's flora. A few blocks away is the **farmer's market**, which comes alive on weekends. Vendors hawk everything from handbags to those famous Puerto Rican coffee beans.

Where to Stay in Old San Juan

Accommodations in Old San Juan don't come cheap, so you may want to consider some of the less expensive alternatives outside the city center. (For information on camping, see "Puerto Rico Specifics" at the end of this chapter.)

Arcade Inn Guest House, 8 Taft St., Condado (just outside of Old San Juan), San Juan, tel 787/725-0668, fax 787/728-7524. This family-run, three-story inn has 19 rooms. It is just 30 meters from the beach and a 15-minute taxi ride from Old San Juan. Rates $50 to $75.

El Morro in Old San Juan

Numero Uno on the Beach Guest House, 1 Calle Santa Ana, Ocean Park, tel 787/726-5010, fax 787/727-5482. This small (12 rooms), delightful, locally owned B&B is right on the beach. All rooms have air conditioning. Rates $55 to $75.

Enrique Castro Guest House, 205 Calle Tanca, Box 947, Old San Juan, tel 787/722-5436. This small, locally owned inn has 12 comfortable but basic rooms, some with a/c. Rates $20 to $40.

Where to Eat in Old San Juan

The streets of Old San Juan are lined with great, inexpensive places to eat. Puerto Rican cuisine blends Spanish and Caribbean flavors in its preparations of local vegetables and seafood. Some restaurants serve Spanish *caldo gallego* (lobster with ham and beans) and paella, a tasty rice dish that contains seafood, chicken, beef, and vegetables.

Café Matisse, 1351 Ashford Ave., Condado (just outside of Old San Juan), is family-run, serving great Puerto Rican dishes such as paella and *ensalada francesca*, a vegetarian salad. Dinner only.

Café Paris, Calle Luna 277, Old San Juan, offers great ambience with checkered-tableclothed tables looking out on the street. A great place for regular or vegetarian lunch or dinner.

El Jibarito, Calle Sol 276, Old San Juan. Features great local cooking.

Maria's, Calle Cristo 204, Old San Juan, is a famous watering hole for celebs and locals alike, serving snacks and sandwiches for lunch.

CARIBBEAN NATIONAL FOREST AND EL YUNQUE

The 11,300-hectare Caribbean National Forest, located in eastern Puerto Rico about 50 kilometers southeast of San Juan, is the smallest and only tropical rain forest in the U.S. National Forest system and contains almost 75 percent of the total forest area in Puerto Rico.

Within the national forest are two main peaks, **El Toro,** the highest, at 1,075 meters, and **El Yunque,** the more famous, at 1,065 meters. It is the latter that attracted the attention of the indigenous Taíno, who named the mountain *yuque* ("white land") because of its consistent cloud cover. The Spanish corruption is *yunque* ("anvil"), which some say the peak resembles when not cloud-covered.

The park was originally founded in 1903 when President Theodore Roosevelt proclaimed about 5,000 hectares of forest the Luquillo Forest Reserve. Since then the park's name has changed to the Caribbean National Forest (in 1935) and the park has expanded. Its name is changing once more, to the Luquillo Experimental Forest and Biosphere Reserve, but it is still referred to as the Caribbean National Forest or El Yunque.

The area contains elements of four types of rain forests. On the lower slopes is the *tabonuco* forest, which takes its name from the immense 45-meter-high, white-barked *tabonuco* tree. Some 200 other varieties can also be found here. The second type of forest is the *palo colorado* forest, which occurs above 600 meters. It is named for an indigenous tree found in the area, some of which are almost 2,500 years old. The *palo colorado* is a slow-growing tree, but some examples in the park have trunks that are seven meters in circumference. Above 600 meters is the palm forest, with its mountain cabbage or *sierra* palms, followed by the dwarf or elfin forest on the highest ridges above 600 meters. At these high elevations, vegetation seldom grows higher than three meters.

Park visitors can see more than 60 species of birds, including the rare bare-legged owl, lizard-cuckoo, and Puerto Rican parrot, whose population once numbered in the millions but dropped as low as 25 birds in 1975. Thanks to an intensive conservation and captive breeding program, the bird is making a comeback (there are about 70 now), and a few can be seen around the picnic area on the slope behind the visitors center. Dusk and dawn are the best times to glimpse them. The endemic elfin woods warbler, a bird found only here and in the Maricao Forest, can sometimes be seen along the El Toro Trail and on the higher dwarf forest ridges.

Visitors can also expect to see many of the 16 varieties of *coquí* tree frogs. Park biologists estimate their numbers at about 20,000 per hectare, and at dawn their incessant chirping is almost deafening.

There is no park admission charge, but three dollars is required to enter the El Portal Forest Center. For more information, visit the El Portal Tropical Forest Center on Highway 191 at the park entrance or contact the Caribbean National Forest Administration, tel 787/888-5609, fax 787/888-5622. Maps are available, and lectures and guided tours are offered through the Palo Colorado Visitors Center in the park.

Things to Do in the Caribbean National Forest

More than 60 kilometers of hiking trails, ranging from easy to difficult, crisscross the park. Some trails have eroded while others are in better shape. With more than 500 centimeters of annual rainfall, it's no surprise that forest erosion is a major concern. Hurricane Hugo also caused severe damage in the forest, but the land is recovering quickly. Some vegetation has actually grown back more densely in some places.

One peculiarity of the park is that many of the trails are hard-surfaced (some even paved) in an effort to combat erosion and to make it easier to access the forest. The local authorities feel that the more accessible the park, the more concern there will be for conservation programs in general. These well-marked "highways" are easy to find and follow, eliminating the need for guides.

The shortest and least difficult trail is the **Big Tree Trail**, which is less than three kilometers round trip and begins at Kilometer 10.4. The Big Tree is not only the most popular trail in the park, but also one of the best for viewing the *tabonuco* forest. The trail is completely paved.

Another popular but steeper trail is three-kilometer **La Mina Trail** (Mine Trail), which starts behind the visitors center. This asphalt-covered trail descends into the rain forest to the picturesque La Mina waterfall and an old, abandoned Spanish gold mine. The waterfall is a popular bathing and picnic spot.

The 10-kilometer round-trip **El Yunque Peak Trail** starts at the visitors center and climbs steeply to the top of El Yunque peak. This is one of the more difficult trails, but popular among the fit. It is paved almost all the way to the top and numerous side trails lead to interesting spots like swimming holes, picnic areas, and stands of *palo colorado* trees where the parrots nest. The main and side trails are well marked.

The most difficult trail in the park is the 20-kilometer round-trip **El Toro Trail**, which winds its way through the four types of forest vegetation on its way to a 1,075-meter summit. The trail is not paved

La Mina waterfall

and depending on the weather can take from 10 to 12 hours to complete. The well-marked trailhead is located between two radio transmission towers just beyond the El Yunque trailhead along Highway 191, the highway that runs through the park. This less-traveled trail affords hikers the best opportunity to observe the diverse flora and birdlife of the region.

Other Regional Nature Reserves
While in this region, two other small nature reserves are worth a visit.

Just east of San Juan along the coast is the **Piñones Forest**, the largest of Puerto Rico's mangrove forests. All four species of mangrove grow here, and a variety of shore birds, including common terns, frigate birds, and pelicans, can be seen. The waters around the mangroves are an excellent place to snorkel. Most trails are fairly obvious, but some are not (see "Outfitters and Guides," below, for information on guides).

The small (127-hectare) **Cabezas de San Juan Nature Reserve**, outside the town of Fajardo on the northeasternmost tip of the island, features mangroves, dry forest, and a few lagoons that are phosphorescent at certain times of the year. The reserve's fringe reef and mangroves offer very good snorkeling. Guided tours in English are offered daily at two in the afternoon. Admission is five dollars. Reservations are required (tel 787/722-5882 weekdays and 787/860-2560 weekends).

Outfitters and Guides for the Caribbean National Forest
Guides are not required for the Caribbean National Forest. For the
Piñones Forest, try **La Lanmcha Paseadora**, tel 787/791-0755. Reserve
guides are provided at Cabeza de San Juan Nature Reserve.

For more organized affairs try:

Aventuras Tierra Adentro, 272-B Ave. Piñero, University
Gardens, Río Piedras, tel 787/766-0470, fax 787/754-7543. Offers all
kinds of adventures.

Tropix Wellness Tours, Apartado 13294, Santuree, tel 787/268-
2173, fax 787/268-5882, email: tropix@msn.com. Offers organized
spelunking, canyoning, cascading, hiking, and kayaking tours.

Beach resorts ring the base of the mountain range along the coastal
plain. There are dozens of places to rent equipment along the coast, and
all of the larger resorts have water-sports shops. For sea adventures, try
either of the following:

Mike Benítes Marine Services, Box 9066541, San Juan, PR
00906, tel 787/723-2292, fax 787/724-6265. The best in deep-sea fishing, this operation will help you catch the big one.

Ocean Sports, 77 Isla Verde Ave., Isla Verde, tel 787/268-2329,
rents an assortment of water-sport equipment including snorkeling gear,
windsurfers, kayaks, and fishing gear.

Where to Stay near the Caribbean National Forest
The forest and nearby sights are within an hour's drive of San Juan, so it
is probably best to stay there. Most accommodations in this region are
located along the coast between San Juan and Fajardo and tend to be the
larger beach resort–type properties.

Casa Cubuy Eco-lodge, at Kilometer 22 on Highway 191, Box
721, Río Blanco, tel 787/874-6221. This intimate 10-room inn on the
southern slope of El Yunque is ideal for those planning a long stay in the
park. Owners Marianne and her son can help out with transportation to
and from the park for a small fee. Rates $70.

Parador La Familia, Highway 987, four kilometers north of
Fajardo, Box 21399, Fajardo, tel 787/863-1193, fax 787/860-5345. This
28-room family-run *parador* has all the comforts of home plus a bar and a
great restaurant. Rates $55 to $65.

Camping in the Caribbean National Forest
Camping is allowed in the park and in other areas along the coast, but
sites get changed depending on usage. It is best to drop into the Sierra
Palm Interpretive Center at Kilometer 11.6 on Highway 191 (open 9 to
5:30 daily) or ask the ranger at the visitors center. The Puerto Rico

Department of Recreation and Sports and the Department of Natural Resources and the Environment can offer more information (see "Puerto Rico Specifics" at the end of chapter for more information on camping).

Where to Eat near the Caribbean National Forest

All the hotels or *paradors* listed above have good restaurants, and there are dozens of places to eat along the coast. Meals are also available at the visitors center in the park.

Don Pepe, on Highway 3 at Kilometer 31 near the entrance to El Yunque, serves international cuisine as well as Mexican dishes.

Las Vegas, on Highway 191 at Kilometer 1.5, tel 787/887-2526, is not far from El Yunque and serves great Puerto Rican delicacies and seafood.

Getting to the Caribbean National Forest

The best way to get around the island is to rent a car. Buses are simply unreliable and travel only on the main roads. Bus companies do run tours to these areas, but their itineraries are limited and rushed, and they are not recommended.

From San Juan: Take either Highway 3 or Highway 187 east to Highway 191, which takes you directly into the Caribbean National Forest. For Piñones Forest take Highway 187 east from San Juan. For Las Cabezas de San Juan, take Highway 3 east to Fajardo; just before you enter Fajardo turn left (northeast) onto 987 and follow the signs for Seven Seas Beach.

From Fajardo: Take Highway 3 west to 191 for El Yunque or Highway 187 for the Piñones Forest.

THE NORTHWEST REGION

Ninety kilometers west of San Juan lies one of the best tracts of karst countryside anywhere in the Caribbean, except maybe for Cuba's western Viñales Valley area. Karst terrain is characterized by limestone hummocks, or *mogotes*, sinkholes, caves, and jagged rocks. The free-standing rock outcroppings called *mogotes* resemble the limestone hills of Quilin in southern China. They are similar to buttes in the United States but more rounded. Most karst terrain in the Caribbean was formed about 160 million years ago when large limestone deposits were uplifted to form huge limestone plateaus. Over time water and wind eroded the plateau carving out high hummocks (some 300 meters high) and steep-sided valleys. The rivers that dissected the plateau sometimes passed through the limestone formations creating cave networks. Sinkholes are the collapsed ceilings of caverns, which open to the surface.

The north coast region is punctuated by haystack-shaped hills, large sinkholes, and the Western Hemisphere's third-largest subterranean cave system. Besides being the spelunking capital of Puerto Rico, this area contains a number of smaller but still interesting parks, forests, and archaeological sites. **Arecibo** makes a great base from which to explore the northwestern region.

Río Camuy Cave Park

This 108-hectare park is definitely the best-kept secret on the island, mainly because most people don't like caves and many visitors usually never get this far afield. Not only is this the third-largest cave system in the Western Hemisphere, but the Camuy River is the third-largest underground river in the world. The 17-kilometer river winds its way through the region about 120 meters below the surface, carving out many massive chambers on its journey to the sea.

The process of erosion also continues on another front. Dense vegetation in the sinkholes and collapsed caverns produce carbon dioxide, which is absorbed by rainwater to form a mild carbonic acid that further dissolves the porous limestone.

The Camuy cave system was first explored by outsiders in the late 1950s by Russell and Jane Gurnee, of *National Geographic* fame. They mapped out almost six kilometers of this extensive subterranean system and were instrumental in the park's creation in 1986. They even discovered a new, blind species of fish, which was named *Alaweckelia gurneei* in their honor. Today, more than 11 kilometers of caverns and some 220 caves have been explored and mapped in the system. The Camuy site has 16 large caverns, including the massive, 60-meter-high Clara de Empalme Cave, which contains huge stalagmites and stalactites.

Visitors to the park are shown a short film about the caverns before they proceed down a pathway to an open-air trolley for the descent into the caverns. The trolley descends through a steep-sided chasm amidst a profusion of graceful ferns, tall mahogany trees, and limestone formations, then through a 60-meter-deep sinkhole before reaching the entrance of the Clara de Empalme Cave. From here visitors are taken on a 45-minute guided tour through the immense cavern network. Tours are bilingual and quite informative.

From here visitors then reboard the trolley for a short ride to the **Tres Pueblos Sinkhole**, so named because it lies at the convergence point of three municipality boundaries (pueblos): the towns of Camuy, Hatillo, and Lares. The hole is gigantic. At almost 200 meters across and 120 meters deep, it is large enough to hold the entire El Morro fortress. A series of viewing platforms, around the rim, allows visitors a good look at the Camuy River some 120 meters below. Beyond Tres Pueblos are a series of steps that descend into another sinkhole to the entrance of

Cueva Espiral (Spiral Cave). After exploring Cueva Espiral visitors board trolleys for a ride back to the parking lot.

The caves are open Tuesday to Sunday and holidays from 8 a.m. to 3:45 p.m., and due to the ecological sensitivity of the site, the number of visitors through the caves is regulated. For more information, call 787/898-3100.

Other cave systems in the area that can be explored on your own include **La Cueva de la Luz** (Cave of Light) and **La Cueva de Pagan Pagan** (Pagan Pagan's Cave). For the more adventurous, a few outfitters offer real backcountry spelunking requiring rappelling down 100-meter sinkholes to reach underground rivers, waterfalls, and caverns. See "Outfitters and Guides," below, for more information.

The park is located on Highway 129, 20 kilometers south of Arecibo or about 1.5 hours from San Juan. Admission is $10 and parking is $2. For more information, contact the Río Camuy Cave Park Puerto Rico Land Administration, HCO3-33504, Box 363767, San Juan, PR 00936, tel 787/723-8194, fax 787/725-4004.

Guajataca Forest Reserve

Of the two forest reserves that lie within karst country, 1,620-hectare Guajataca provides the best example of this dramatic landscape. The most remote of the island's parks and reserves, it has the largest hiking trail system of all the parks and forest reserves.

More than 40 kilometers of fairly well-maintained hiking trails meander through the rugged topography. While the majority are moderate in difficulty, the jagged limestone will surely destroy most shoes, so make sure you have a hardy pair of hiking boots.

Many of the trails are long but relatively flat, and most tend to skirt the haystack-shaped limestone outcropping and sinkholes that characterize the area. One of the longer trails, **Cabralla**, runs from just beyond the ranger station and meanders 13 kilometers up the lush Río Guajataca valley to Lago Guajataca. The lake, a five-kilometer-long manmade reservoir, is a popular freshwater fishing spot and great for an invigorating swim after the long hike.

On many of the trails, the vegetation is so dense, you don't get a good view of the area, but a shorter trail, which leads from the ranger station to a lookout tower, offers great views of the surrounding countryside. In the southwest corner of the park is a small cavern, **Cueva del Viento**, which can be reached by a combination of trails. Maps of the reserve and trails are available at the ranger station and are required for some of the more remote hikes. Within the park boundaries are large tracts of blue mahoe trees, part of a number of old tree plantations in the region.

Santero: Saint Carver

In small workshops high in the Cordillera Central range of Puerto Rico are a group of master carvers called santeros. *These unique artists turn shapeless hunks of tropical wood into elaborately detailed and brightly colored statues called* santos, *religious icons that are a traditional fixture in most homes on the predominantly Catholic island. Some artists, such as 83-year-old Don Ceferino, even make tiny clothing for their statues.*

The faithful believe that the statues possess spiritual powers capable of granting wishes or performing certain good deeds. The most popular statues are those depicting St. Anthony, revered for his matchmaking ability. Throughout the island single girls of marrying age hang his image upside down from their dresser mirrors until they are wed, after which the statue is placed right side up on their dressers to bring good luck and longevity to the marriage.

Over the years these unique statues have not gone unnoticed. Many now grace the shelves of collectors in Europe and the United States. The work of some santeros is in such demand, they carve exclusively for collectors, taking orders years in advance. Visitors to the island can find santos in most upscale souvenir shops and some jewelry stores, but the best selections are found in religious gift shops.

The park is located between Aquadilla and Arecibo off Highway 2, about 30 kilometers west of Arecibo. Admission is free. More information about visiting is available at the ranger station near the park entrance, off Highway 446.

Arecibo Observatory

About 16 kilometers south of Arecibo off Highways 129 and 635 is the Arecibo Observatory, the largest radio dish telescope in the world that is actually embedded in the ground. The 8-hectare, 636-metric-ton dish is 304 meters in diameter and 50 meters deep and sits in a gigantic sinkhole depression between adjoining hills. Part of the SETI (Search for Extra-terrestrial Intelligence) network, it is used by Cornell University scientists to study pulsars and quasars. Tours are held Tuesday through Friday at two in the afternoon (tel 787/878-2612). Visitors can view monitors displaying audio and radio signals that have been converted into digital images and fre-quency charts and learn about the history of the dish and recent discoveries related to pulsars and quasars. Some tours take visitors on top of the dish.

Río Abajo State Forest

This forest, located 15 kilometers south of Arecibo along Highway 10, covers some of the most dramatic karst formations in the area. The for-est is not well developed as far as trails and amenities are concerned; exploring is done via a series of old logging roads and four-wheel-drive paths. The 2,050-hectare forest is part of the island's managed forest program, producing balsa, southeast Asian teak, West Indian mahogany, and Australian pine. At an average elevation of 450 meters, the forest gets enough rain to support a wide variety of birdlife, and was one of the last wild habitats of the rare Puerto Rican parrot. Just west of the main forest is **Laguna Dos Bocas**, a long narrow lake accessible from Highway 612, an old logging road. A ferry makes the two-hour round trip around the lake four times per day starting at seven in the morning. Although it is basically used by people living around the lake, visitors are welcome and the trip is worthwhile. You can board at numerous loca-tions along the lake.

Caguana Indian Ceremonial Park and Museum

Twenty-two kilometers south of Arecibo along Highway 10 is the village of Utuado, and 12 kilometers west of this village along Highway 111 is the Caguana Indian Ceremonial Park and Museum. Dating back to A.D. 1200, it is one of the more important archaeological sites in the Caribbean. The area was first excavated by J. A. Mason in 1915, and little has been done to it since besides keeping the vegetation from engulfing the five-hectare site. The park contains 10 Taíno *bateyes* (ball courts), which many historians believe to be the forerunner to soccer. Wide ravines surround the courts, which are lined with walls constructed of huge monolithic slabs of granite, some weighing tons. Etched into these massive slabs are ancient face carvings and other petroglyphs. The museum contains exhibits of Taíno artifacts such as tools and utensils and plaques describing what archaeologists believe were the first ball games played in the Caribbean. The site is open daily nine to five, and the museum is open on weekends ten to four (admission is free).

Outfitters and Guides for the North Coast Region
Several outfitters offer high-adventure spelunking, canyoning, cascading, and body rafting or tubing on underground rivers in karst country, particularly in the Río Camuy system. The highly experienced staffs of **Aventuras Tierra Adentro**, 787/766-0470, and **Tropix Wellness Tours**, 787/268-5882, are best for these types of adventures.

Where to Stay in the Northwest Region
There are dozens of small inns, or *paradors*, throughout the area between Manati and Quebradillas and south from Arecibo to Utuado. (For information on camping, see "Puerto Rico Specifics" at the end of this chapter.)

Parador Casa Grande, off Highway 612 close to Laguna dos Bocas, Box 616, Utuado, tel 787/894-3939, Web site: www.motel-casagrande.com, is located in the mountains near Laguna dos Bocas. This quiet, 20-room restored coffee plantation house is surrounded by great scenery and has all the comforts of home. Rates $55 to $85.

Parador El Buen Café, on Highway 2 in Hatillo, #381, Carr. 2, Kilometer 84, Bo. Carrizales, Hatillo, tel 787/898-1000, fax 787/898-7738, is a small, 20-room motel-like property near the beach in town with a renowned restaurant. Rates $75 to $95.

Parador El Guajataca, on Highway 2 in Quebradillas, Box 1558, Quebradillas, tel 787/895-3070 or 800/964-3065, fax 787/895-3589, is a larger, more modern motel (38 air-conditioned rooms) with a large pool overlooking the Atlantic Ocean. Rates $75 to $95.

Where to Eat in the Northwest Region
The above *paradors* have excellent restaurants, but there are dozens more scattered along the coastal road between Arecibo and Quebradillas and at the Río Camuy Caves.

La Parillada Restaurant Argentino, Av. Rotarios 522, Arecibo, tel 787/878-7777, specializes in Argentinian meat dishes and some seafood.

Restaurant Brisas de Guajatacas, 750 Calle Estación at Los Merenderos, Quebradillas, tel 787/895-5366, serves up tasty local dishes for reasonable prices.

Taco Rico Restaurant, Av. Fernando L. Rivas, Utuado, serves great Mexican dishes in a casual atmosphere. Lunch and dinner.

Getting to the North Coast Region

There are buses *públicos* running from San Juan, but rental cars are the way to see the island. Highway 22 runs along the north coast from San Juan to just west of Arecibo. Branch off at Highway 10 north to Arecibo or south to Utuado. For Río Camuy take 129 south from Arecibo or Highway 486 south (off Highway 2) from Hatillo and Quebradillas. Guajataca Forest is south on Highway 446 south (off Highway 2 just east of Quebradillas). For the Arecibo Observatory take Highway 129 south (from Arecibo) to Highway 134 south, then Highway 635 east and follow the signs. Highway 10 south (from Arecibo) takes you through Río Abajo Forest, Utuado, and the Indian ceremonial site.

THE SOUTHERN REGION

The drier southern side of Puerto Rico is in the rain shadow of the Cordillera Central Mountains but still gets enough rain to support four smaller, unique forest reserves: Toro Negro, Maricao, and Guanica. The first three are located on the southern slopes of the Cordillera Central while Guanica lies on the coast. Combined, they nourish most of the island's flora and fauna species.

The city of **Ponce** (114 kilometers southwest of San Juan on the south-central coast) is an ideal location from which to explore this region. Ponce is Puerto Rico's second largest city and is just as rich in colonial architecture as San Juan. Its cobblestone streets, century-old buildings, and quiet demeanor has prompted people to affectionately refer to it as La Perla del Sur (The Pearl of the South).

Ponce is just over an hour's drive from San Juan; go south along the San Juan to Ponce (Highway 52).

Guáncia Forest Reserve

The Guáncia Forest Reserve, on the site where the Americans landed in 1898 during the Spanish-American War, is one of the best examples of subtropical dry forest and scrubland found anywhere in the world. More than 200 tree and plant species have been recorded in the 1,620-hectare reserve, including the ever useful *lignum vitae*, dubbed the "tree of life" because of the many uses for its wood and leaves. In fact, so important is this small parcel of habitat, in 1975 it was designated a Man and the Biosphere Reserve by the United Nations.

The biggest attraction here is the birdlife. Almost half of the island's species frequent these woodlands, and early morning birders are rewarded with sightings of such rarities as the Puerto Rican emerald hummingbird, the Puerto Rican bullfinch, and the Puerto Rican nightjar. Though the nightjar was thought to be extinct years ago, the reserve now supports a

Fountain and cathedral in Ponce

population of more than 900. The rare *guabario*, or Puerto Rican whip-poorwill, is found only here on the entire island. In all, about 14 endangered species make their home here.

Besides birds, green and leatherback turtles nest along the reserve beaches, and black *Ameiva wetmori* ground lizards can be seen everywhere. A program is underway to curtail mongoose predation on lizard and turtle eggs and juveniles. Some visitors may even be lucky enough to spot a manatee in the fringing mangroves.

More than 57 kilometers of abandoned dirt roads and trails crisscross the reserve, making it one of the more popular nature spots on the island. Vehicles are not permitted in most of the park but the trails are well marked, making it easy to find your way around. There are 10 main trials outlined in Beth Farnsworth's booklet *A Guide to the Trails of Guánica*, which is available at either of the two ranger stations. The one-kilometer **Velez/Vigía Trail** up to the highest point in the reserve, **Criollo II**, is the shortest trail, while the 5.5-kilometer **Fuerte Trail**, which leads to the ruins of an old fort, is the longest.

Visitors should be aware that this area gets less than 50 centimeters of rain annually and daytime temperatures can reach 40 degrees Celsius (over 100 degrees Fahrenheit).

The reserve is 30 kilometers west of Ponce off coastal Highway 2. There is no park admission fee. Visitor information can be obtained at ranger stations located at both ends of reserve, on Highway 335 and Highway 334.

Toro Negro Forest Reserve

The Toro Negro Forest Reserve, 32 kilometers northeast of Ponce in the southern Cordillera Central, flanks the highest peaks on the island, including Cerro de Punta (1,338 meters), and is home to Puerto Rico's highest lake, Guineo Reservoir. The 2,833-hectare reserve protects Puerto Rico's most important watershed and is the headwaters for several of the island's main rivers. It is also the coldest place on the island, with nighttime winter temperatures hovering around five degrees Celsius.

A steep road followed by a 20-minute climb gets you to the top of **Cerro de Punta**, where on a clear day you can almost see forever. Once you get over sharing this lofty perch with a number of transmission towers, the view is fantastic. For those who require a more difficult workout, the steep, three-hour climb through old coffee plantations from the **Parador Hacienda Gripinas** (off Highway 527) is most rewarding. There are dozens of trails ranging from one to three hours leading to waterfalls and scenic lookouts. Most are marked and there is a map of the region at the Doña Juana Recreation Area within the reserve. In addition to hiking and birding, there are a few small lakes suitable for swimming.

From Ponce head east on Highway 52, then turn north onto Highway 149 and follow the signs to the forest. Park admission is free. For visitor information, inquire at the ranger station at the park entrance, off Highway 143

Maricao Forest Reserve

This reserve is one of the least visited of the 14 in Puerto Rico, and many of its trails lead into seldom-visited expanses of forest. The area has a prolific bird population with more than 50 species recorded, many of which are endemic. Avid birders will find the scaly-naped pigeon, Puerto Rican lizard-cuckoo, and the rare and elusive elfin woods warbler. This is also the prime nesting area for the sharp-shinned hawk.

The 3,508-hectare reserve on the southwest slopes of the Cordillera Central, 65 kilometers northwest of Ponce, is characterized by porous, bluish-green serpentine soil of submarine volcanic origin, which creates a topography similar to karst, even though the area gets almost 300 centimeters of rain annually. These unique soil conditions contribute to the most exceptional diversity of trees within any of the reserves—278 species in all, including 37 endemic to this reserve only.

One of the best hiking trails on the island begins at Kilometer 14.8 on Highway 120 and takes approximately seven hours to hike. This 16-kilometer trail is not for the meek. It runs from the forest's main ridge down to the fish hatchery 300 meters below on the Maricao River, just south of the town of Maricao. The stretch through the Maricao River valley is especially difficult as it passes through jungle-like vegetation and the trail disappears in some places. Don't try to hike this trail without a compass and good topographical map. If you get lost, find the river and follow it west. Better yet, hire a guide (f see "Outfitters and Guides," below).

To get to Maricao from Ponce, head west to Sabana Grande, then take Highway 120 north to the reserve. Admission is free. The ranger station off Highway 120 can provide more information, or contact the Puerto Rico Department of Natural Resources and Environment, Box 90066600, Puerto de Tierra Station, San Juan, PR 00906-6600, tel 787/723-1717, fax 787/723-1791.

Outfitters and Guides in the Southern Region
Except for Maricao you will have no problems navigating the southern reserves. But ask at the ranger post or fish hatchery about a local guide before attempting the ridge-to-hatchery trail in the Maricao forest. Another option is to contact one of the outfitters listed in the previous sections.

Where to Stay in the Southern Region
Ponce is a perfect base for exploring these reserves, but there are *paradors* located closer to the reserves. The tourism department can provide a list.

Hotel Bélgica, Calle Villa 122, Ponce, PR 00731, tel 787/844-3255, offers 20 large clean rooms, most with air conditioning and balconies overlooking the busy street. Rates $50 to $60.

Hotel Melía, Calle Cristina 2, Ponce, PR 00731, tel 787/842-0260, fax 787/841-3602. This larger, but nice 78-room hotel in an old restored building has great atmosphere but smaller rooms. All amenities except pool. Rates $75 to $85.

Parador Hacienda Juanita, Kilometer 23.5 on Highway 105 near Maricao, Box 777, Maricao, PR 00606, tel 787/838-2550, fax 787/838-2551. This old restored coffee plantation house tucked into dense vegetation has 21 rooms, excellent restaurant, and pool. The host can help you find a guide for the Maricao Reserve hike. Rates $75 to $85.

Where to Eat in the Southern Region
Like other areas of Puerto Rico there is no shortage of good inexpensive eateries along the south coast and in Ponce. The hotels listed above all serve great food.

Lupita's Mexican Restaurant, Calle Reina Isabel 60, Ponce, tel 787/848-8808, is located in a nineteenth-century building with adjoining courtyard. They serve great Mexican dishes and blue and green margaritas. A live mariachi band plays on weekends.

Getting to the Southern Region
The easiest way to get to Ponce is to drive south along the San Juan to Ponce Highway 52, just over an hour's drive. For Toro Negro Forest head east from Ponce on Highway 52, turn north onto Highway 149, and follow the signs. West from Ponce along Highway 2 before entering Guanica are Highways 333 and 334, turnoffs into the park. For Maricao head west from Ponce to Sabana Grande, then take Highway 120 north to the reserve.

PUERTO RICO SPECIFICS

Getting There
Puerto Rico is served by every major North American airline and by LIAT and American Eagle from within the Caribbean. While there are seven airports on the island, all international flights and most regional flights arrive at the Luis Muños Marin International Airport just outside of San Juan. There are daily flights to Ponce from JFK on American.

Getting Around
Nobody likes to admit it, but local transportation outside of San Juan is poor at best. Minibuses called *públicos* have license plates that end in *P* or *PD*. Stops seem to be where anyone stands and most tend to stick to the main roads (not much help where you will be going). Another way to get around is to sign up for tours with one of the outfitters mentioned in the "Outfitters and Guides" sections earlier in this chapter.

Despite all you may have heard about crazy Puerto Rican drivers, renting a car is really the only way to go. Just drive slow and beep your horn around narrow curves. All of the major American rental car companies (**Budget, Avis, National, Hertz**, and so on) are represented on the island, and it's best to stick with them. Local agencies offer no real savings. Use their toll-free numbers to book reservations and expect to pay about $200 a week.

Tourist Information
San Juan, #2 Paseo La Princesa, Old San Juan, PR 00902, tel 787/721-2400, fax 787/725-4417

East Coast U.S.A., 575 Fifth Ave., 23rd floor, New York, NY 10017, tel 212/599-6262, 800/223-6530, fax 212/818-1866

West Coast U.S.A., 3575 W. Cahuenga Blvd., Suite 560, Los Angeles, CA 90068, tel 213/874-5991, 800/874-1230, fax 213/874-7257

Canada, 41-43 Colbourne St., Suite 301, Toronto, Ont. M5E 1E3, tel 416/368-2680 or 800/667-0394 (within Canada only), fax 416/368-5350

Web sites: For information try www.discoverpuertorico.com and www.travelfile.com/get?prtorico.

Camping on the beach in Puerto Rico

Camping in Puerto Rico

There are numerous places to camp on the island. Most reserves allow camping, but few have established campsites so be prepared to rough it. There are also a few private camp-sites but they are no better. The two outfitters listed under "Outfitters and Guides" earlier in this chapter can assist with camping, including supply-ing equipment. For information on camping around the island contact **Puerto Rico Department of Natural Resources and Environment**, Box 90066600, Puerto de Tierra Station, San Juan, PR 00906-6600, tel 787/723-1717, fax 787/723-1791; or **Puerto Rico Department of Recreation and Sports**, Box 2089, San Juan, PR 00902, tel 787/721-2800, fax 787/721-8012.

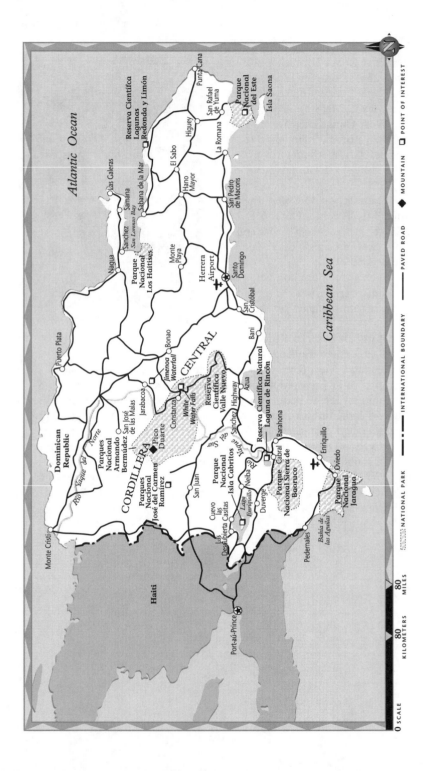

DOMINICAN REPUBLIC

7

Located 112 kilometers due west of Puerto Rico, the Dominican Republic is the Caribbean's second largest nation in size and population. It shares the island of Hispaniola with Haiti, making it one of only two divided islands in the Caribbean (the other is St. Martin/Sint Maarten). The Dominican Republic, with an area of 48,000 square kilometers, occupies the eastern two-thirds of Hispaniola and boasts more than 400 kilometers of soft white-sand beaches along with Pico Duarte, at 3,174 meters the Caribbean's loftiest peak, and Lago Enriquillo, the largest natural lake and lowest point in the Caribbean (40 meters below sea level).

The land rises from the broad eastern lowlands to the Cordillera Central range in the west, which occupies almost 40 percent of the total land mass. One-third of the predominantly Spanish speaking and Catholic population (almost 2.3 million) live in the country's capital city, Santo Domingo, the oldest city in the Western Hemisphere.

In terms of activities, the Dominican Republic has it all: fantastic hiking, bird watching, cycling, horseback riding, snorkeling, and spelunking. It is also one of only two Caribbean destinations where the rivers are large and fast enough for tubing, kayaking, and white-water rafting.

The Dominican Republic has been largely deforested for agriculture, lumber, and fire wood. Only about 15 percent of the original forests remain and these, for the most part, are relegated to the higher elevations and more inaccessible areas. Not wanting to repeat the plight of its neighbor, Haiti, where almost every tree has been cut down and erosion has devastated the land, the Dominican Republic, in the mid-1950s, took action to save its remaining forests. In the last 45 years it has established 14 national parks and 7 nature reserves.

Almost 10 percent of the country is now protected, and a number of reforestation programs are in full swing. Additionally, government and local groups actively promote the Dominican Republic as an ecotourism destination. They now realize that there is "gold in them there hills" and have set up park offices close to all parks. Admission fees vary, but five dollars is average. The fees collected are used to fund park programs and pay rangers to protect the park and wildlife. A permit from the National Parks Office, obtained personally or through an outfitter or guide, is required in advance for all park visits. Thanks in part to the country's proximity to the ecological devastation in Haiti, the people's conscious-ness about maintaining their natural environment is growing steadily.

Unfortunately, the Republic's awareness of the need to preserve land resources has not yet spilled over to the island's surrounding waters, where coral reefs are under daily attack from inexperienced visitors and locals alike. The use of dynamite to fish is still an all-too-common prac-tice and, although illegal, difficult to police. The recent creation of the La Caleta National Underwater Park is a small step in the right direction, and as more private diving and snorkeling operators spring up to handle the increased demand, more pressure will be put on the government to designate other areas as marine parks or sanctuaries.

With distinct geographic regions and tropical, subtropical, and semi-arid vegetation zones—all together nine different and transitional zones—the Dominican Republic supports a wide variety of flora and fauna. More than 5,500 varieties of flora and 5,500 species of fauna are found on the island. Twenty species of cactus share the dry areas with some 300 vari-eties of orchids. Trees vary from the coastal mangroves to the 40-meter-high mahogany and *capá* trees used for shipbuilding. Twenty-four of the island's 258 species of birds are endemic and include the white-winged dove, Hispaniolan trogon, Leselle's thrush, Hispaniolan palmchat (the national bird), endangered parrot, *cotica*, and flamingo.

As on the other islands, mammals are scarce, but the *solenodon* (a rat-like insectivore) and the *hutia* (also known as agouti) are plentiful, as well as 18 species of bats. A few manatees swim in Samaná Bay, and a few crocodiles lurk in the waters of Lago Enriquillo. All four varieties of sea turtles nest on many beaches on the island.

Dominican Republic History

Columbus landed on the island the Taíno Indians called Quisqueya ("mother earth"), on December 6, 1492, and named it La Isla Española (or Hispaniola, meaning "little Spain"). Like many of the other Caribbean islands, it had been rocked by violence over the years. The first settlement Columbus built in the north was destroyed by the Taíno, then his second settlement, in the south, La Nueva, was destroyed by a hurricane in 1502. By 1509 the new settlement of Santo Domingo was flourishing as Spain's base for conquests in Central and South America. In 1586 Sir Francis Drake pillaged the city and burnt most of it to the ground.

The following four centuries saw attacks by the French, Haitians, and British with the land changing hands a few times. In 1822 the country was occupied by Haiti and remained under Haitian rule until February 27, 1844, when revolutionaries, led by Juan Pablo Duarte, overthrew the Haitians and paved the way for the country's independence. The late 1800s were racked by civil wars, assassinations, and controversy, but the bloodiest time was during the 1930 to 1961 dictatorship of Rafael Leonidas Trujillo y Molina, during which time 10,000 Haitians and a similar number of Dominicans were slaughtered. Over the last 20 years, however, the island nation has embraced democracy and, although still considered a poor nation, it is moving forward with tourism as the island's major industry.

SANTO DOMINGO

Although there are three international airports on the island, many flights arrive in Santo Domingo. A visit to the city's Colonial Zone is a must. Somewhat similar to Old San Juan or Old Havana, the Colonial Zone contains the oldest buildings in the Western Hemisphere. Founded in 1496 by Columbus' brother, Bartolomé, Santo Domingo holds the title of "first" for so many things that UNESCO designated it a World Cultural Heritage Site. Many sixteenth-century buildings dot the landscape and recent restoration projects have made the old city even more attractive.

Things to See and Do in Santo Domingo

In the center of the old town are **Parque Colón** (Columbus Square), the **Cathedral of Santa Maria la Menor**, completed in 1523, and the **Tower of Homage**, completed in 1503. Of course, one of the main attractions in the old city is the new **Christopher Columbus Lighthouse Monument**, opened in 1992 to honor Columbus' quincentenary. The seven-story cross-like structure holds what many believe to be the remains of Columbus himself, although at least two other countries claim they have the great navigator's remains. The monument houses displays of fifteenth-century pottery and countless exhibits about Columbus.

The centerpiece of the old city is the palace **Alcazar de Colón**, former home of Don Diego (son of Columbus) and first viceroy of

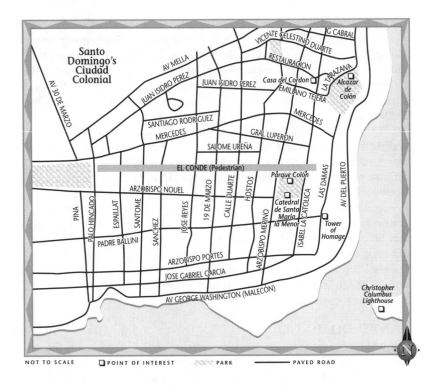

NOT TO SCALE   ☐ POINT OF INTEREST   ░░░ PARK   ——— PAVED ROAD

Hispaniola. Built in 1510 without the use of a single nail, it is a short walk from the **Casa del Cordon**, the oldest building in the Western Hemisphere. Built in 1508 it was home to Don Diego and his family during construction of the palace.

Where to Stay in Santo Domingo

Because Santo Domingo is also the business center of the country, downtown hotels tend to be large affairs. There are, however, a few smaller, locally owned ones.

Hostal Nicolás Nader, corner of Luperón and Duarte, tel 809/687-6674, fax 809/687-7887. Located in a sixteenth-century colonial building, this hotel has 20 basic, comfortable rooms with air conditioning and great atmosphere. Rates $40 to $55.

Hotel Napolitano, George Washington Ave. #51, Santo Domingo, Dominican Republic, tel 809/687-1131, fax 809/687-6814. Along the ocean about three blocks from the Colonial Zone, this 72-room hotel has air conditioning, a swimming pool, and a restaurant. Rates $50 to $65.

Hotel Palacio, 106 Calle Duarte, Santo Domingo, Dominican Republic, tel 809/682-4730, fax 809/687-5535. This hotel has 10 attractive, small, and intimate rooms in a nineteenth-century building that was home to Buenaventura Baez, former five-time president of the Dominican Republic. Rates $50 to $60.

Where to Eat in Santo Domingo

The hotels listed above have great restaurants, but there are hundreds more in the Colonial Zone or along George Washington Avenue.

Alcazar de Colón in Santo Domingo

Fonda Atarazana, Calle Atarazana #5, tel 809/689-2900. Near the Alcázar in the Colonial Zone, this charmer serves tasty local dishes such as curried goat in sherry sauce.

Il Buco, Arizobispo Meriño 162A, tel 809/685-0884. One of the most popular eating spots in the Colonial Zone, Il Buco serves great seafood and local creole dishes.

La Parilla, George Washington Ave. #533, tel 809/688-1511. This restaurant serves delicious local creole dishes.

PARKS OF THE SOUTHWEST REGION

Often referred to as the arid southwest, this region of the country lies in the rain shadow on the drier, leeward side of the Cordillera Central. It contains the Valle de Neiba (an old rift valley), between the Sierra de Neiba, in the north, and Sierra de Bahoruco, on the south, where you'll find Lago Enriquillo and Parque Nacional Isla Cabritos. Occupying almost the entire southwest Pedernales peninsula is the great thorn forest of Parque Nacional Jaragua, the country's largest national park.

The best base from which to explore these parks is **Barahona,** on the east coast of the peninsula. The city is small (population 50,000) and relatively young by Dominican standards (founded in 1802). It is, however, becoming a popular spot for those planning on exploring the region. Six kilometers west of Barahona, just outside the even smaller village of **Cabral,** is the **Reserva Científica Natural Laguna de Rincón,** the country's largest freshwater lagoon. The 47-square-kilometer lagoon has abundant wildlife, including the *jicotea*, a freshwater slider turtle, masked and ruddy ducks, sora crake, and flamingos. A marked hiking trail rings the lake.

Parque Nacional Jaragua

The 1,350-kilometer Jaragua, named after the Taíno chieftain *Xaragua*, covers almost the entire southwest peninsula, 700 square kilometers of offshore waters, and the small islands of Alto Velo and Beate. It is the largest, driest, and most undeveloped of all the Republic's parks. The park stretches from Ovieda on the west side of the peninsula to Pedernales on the eastern border with Haiti, and is bordered on the north by the Sánchez Highway (which runs all the way from Santo Domingo).

The compact limestone soil is filled with ferrous oxide, which gives the region its reddish appearance. Much of the limestone has been eroded to form a jagged "dogtooth" terrain covered with thorny forest, aloe, and cacti. The forest contains drought-resistant varieties like the copey, the stunted Hispaniola mahogany, *lignum vitae* ("tree of life"), wild frangipani senna, and gumbo-limbo. The coastline is fringed with seagrape, red and button mangrove, and a few stands of the rare white mangrove lining the salt marshes.

Within the park boundaries is Lago Ovieda, a 10-kilometer-long salt-water lake situated just southeast of the east coast town of Ovieda, an area known for its birdlife. This area contains more than 130 species of birds, including the Don Juan grande (a common potoo so named because of its arrogant demeanor), burrowing owl, Antillian palm swift, sooty tern, and the endemic green-tailed warbler. Also frequenting the salt lake and the bordering sandbars is the nation's largest concentration of greater flamingos. Just offshore, Beate island is an ideal place to see flamingos, roseate spoonbills, Ridgeway's hawks, willets, and frigate birds.

Land animals include *solenodons*, *hutias*, 11 bat species, and 2 endemic iguanas—the Ricord's and rhinoceros. All four Caribbean sea turtles species nest along the region's fantastic white-sand beaches, which include one of the most spectacular undeveloped beaches in the country, **Bahía de las Aquilas**. The area is also noted for its large variety of butterflies.

The region's porous limestone foundation has led to the creation of a number of caves, including Guanal, La Cueva la Poza, Cueva Mongó, and, the most accessible, Cueva de Abajo, on the southern tip of Bahía de las Aquilas. The area was sacred to the Taíno, evidenced by the ancient petroglyphs and pictographs found in many of the caves.

There are no marked trails and only a few operators offer guided trips into the park. A more convenient way to see the park is by boat; a few fishermen in the small village of Trujille will be happy to take you for a tour. A few shorter trails also exist in the park, but a guide is a must and a Parks Department requirement.

Remember to get advance permission from the Parks Department before attempting any excursions into the park. Entry to the park costs five dollars per person.

Lago Enriquillo and Parque Nacional Isla Cabritos

Parque Nacional Isla Cabritos, which comprises Lago Enriquillo and its shoreline plus the three islands within the lake, is one of the few Caribbean parks where there are no towns, people, restaurants, or lodgings—nothing but scrub forest and an abundance of wildlife, including the largest concentration of crocodiles in the world. The area, northwest of Barahona almost on the border with Haiti, is as unique and beautiful as are Death Valley or the Mojave Desert. As in those desert areas, there are no handy sources of food or water.

Lago Enriquillo is the Caribbean's largest natural lake as well as the lowest point in the entire region, 40 meters below sea level. It is estimated that the waters here are four times as salty as the sea and the area's daytime temperature seldom drops below 40 degrees Celsius. The lake is all that remains of an old sea channel that ran through the island between Barahona and the Bay of Port-au-Prince in Haiti.

The lake gets it name from a famous Taíno rebel leader, Enriquillo, who fought the Spanish in the mid-1500s. The Spanish were never able to defeat him and his followers, so they signed a peace treaty, made him a Don, and granted his people reservation land wherever they wanted to settle. Enriquillo and his people were the last Taínos on the island.

Isla Cabritos (Little Goats Island) is the largest of three islands in the salt lake, and rumored to be the place the Spanish peace treaty with Enriquillo was signed. Despite its name, all the goats have been removed and the island has become home to a number of the Republic's endangered species, including the American crocodile, Ricord's and rhinoceros iguanas, slider turtles, Hispaniola parrot, and flamingo. The lake and island are said to have one of the largest populations of crocodiles in the world—recent estimates put their numbers at about 10,000. The island is mainly crushed coral on a limestone base, but supports some thorny bushes such as cayuco and cholla, cacti, and aloe.

Isla Cabritos is accessible only by boat from the National Park Office just outside La Descubrieta. A round trip costs about $30 (arrange the rate before getting into the boat). Well-worn trails crisscross the island, allowing visitors to explore and enjoy wildlife viewing.

Amber

The Greeks called amber elektron *(the word from which we get "electron" and "electricity") because of its ability to generate static electricity when rubbed on silk. Its static qualities earned it the nickname "touchstone," but the movie* Jurassic Park *elevated it to new gem status. In the last few years scientists have examined the DNA of insects and vegetation trapped in amber for clues to origins of the species. Everywhere you go in the Dominican Republic you will see hand-crafted amber jewelry.*

The Dominican Republic has some of the world's largest deposits of this semiprecious gem. It is not a mineral or stone, but prehistoric tree resin or sap petrified millions of years ago. As many varieties of amber exist as there were varieties of trees. Its color varies from the familiar orange-yellow to deep red. The rarest hue is white. Its value is determined by color and composition; the closer to red the higher the price. However, the most expensive pieces, regardless of color, are those containing "inclusions," fossilized insects or plants trapped inside. The largest piece of amber ever unearthed, eight kilograms, was found near Sabana de la Mar in 1979.

The Joyas Criollas Museum at the Plaza Criolla in Santo Domingo has a good collection of amber on display, and there are two mines, just north of Santo Domingo in El Valle, which offer guided tours. Be careful to buy only crafted amber; it is illegal to export or remove raw amber from the country.

Birds common to the area are the endemic gray-headed quail-dove, Hispaniola trogon, and Antillean siskin. In the mountains surrounding the lake, bird species such as the grasshopper sparrow, golden swallow, yellow-billed cuckoo, and yellow-bellied sapsucker are common while the lake's shoreline teems with birds such as the clapper rail, tern, spoonbill, and nighthawk.

On the northwest shore of the lake, just outside the village of La Descubierta, is the **Cuevo las Caritas** (Cave of the Little Faces), named for the petroglyphs found on the cave walls. On the northeast corner of the lake, between the villages of Neiba and Galvan, are the refreshing cold water pools of **Las Brias** and hot sulfur springs called **Las Marias**, popular with locals who use them to cure all manner of ailments.

A ring road circles the lake and takes about two hours to drive around. Many of the sites listed are found along this loop road. You can obtain park permits (five-dollar fee) and arrange boat rides at the National Park Office just west of the small village of Las Caritas, on the north side of the lake.

Parque Nacional Sierra de Bahoruco

Sandwiched between Lago Enriquillo and Parque Jaragua, this 309-square-kilometer park offers a bit more vegetation and wildlife. This range of mountains, rising to 2,367 meters, was the place where the Taíno chieftain Enriquillo made his last stand. The mostly limestone formation, being higher than the surrounding landscape, tends to capture more rainfall and therefore supports a few larger tree varieties, including the creolean pine, laurel cherry, myrtle, West Indian sumac, and mahogany. About 160 species of orchids are found here, including 20 endemic varieties. Fifty bird species have been recorded in the park, including the peewee, Vervian hummingbird, and the rare white-necked crow.

With a four-wheel-drive vehicle it is possible to drive straight over the mountains to the Sánchez Highway in the south. The road passes Loma del Torro, the highest peak in the park, at 2,367 meters. Another road leads south along the Haitian border to Pedernales, but it is not advisable given the unrest in Haiti and the ongoing border disputes.

For more information, visit the National Park Office 11 kilometers south of Duvergé in Puerto Escondido. Admission to the park is five dollars per person.

Outfitters and Guides in the Southwest Region

Delia's Tours, Santo Domingo, tel 809/682-1086, offers custom guided tours to all the parks in the southwest region.

Ecoturisa, Calle Santiago #203-B, Santo Domingo, tel 809/221-4101, fax 809/685-1544, is your best bet for trips to any of the Dominican Republic's national parks or reserves. This quasi-governmental, centralized tour organization can arrange any tour you want and takes care of guides and permits. Part of the organization's profit goes to the Fundación Prospectiva Ambiental Dominicana, a nonprofit organization promoting education and protection of the environment.

Rancho Baiguate near Jarabacoa

Elena Nunciatini, tel 809/537-5831 or cel 809/224-9625, offers guided trips to Isla Cabritos National Park.

Iguana Mama Adventure Tours, Cabarete, tel 809/571-0908 or 800/849-4720 (U.S.A.), fax 809/571-3346, email: iguana-mama@codetel.net.do, web site: www.iguana-mama.com, offers guided biking, hiking, and rafting trips all over the island. They take care of everything.

A few **private tour operators** have opened their own central booking service at Avenue Central #32, Apto. 5, Ens. Carolina, Santo Domingo, tel 809/532-7920, fax 809/532-8323.

Rancho Baiguate, Jarabacoa, Dominican Republic, tel 809/574-6890 or 809/696-0318, fax 809/574-4940, email: rancho.baiguate @codetel.net.do. Besides guided hikes and cycle trips, they offer rafting and just about anything else you can imagine, including cascading, canyoning, and ATV adventures. The Rancho Baigute also has 17 guest rooms.

Where to Stay in the Southwest Region

Barahona offers a variety of accommodations. For information on camping, see "Dominican Republic Specifics" at the end of the chapter.

Hotel Caribe, Ave. Enriquillo y Playa Saladilla, Barahona, tel 809/524-4111 or 524-2185, fax 809/524-5115. This small hotel has 23 comfortable rooms with bath and a great restaurant. Rates $25.

Hotel Las Magnolias, Calle Anacaona #13, Barahona, tel 809/524-2244. Near the bus station, this hotel has 20 simple but comfortable rooms with air conditioning. Rates $15 to $20.

Riviera Beach Hotel, Ave. Enriquillo #6, Barahona, tel 809/524-5111, fax 809/524-5798. A great local 108-room hotel just outside of town is larger and more touristy than others but offers great amenities for those wanting more comfort. Rates $75 to $85.

Swiss Hotel, 10 kilometers south of Barahona along the main road, tel 809/545-1496. A real charmer with 17 spacious, clean rooms with views of the sea. Rates $35 to $45.

Where to Eat in the Southwest Region

There are small cafés in most of the small towns in the area, and the hotel restaurants are also a good bet. Local favorites in these parts include all kinds of paella, *pica-pollo* (crispy fried chicken), *sanchoco* (a rice dish with seven meats), *cocido* (spicy cow's feet and garbanzo beans), *chimichurri* (spicy sausage), spicy conch chowder, and curried goat.

Brahamas, in La Descubierta, serves good local meals.

Brisas del Caribe, Avenida Enriquillo, near the airport, Barahona, serves everything from local to Chinese.

La Rocco, next to the Hotel Caribe in Barahona, serves great inexpensive seafood.

Getting to the Southwest Region

Barahona is about three hours by car and four by bus from Santo Domingo. Buses leave the main bus station in Santo Domingo four times a day for Barahona. You can also fly into Barahona from Santo Domingo via **Columbus Air**, but service is spotty at this time. The best way to see this region and the Dominican Republic in general is by car. At $60 per day for a four-wheel-drive vehicle it's not cheap, but the roads are good and there are plenty of gas stations.

To get to Barahona just head west on the Sánchez highway from Santo Domingo and follow the signs. For the Natural Laguna de Rincón, head west on Highway 46 from Barahona towards Cabral. For Lago Enriquillo, head west on Highway 48 from Barahona towards Neiba and follow the signs to La Descubierta.

CORDILLERA CENTRAL REGION

Probably the closest thing that Dominicanas have to the last frontier, and the farthest thing from most visitors' minds, is the Cordillera Central, cherished by the local population as *the* place to get away from it all. Not only is it the Republic's vacation playground, it plays an integral part in the island's economy. The great rivers spawned in these mountains are the life blood of the island's agricultural and manufacturing sectors (by providing hydroelectricity). This range also contains the four highest peaks in the Caribbean.

Occupying more than 2,000 square kilometers, it is the single most important resource the island has, except for maybe its beaches. So important is its watershed, it was the first area to be declared a national park. In fact, almost 75 percent of the total area has been designated the Armando Bermúdez and José del Carmen Ramírez National Parks. Two other smaller scientific reserves, Valle Nuevo and del Ebano Verde, account for another 500 square kilometers.

The best place from which to explore this great region is the small mountain community of **Jarabacoa** (population 45,000), situated 30 kilometers off the main Santo Domingo-to-Santiago highway, high on the eastern slopes of Pico Duarte.

Parques Nacionales Armando Bermúdez and José del Carmen Ramírez

The twin parks of Armando Bermúdez and José del Carmen Ramírez are divided by the Río La Compartición. Armando Bermúdez was created in 1956 and José del Carmen Ramírez in 1958 to protect the watershed for Santo Domingo and the great fertile plains of the San Juan Valley. The Cordillera Central gives rise to 14 rivers, all of which play an important part in sustaining the island's agricultural industry. The island's two largest rivers, the Ríos Yaque del Sur and Yaque del Norte, along with three others have dams that provide most of the island's electrical power.

Because of the many vegetation zones found within these parks, visitors will be treated to almost every variety of flora and fauna found on the island, except arid zone species. The vegetation is specific to elevation. Up to 1,000 meters it is tropical rain forest with canopies over 40 meters. West Indian mahogany, white cedar, and walnut share the slopes with

Armando Bermúdez mountains in Cordillera Central

more exotic varieties like wild mountain olive, *petitia*, and *palo amargo*. At elevations between 1,000 and 2,000 meters, the tall canopy is replaced by much smaller, more compact varieties such as myrtle, laurel cherry, sierra palm, and wild avocado. Above 2,000 meters the vegetation becomes even more sparse, with varieties such as *palo de viento*, wild brazilleto, cyrilla, and creolean pines.

Besides containing many of the island's bird species, the parks support many rare varieties such as the Hispaniola parrot and woodpecker, white-necked crow, palm chat, rufous-throated solitaire, Greater Antillean elania, and peewee. *Hutia, solenodon,* mongoose, and iguana are also common in the parks. The government has introduced wild boars into Armando Bermúdez in hopes of establishing a hunting program. Perhaps they should have consulted with the Hawaiians before doing so. Wild boars are devastating Hawaiian forests.

The highlight for most visitors to the parks is an ascent of 3,174-meter **Pico Duarte**. The mountain was first climbed in 1944 as part of the 100th anniversary celebration of the island's independence. The peak was named after the father of Dominican Republic independence, Juan Pablo Duarte, and is usually climbed in the winter months when it is drier, but also much colder. Snow and frost have been recorded on the mountaintop on many occasions, and numerous climbers have succumbed to hypothermia. The 23-kilometer eastern approach, **La Ciénaga Trail**, starts in La Ciénaga at 1,350 meters and is all uphill. At 2,500 meters, about halfway up the mountain, is La Comparticíon, where hikers will find a few cabins in which to spend the night. From here the summit is a strenuous three-hour climb. Most do the climb in four days, but the really fit ones can make it in three. Use a guide.

Also ascending Pico Duarte, the **Mata Grande Trail**, from the north, and the **Sabaneta Trail**, from the south, are shorter but more difficult, without an established overnight point. What makes this trek difficult is that everything must be packed up the slope, including food, water, warm clothes, and bedding. Many hikers rent mules to carry the bulk of their provisions and equipment. For their own safety all hikers must be accompanied by a trained guide and must provide details of their trip to the National Park ranger station in La Ciénaga. For this reason, it's best to go with an organized tour that will make all the arrangements, including securing a park permit. *Under no circumstance should a trip up Pico Duarte be attempted without a guide*, whichever of the three trails you take. Over the last few years, there have been some unpleasant stories involving "stupid gringos" who have lost their lives here.

Other activities in the area include white-water rafting, rock climbing, horseback riding, and mountain biking in the park. Rancho Baiguate (see Outfitters and Guides in the Southwest Region," above) includes all these activities when you stay at their ranch.

Admission is $10 per person per park. For more information, contact the National Parks Department at Santo Domingo, tel 809/221-5340.

Reserva Científica Valle Nuevo

Designated in 1983, this 409-square-kilometer reserve in the southeast Cordillera is one of the most isolated and undisturbed places on the island. About a third of the western slopes were destroyed in 1983 by forest fires, and the reserve was established to protect the remaining stands of montane and oceanic forests threatened by logging and farming. A few logging roads off Highway 41 push deep into the reserve, and regulated logging operations are underway in the area. The reserve is bordered on the north by Constanza and on the west by Highway 12, which runs from Constanza to San Jose. Highway 41 from Constanza runs south through the heart of the forest. White Water Falls is within the park (see next section).

Most of the reserve is at 2,000 meters elevation, but the road from Constanza climbs to about 2,400 meters at its highest point, about 16 kilometers to the south, near the settlement of El Convento. From here the road descends into the upper Río Ocoa valley. Most of the forest species found on the reserve are similar to those of other highland forests in the area, with the exception of holly and lyonia, which are found nowhere else in the Caribbean. It is thought that these two temperate species, more common in North America, got here by migrating birds dropping their seeds. The forest environment proved ideal and the species were established. The lower slopes, approaching the Río Ocoa valley, have thick stands of pine. The government is actively reforesting slopes damaged by the fires.

Of the 250 plant species found in this reserve, almost half, including the Dominican magnolia, are endemic. The lower, drier areas of the reserve support mahogany and mesquite. The reserve offers some of the best birding on the island, with common sightings of Antillean euphonia, palm crow, black-crowned palm tanager, narrow-billed tody, and white-winged warbler.

Though the road is bad at the best of times, the trip from Constanza to San José is quite spectacular. The one-day trip is best attempted in a four-wheel-drive vehicle with a full tank of gas and some emergency provisions. The drive from San José to Santo Domingo takes about two hours.

Visitors to the park will be charged a $10 admission fee. For more information, contact Rancho Baiguate (tel 809/574-6890 or 809/696-0318, fax 809/574-4940) or the National Parks office in Jarabacoa.

Other Things to See and Do in the Cordillera Central Region

There are a couple of waterfalls in the Cordillera worth seeing. The 32-meter-high **Jimenoa Waterfall** is located about 10 kilometers south of Jarabacoa off the road to Constanza. The trailhead to the falls is located on the edge of the small hamlet of El Salto and difficult to find, but there is always someone around to point it out for you. **White Water Falls** (Aguas Blanco) is 10 kilometers south of Constanza off Highway 41 near the settlement of El Convento. Ask someone to point out the trailhead, then hike two kilometers up to the falls. Keep a sharp eye out for the rare sharp-shinned hawk and the gray-headed quail-dove, both common in the area.

Another point of interest is **Constanza**. In the mid-1950s, the island's dictator convinced about 50 Japanese farm families to settle in Constanza and train the locals in the art of Japanese farming. Today, Constanza is a thriving Japanese community, resembling any farming community in Japan, and worth a quick visit.

Outfitters and Guides in the Cordillera Central Region

Most of the parks mentioned in the Cordillera Central Region require a guide. Many towns and privately owned lands fall within the park boundaries, and sometimes you'll need to walk through private property to get to an attraction. Outfitters make yearly payments to private land owners for access rights. If you go alone you may be confronted by a Spanish-speaking local waving a cutlass demanding money. So use a guide.

The best operator in the Cordillera is **Rancho Baiguate**, based in Jarabacoa. **Iguana Mama Adventure Tours** and **Ecoturisa** are good backups (see "Outfitters and Guides in the Southwest Region," above). A four-day trip to Pico Duarte will run about $400 and includes everything.

Where to Stay in the Cordillera Central Region

Pinar Dorado, one kilometer south of Jarabacoa on the Jarabacoa-Constanza highway, tel 809/574-2820 or 800/843-3311 (U.S.A. only), fax 809/687-7012. This 77-room hotel is popular with European tourists visiting the mountains. It has all the amenities. Rates $35 to $50.

Rancho Baiguate, Jarabacoa, Dominican Republic, tel 809/574-6890 or 809/696-0318, fax 809/574-4940, email: rancho.baiguate@ codetel.net.do, offers one-stop shopping at its best. Not only does the ranch have 17 great rooms, but they are probably the best outfitter in the region. Room rates vary because they include trips, but the average is $45.

For information on camping, see "Dominican Republic Specifics" at the end of the chapter.

Where to Eat in the Cordillera Central Region

Along with the hotels listed above are dozens of smaller local establishments offering good food. (The hotel restaurants do offer much better service.)

Hotel Lorenzo, Calle 16 de Agosto, Constanza, is a great place for local steak and chicken creole.

Restaurant Brasilia, Calle Colón #26, Jarabacoa, serves great local dishes.

Getting to the Cordillera Central Region

Jarabacoa is a four-hour drive from Santo Domingo, just 24 kilometers off the main Santo Domingo–Santiago expressway. **Caribe Tours** (27 de Febrero, Santo Domingo, tel 809/687-3171) runs a daily bus from Santo Domingo to Jarabacoa. You can also fly into Santiago from Puerto Rico or Santo Domingo and rent a car there for the two-hour drive to Jarabacoa.

PARQUE NACIONAL LOS HAITISES

The Samaná peninsula is another of the "most beautiful" places on the island, characterized by lush rain forests, deep bays, and fantastic beaches. It is situated on the northeastern coast about 120 kilometers northeast of Santo Domingo. The peninsula is about 50 kilometers long and 15 kilometers wide, occupying a total of 1,000 square kilometers. Stretching along the length of the peninsula are the Cordillera Samaná, which rise abruptly from Bahia Samaná to about 500 meters. The peninsula's topography, combined with the colder Atlantic currents mixing with the bay's warmer waters, creates ideal conditions for marine life. Each year between 1,000 and 2,000 humpback whales enter the bay's quiet waters to give birth and take advantage of the abundant food.

On the south side of the Samaná Bay is the 208-square-kilometer Parque Nacional Los Haitises and the two smaller lagoons that make up the Reserva Científica Lagunas Redonda y Limón. Due to the remoteness of the bay, these parks are very difficult to get to and remain in a very wild state. The lack of people traffic means these areas are unbelievably rich in wildlife and a paradise for avid birders. This is also the karst country of the Dominican Republic. The area is riddled with caves and *mogotes* (limestone hummocks). One of the last refuges for the Taíno, traces of their history can be found on cave walls throughout the park.

The small coastal community of **Santa Bárbara de Samaná** is the best base from which to explore the natural places in this region. Located on the bay side of the peninsula, it feels more like a town of 5,000, but actually is much larger (pop. 50,000). From here ferries and charter boats cross the bay to the lagoons and park, as well as make trips out to the whales.

The rugged park is accessible only by boat from Samaná or from Sabana de la Mar, on the south side of the bay. The park's 30-kilometer coastline is thick with all the mangrove species crowding the mouths of estuaries running deep into the park. In some places the shoreline rises steeply to limestone cliffs and a system of caves. The interior of the park is a raised sediment limestone shelf put down about 40 million years ago. Over the years the rains, which average about 230 centimeters annually, eroded the shelf forming a karst topography of deep caves, 300-meter-high hummocks, and *dolines* (sinkholes). Most of caves have petroglyphs or pictographs.

Under most conditions karst regions do not support great varieties of flora and fauna, but the heavy annual rainfall and incessant cloud cover have combined to make an exception. The knolls and valleys are densely covered with montane and lowland forests varieties including balata, copey, mountain palm, silk-cotton, Hispaniola mahogany, and the American muskwood, with lianas and begonias offering colorful diversion. Visitors to the park should watch out for the dangerous *pringamoza* plant that, if touched, causes a terrible rash that can last for days.

Along the park's coastline are dense stands of red mangrove that, at low tide, give some indication of the bay's rich sealife. The roots, exposed at low tide, are totally covered with oysters, mussels, and other marine crustaceans while the crystal clear waters between the roots support clouds of small fish fry. Feeding in the mangroves and estuaries along the coast are rare double-crested cormorants, northern jacanas, ibis, snowy egrets, snowy terns, blue herons, and brown pelicans. Ruddy ducks, white-cheeked pintails, least grebes, northern bobwhites, and killdeer are also common in the estuaries.

A guide is not really necessary in the park, and the person who brought you across the bay usually will tell you where to head. Tell your boatman where you want to go and he or she will drop you off and show you where the trail starts. The more established outfitters (see "Outfitters and Guides," below) can provide knowledgeable guides who know the history and flora and fauna of the region.

The park admission fee is five dollars. For more information, contact the park offices in Samaná and Sabana de la Mar at 809/556-7333.

Things to See and Do in Parque Nacional Los Haitises

Near San Lorenzo Bay are three caves that are easy to get to and worth exploring. Two of them, **Cueva de Willy** (Willy's Cave) and **Cueva de la Arena** (Sand Cave), are closer to the bay. Both have interpretive trails, handrails, and steps leading down into the depths. **Cueva del Ferrocarril** is further down the coast. A trail along the shoreline called the Arrozal

Path leads to all the caves, but you can get to it only by boat. Another group of caves including those at **San Gabriel** and **La Línea**, while more difficult to reach, contain well-preserved pictographs and petroglyphs.

At present there is only one marked trail heading inland. The **Inland Trail**, marked with some 17 interpretive plaques, runs deep into the interior of the park. The three-hour walk can be difficult, especially if it rains—when the ground instantly turns to mush—so it is advisable to take a guide and plenty of water.

The **Reserva Científica Natural Lagunas Redonda y Limón** consists of two large, muddy, brackish lagoons, about 30 kilometers east of the main park. They are both shallow (less than two meters deep) and abound with bird and marine life. This is by far the most remote park or reserve on the island and obviously the abundant bird population prefers it that way. Besides millions of mosquitoes visitors will find pied-billed grebes, great egrets, roseate spoonbills, ibis, black-crowned night herons, and dozens of water fowl species including ruddy ducks and northern pintails. The reserve is accessible only by boat.

Whale watching between January and March is another popular activity. Almost 30 percent of the world's remaining humpbacks congregate in the waters off the island's northeast coast to calf and mate. Although you can get almost anyone with a boat to take you out to the whales, it is better for all concerned, especially the whales, to use one of the two ecologically friendly operators that conduct themselves according to the new Whale Watching Regulations.

Outfitters and Guides in Parque Nacional Los Haitises

Trips to the park and lagoons can be arranged through **Ecoturisa**, Calle Santiago #203-B, Santo Domingo, tel 809/221-4101, fax 809/685-1544, but most of the hotels in Samaná, or across the bay in Sabana de la Mar, can arrange trips and guides. Since there are no extensive trails in the park or reserve, and evening rain showers are common, camping is not a good idea. It is permitted, but definitely not practical. Most trips can easily be handled from Samaná in one long day. Many boat owners offer trips across the bay to the park and reserves, but be careful: Many are just kids and the boats have no safety gear. It is best to deal with someone the hotel recommends. The National Parks office in Sabana de la Mar, tel 809/556-7333, can assist with a boat and a guide.

Complejo Turístico Villa Suiza, Calle Monción, Sabana de la Mar, tel 809/566-7609 or 809/547-2278, fax 809/532-8164, is actually a hotel but also a great place to arrange tours.

Gary Hurtado, Samaná, tel 809/538-2152 or 809/240-6100, handles all kinds of tours.

Nadime Bezi, Samaná, tel 809/538-2556, handles guided tours of the park.

Prieto Tours, Samaná, is a good choice and can be contacted through any of the hotels.

Wega Tours, Sabana de la Mar, tel 809/556-1197, offers trips to both the lagoons and park.

WhalesMarine, Avenida le Malecón, Samaná, tel 809/538-2494, offers, you guessed it, whale-watching tours.

Where to Stay in Parque Nacional Los Haitises

Samaná is probably the best place to stay because it is large and has more infrastructure for those planning a variety of adventures. If you are interested only in the park, Sabana de la Mar is another option.

Complejo Turístico Villa Suiza (see "Outfitters and Guides," above) offers 14 clean rooms. Rates $35 to $50.

Cotubanamá, right downtown, Samaná, tel 809/538-2557, is a clean, very basic 20-room hotel with a good restaurant. Check first before taking a room; some are tiny. Rates $25.

Tropical Lodge, Avenida Marina, on the east side of town, Samaná, tel 809/538-2480, fax 809/538-2068, is a comfortable eight-room inn overlooking the bay. Rates $40 to $50.

Where to Eat in Parque Nacional Los Haitises

By far the best food and service is found at the hotel restaurants, but there are a few other good ones along the Malecón, facing the bay.

Black and White, Avenida Malecón, near Café de Paris, serves meals at any hour of the day.

Café de Paris, Avenida Malecón, offers light lunches, pizza, crêpes.

Captain Morgan's, across the street from the King's Hotel, is an American-style sports bar.

Getting to Parque Nacional Los Haitises

Caribe Tours, 27 de Febrero at Leopoldo Navarra, Santo Domingo, tel 809/687-3171, offers three daily buses to Samaná from Santo Domingo; the trip takes about six hours. **Metro Tours**, Santo Domingo, tel 809/566-7126 or 809/566-6590, also offers regular island bus service. If you plan on spending some time on the peninsula, this is a good alternative to renting a car, driving it there, and having it sit around most of the time while you're off on your boat-related adventures. If you decide to rent a car, be prepared for the five-hour drive north up the Duarte highway, then east at La Vega to San Francisco and Nagua. From Nagua you head east along the coastal highway to Samaná. Another way is to fly into

Punta Cana on the eastern side of the island, then bus it to Sabana de la Mar, then take the ferry across. Three ferries cross the bay each day between Samaná and Sabana de la Mar, but they fill up early.

DOMINICAN REPUBLIC SPECIFICS

Getting There
The Dominican Republic has five international and three regional airports. Most North American carriers have daily flights into the Dominican Republic. Although most visitors arrive via Santo Domingo, in the south, you can also enter through Puerto Plata, in the north, and Punta Cana, in the east. Flying into or out of certain airports may require going through San Juan, Puerto Rico. You will need a $10 tourist visa to enter the country. It can be purchased through your travel agent or at the airport.

Getting Around
A popular way to see the island is to land in Santo Domingo, see the southern sights, then bus or drive to Jarabacoa and the Cordillera Central. From there, bus or drive to Samaná via Puerto Plata, then back to Puerto Plata to fly home. It sounds hectic, but it can easily be done in 10 days. However, if you can afford it, a car is by far the best way to see the Dominican Republic. A four-wheel-drive vehicle rental will cost about $500 per week.

The major rental car companies (**Avis, Hertz, Budget, National,** etc.) are all in attendance at the major airports. A local company, **Nelly** (at all airports), is also good and more likely to negotiate a lower drop-off fee if you decide to enter and depart the country from different airports. The major North American car agencies don't negotiate.

It is important to get a map of the Dominican Republic before you leave home. Most of the maps available on the island are not detailed enough, especially if you plan on driving. Buy the *Hildebrand's Travel Map of Hispaniola* and use it in conjunction with a local map.

Tourist Information
Tourist information booths are located at Los Américas International Airport in Santo Domingo and at Launion Airport in Puerto Plata.

Santo Domingo, corner of Avenidas Mexico and 30 de Marzo, Apt. 497, tel 809/221-4660, fax 809/682-3806

Puerto Plata, Avenida Hermanas Mirabel, tel 809/586-3676

Santiago, City Hall, Avenida Duarte, tel 809/582-5885

East Coast U.S.A., 1501 Broadway, Suite 410, New York, NY, 10036, tel 212/575-4963 or 4966 or 888/374-6361, fax 212/575-5448

Canada, 2080 Crescent St., Montreal, Quebec H3G 2B8, tel 514/499-1918 or 800/563-1611, fax 514/499-1393

Web sites: www.dri.com/travel/english/ecosports.html and www.dominicana.com.do/

Email: sectur@codetel.net.do

Camping in the Dominican Republic

There are no camping facilities in the Dominican Republic, although the Tourism Offices and the National Parks Department say you are welcome to camp in any of the national parks or reserves. Most of your hiking will be with a guide or tour operator, and they usually take care of everything. Camping by yourself may not be safe in certain outlying areas, and since you never know whose land you may be on, you run the risk of upsetting someone. Instead, find yourself a comfortable, inexpensive inn in which to hang your hat.

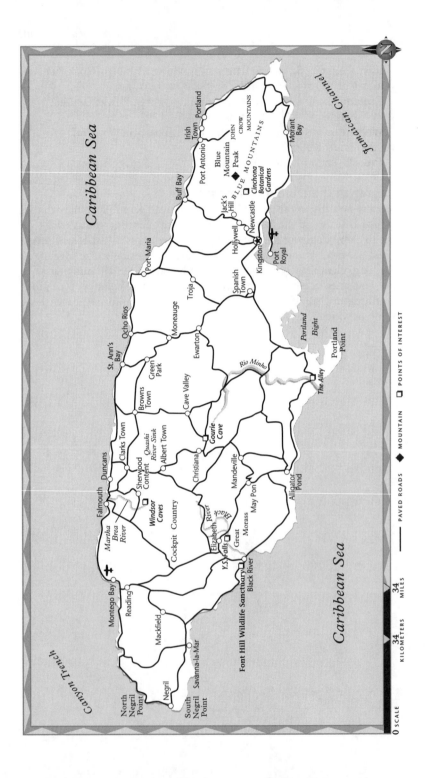

8

JAMAICA

Lying 145 kilometers south of Cuba, Jamaica is the third largest island in the Caribbean, with a population of 2.6 million. At 11,425 square kilometers it is about the size of Connecticut, only a bit more mountainous and with a few more palm trees. The island is 234 kilometers long and 82 kilometers wide, with 50 percent of its land mass rising more than 300 meters. A ridge of mountains running the length of the island rises from the west coast, reaching its highest point, Blue Mountain Peak, at 2,256 meters in the east. The country is divided into three regions: Cornwall (west), Middlesex (central), and Surrey (east). These regions are then subdivided into 14 parishes or districts, including the district of Kingston.

Jamaica is one of the islands that developed a mass tourism industry, which still thrives along the west and north coasts, Negril and Montego Bay. Only recently have officials given a thought to conservation and ecotourism. In the early 1990s, two governing bodies were created to preserve the island's remaining natural resources and to heighten local awareness in the environment. The Protected Areas Resource Conservation Project (PARC), created in 1991, was given the mandate to establish and develop national parks for tourism using sound conservation methods. In 1993, in a joint venture with the United States Agency for International Development (USAID), it established the 81,000-hectare Blue Mountain and John Crow Mountain National Park. It was established to save the remaining stocks of endemic forest and to serve as a springboard for an ecotourism industry.

The other group, the Natural Resources Conservation Authority (NRCA), created in 1992 by the Natural Resources Conservation Authority Act, had a mandate to manage the established parks and to promote public awareness of the ecological systems of Jamaica. Together these groups, along with a number of private groups, are making great strides in ecotourism and land reform. Proposals for seven more land-based parks and four marine parks are in final reading in the government and should be formally decreed within the next five years. Montego Bay Marine Sanctuary has already been informally established to protect the bay's great marine diversity.

Jamaica boasts more than 3,000 species of flowering plants, including some 800 endemic varieties. More than 200 species of orchids (of which 30 are endemic), 550 species of ferns, and 10 varieties of cacti are also found here. Although much of Jamaica's flora is now of the imported variety, 405 of the higher plant species are endemic and the island ranks fifth in the world in endemic species. Jamaica is famous for its hardwood species, such as Jamaican mahogany, cedar, blue mahoe (the island's 25-meter-high national tree), and the West Indian cottonwood. This last species, the tallest and straightest tree in the forest, was used by the Arawaks for their dugout canoes.

The main forests support a variety of bird, animal, and insect life. More than 250 bird species, of which 27 are endemic, call Jamaica home. Most endemic birds are found in the Blue Mountain region, including the Jamaican doctor bird, a swallowtail hummingbird and Jamaica's national bird, which derives its name from its needle-like bill. Other endemic birds include the Vervain hummingbird (the world's second smallest bird), black-billed parrot, and Jamaican tody.

Jamaica is also noted for its magnificent butterflies, such as the unique swallow-tailed *papilio homerus*, with a 14-centimeter wingspan, found nowhere else in the world. Loss of habitat and poaching—collectors will pay $3,000 for a good specimen—have reduced its numbers to about 500. It is now found only in the Blue Mountain and John Crow National Park. Except for a few bat species and the common *hutia*, a rodent-like animal, there are few mammals. About 100 West Indian manatee and 300 American crocodiles share the swamps of Long Bay and Black River.

As far as natural activities go, Jamaica has it all: bird watching, hiking trails, white-water rafting, spelunking, and mountain biking as well as great diving and snorkeling along the north shore. A number of new outfitters, in conjunction with government groups, have established some great outdoor adventure tours, and since ecotourism is relatively new to the island, much of these activities will occur in seldom-visited habitats.

Most natural adventures and activities are found in three locations: the Blue Mountain and John Crow National Park in the east, the Cockpit Country in the north-central, and the Great Morass and Black River swamps in the southwest. They are all easily reached from Montego Bay ("MoBay"), thereby eliminating the need to stay in over-crowded and busy Kingston.

Located northeast of the capital, Kingston, the Blue and John Crow Mountains dominate the eastern parishes of Jamaica. The area is known worldwide for producing some of the world's most expensive coffee and some of the best *ganja* (marijuana).

Jamaica History

Although Columbus sighted the island in 1492, it was not until May 5, 1494, that he actually landed and named the island Santo Jago. Many years later the island's name was changed to Jamaica, a name closer to the original Arawak *Xamayca*, meaning "land of wood and water." But Columbus' log entry of the "fairest isle eyes have ever seen" did not prepare him for the hostility he faced from the Arawaks. Before being settled by the Spanish, Jamaica came under repeated attacks from the British, who finally took control of the island in 1655. Following Britain's takeover, Henry Morgan built his base in Port Royal on the south coast, and declared it a safe haven for buccaneers, pirates, and privateers raiding Spanish territories. By 1680 Port Royal had earned the reputation of being "the wickedest city on earth," a title that ended in 1692 when 80 percent of the city slid into the harbor during a violent earthquake and tidal wave. In 1872 Kingston was made the official capital of the island.

Since the first day Columbus set foot on the island, Jamaica's history has been a violent one. Violent clashes between the Spanish and English were replaced by marauding Spanish and French pirates and buccaneers. During this time the land was also racked by the Maroon Wars, which lasted until the late eighteenth century. The Maroons were free or runaway slaves who formed guerrilla armies in the mountains and attacked the British at every turn. They got their name from the Spanish, *cimarron*, meaning "wild" or "savage."

By the beginning of the nineteenth century, peace had been established with the Maroons, but the land was racked by violent slave rebellions that lasted until emancipation in the late 1800s. Violence again reared its ugly head in the early 1900s in the form of labor and political unrest, and continued until Jamaica was granted a new constitution in 1944. The new constitution permitted local government representation and elections, which in turn led to full independence in 1962.

Since independence each subsequent election has been rocked by violence, reaching a peak in the 1980 elections, when more than 700 died in bipartisan campaign violence. The last two elections, in 1989 and 1993, were peaceful, a trend most Jamaicans hope will continue.

BLUE MOUNTAINS AND JOHN CROW MOUNTAINS NATIONAL PARK

Stretching over 45 kilometers on the eastern side of Jamaica and reaching an elevation of 2,256 meters, the Blue Mountains form one of the longest and highest continuous ranges in the Caribbean. They are flanked on the east by the lower John Crow Mountains and on the west by the much lower Port Royal Mountains. The 81,000-hectare John Crow National Park was established on February 28, 1993, to protect the remaining stands of primary forest and the unique wildlife they support. The northern slopes of the mountains still contain mainly primary forest, but the southern slopes have been dramatically deforested. Coffee planters, farmers, charcoal producers, and Hurricane Gilbert, in 1988, have destroyed great patches of forest.

The park boundaries encompass the entire two ranges. It covers the eastern third of St. Andrew's parish, the southern half of Portland parish, and the northern half of St. Thomas parish. It occupies the central portion of the eastern third of the island stretching east from the north-south A3 highway connecting Kingston with the north shore all the way to the east coast. The John Crow Mountains are the easternmost of the chain.

Today, park rangers patrol the park in an effort to stop illegal destruction of park resources and the growing of *ganja*. People from the neighboring communities are being trained as park guides, and PARC and NRCA actively promote ecotourism within these very poor communities.

The mountains get their name from the bluish haze that seems always to hang over the range. In deep contrast is the dark green tropical rain forest, nurtured by almost 200 centimeters of rainfall annually. More than 500 species of plants, most of them endemic, blanket the slopes. In all, the park contains more than 65 species of orchids and 50 fern species, including primeval-looking Cyathea, which can grow to 10 meters. One of the most unique trees found here is the *Chusquea abietifolia*, a prickly vine-type bamboo that flowers only once every 33 years, due again in 2017. On the lower slopes coffee and wild fruit trees, such as rose apples, abound.

Birdlife is prolific in the park. Besides the common but dramatic long-tailed doctor bird, there are such species as the rare Jamaican blackbird, rufous-throated solitaire, crested quail, and Jamaican tody. The higher elevations are also home to the transparent glass-wing butterfly while the lower slopes are home to the large, very rare swallow-tailed butterfly. Some wild pigs and the almost extinct coney (a.k.a. *hutia* or agouti) share

Jamaican Music: Reggae

The first pop music native to Jamaica was mento, a syncopated African rhythm that originated from slave drum music. It was popular throughout the 1940s and '50s, but soon was overpowered by jazz and rhythm and blues beamed in from radio stations in the American South. By the early '60s mento had combined with the American beats and come back as ska.

Within a few years ska had faded and a new, more impulsive local beat found its way onto Jamaican airways. After independence, the difficulties associated with self-government and the resulting dissatisfaction among the people found expression in music. The lyrics grew angrier and took on a political tone, eventually becoming the political voice of the people.

Toots Hibbert, one of the first performers of the new music, named it reggae because it came from the voices of "regular" people. A few years later Jimmy Cliff recorded "Many Rivers to Cross," a despondent ballad about the harsh realities in Jamaica, followed by his international hit, "The Harder They Come." Cliff's success inspired Bob Marley, Peter Tosh, and Bunny Wailer, three Rastafarians raised in Kingston's notorious "trench" slum, to form the highly successful Wailers. Marley left the group to pursue a solo career and eventually went on to become a cult legend until his death in 1981, when he was 36. A museum commemorating Marley's contribution to reggae is located in a northern suburb of Kingston.

the forest floor of the lower slopes with the three-meter-long Jamaican yellow boa and ground lizards.

Entrance to the park is free at present, but a proposed five-dollar permit fee will soon be enforced. For more information, contact the park office at Guava Ridge, tel 876/997-8044, or inquire at one of the ranger stations at Hollywell, Portland Gap and Millbank, or Maya Lodge (see "Outfitters and Guides" and "Where to Stay," below).

Things to See and Do at Blue Mountains and John Crow Mountains National Park

Dozens of trails, some carved by the Windward Maroons and British soldiers more than 100 years ago, crisscross the ridges of the park. Others, kept clear by coffee-laden mules and local farmers, still provide valuable communication links for local residents. The trails within the park are categorized as guided, non-guided, and wilderness, with those on the northeastern slopes being of the last variety. Nearing completion is the **Grand Ridge Trail**. Jamaica's answer to the Appalachian Trail, it will eventually run almost 25 kilometers from Morces Gap, in the west near Jack's Hill, to Corn Puss Gap in the eastern John Crow Mountains. The ridgetop trail will have various entrance and exit points and sleeping huts.

Various trails originate in the many villages scattered throughout the park, such as the **Vinegar Hill Trail** at Jack's Hill or **Woodcutters Gap** and **Fairy Glade Trails** around Hollywell. The best hike on the island, and one of the Caribbean's finest, is the **Blue Mountain Peak Trail**. The official trail starts in Mavis Bank and climbs steeply up to Whitfield Hall, then to the peak, a 34-kilometer round trip. Many skip the Mavis Bank to Whitfield leg and opt for the shorter 22-kilometer Whitfield to peak hike. Since the peak is covered in mist by nine in the morning, a start time of two in the morning is recommended if you want to get to the summit for a spectacular daybreak and great views.

Since most trails are not marked, topographic maps and a compass are a must when hiking these mountains. The excellent *Hiker's Guide to the Blue Mountains*, by Bill Wilcox, is also a must. Maps and the guidebook can be purchased at the Maya Lodge at Jack's Hill.

There are dozens of interesting coffee plantations within the park that are worth exploring, such as **Clydesdale**, **Old Tavern Estate**, and **Flamstead**, one-time home of Admiral Horatio Nelson. Just north of Mavis Bank is the small but most interesting **Cinchona Botanical Gardens**. Its name comes from the cinchona plant from which quinine is extracted. The plants were imported from Peru by the British to extract malaria-fighting quinine. The gardens offer spectacular views of the Green and Yallahs Valleys, as well as Sir Johns, High, and Farm Hill peaks. The gardens contain a large selection of imported and endemic flora.

The **Río Grande Valley**, most of which lies within the park, divides the John Crow and Blue Mountains and runs from Port Antonio up to the small town of Castle Comfort in the Blue Mountains. Hiking trails follow the winding Río Grande and offer some great hikes and spectacular water-

Lower Sommerset Falls in the Río Grande Valley

falls. Another popular activity is running down the river on a bamboo raft; day or torch-light trips are available. If you stay on the north shore or have some extra time, contact **Valley Hikes** for one of their valley hikes or river rafting trips (see "Outfitters and Guides," below).

Outfitters and Guides near Blue Mountains and John Crow Mountains National Park

It is advisable to utilize guides whenever you go into the wilds of Jamaica. Jamaica's ecotourism is still in its infancy, and you can run into difficulty on your own. Most trails are not marked and are frequently altered by rains. Also, most wilderness areas are a favorite of marijuana growers. You don't want to end up somewhere you should not be—like in some-one's *ganja* plot. Under *no* circumstances should you hire someone who approaches you to be a guide; use only a recognized guide service or a guide arranged by a hotel. Most hotels in the region can arrange any tour you want. Negotiate prices in advance.

Blue Mountain Adventure Tours, 152 Main S., Ocho Rios, Jamaica, tel 876/974-7075, fax 876/974-0635, offers various bike tours through the Blue Mountains region. Customized hiking trips are also available. Guided trips run $80 per day. Pick-up at your hotel is included.

Eco Tours, Fairy Hill, Portland, Jamaica, tel 876/993-8455 or 876/993-4799, offers great biking and white-water rafting adventures. A full-day combo package includes 14 kilometers of white-water rafting on the Río Grande followed by a half-day bike trip to Somerset Falls. Blue Mountain bike trips are also offered. Rates are $50 to $150 and include everything.

Lady G Diver, Port Antonio, tel 876/993-3284 or 800/433-7262, fax 876/935-6024. This four-star PADI operation offers scuba diving and snorkeling along the north coast. One tank dive costs $50 and snorkeling is charged by the hour.

Sense Adventures, Box 216, Kingston 7, Jamaica, tel 876/927-2097, fax 876/929-6967, is the leading guide service on the island. This should be your first choice for touring in the Blue Mountain region. Owner Peter Bentley (also owns Maya Lodge) can make guide and accommodation arrangements for hikes and bike trips of from four hours to nine days. He can also arrange equipment rentals. Guides are $25 to $100 per day depending on specialty; the fee includes all transportation. He charges a $15 fee to plan your entire trip, complete with maps and itinerary.

Sun Venture Tours, 31 Balmoral Ave., Kingston 10, Jamaica, tel 876/960-6685, fax 876/929-5694 or 7512. This outfitter offers day or night trips to Blue Mountain peak and an assortment of other trips including a three-day hike along Grand Ridge. Tours cost $50 to $70 per day and include transportation.

Touring Society of Jamaica, c/o Strawberry Hill Hotel, Irish Town, Jamaica, tel 876/944-8400, or in USA 800/OUTPOST, fax 876/944-8408. This company specializes in all-inclusive custom-designed tours for bird watchers, hikers, and coffee connoisseurs. Day rates are from $55 to $250 depending on accommodations, food, etc. Transportation from regional hotels included.

Valley Hikes, c/o Mocking Bird Hill Hotel, Box 254, Port Antonio, Jamaica, tel 876/993-7134, fax 876/993-7133 or tel/fax 876/993-3881, email: mockbrd@cwjamaica.com. This operator offers great hikes up the Río Grande Valley and river rafting on bamboo rafts. It also offers longer Blue Mountain trips and horseback riding. One-day tours start from $50; three-day Blue Mountain trips run $180.

Where to Stay near Blue Mountains and John Crow Mountains National Park

Most of the hotels in the Blue Mountain area are small and basic, and some even offer camping on their grounds. Of the hotels listed here, two are in the mountains and the other two are nearby along the coast, within

Hotel Mocking Bird Hill

easy reach of day excursions into the mountains. (For information on camping in this area, see "Jamaica Specifics" at the end of the chapter.)

Fern Hill Club, San San, Box 100, Port Antonio, Jamaica, tel 876/993-7374, fax 876/993-7373. This small 31-room inn is on the north shore. Amenities include a pool, air conditioning, and restaurant. Rates $75 to $100.

Hotel Mocking Bird Hill, Box 254, Port Antonio, Jamaica, tel 876/993-7134, fax 876/993-7133, email: mockbrd@cwjamaica.com. This elegant 10-room great house is tucked into the lower northern slopes of the Blue Mountains overlooking the Caribbean. Rates $100 to $130.

Ivor Guest House, Skyline Drive, Jack's Hill Kingston 6, Jamaica, tel 876/927-1460, fax 876/977-0033. Up the hill from the Maya Lodge, this slightly more upscale property consists of a great plantation house built in the 1870s. Owner Hellen Aitkin is a treasure house of information. Rates $80 to $95 include breakfast and daily shuttle to Kingston.

Maya Lodge, Box 216, Kingston 7, Jamaica, tel 876/927-2097, fax 876/929-6967. Owner Peter Bentley runs the best-known lodge on the island and can help you plan your entire tour of the region or island. The lodge is located at 700 meters in the Jack's Hill area. There is a mix of campsites and rooms in cabins. Rates: campsites $10, cabins $25.

Where to Eat near Blue Mountains and John Crow Mountains National Park

Restaurants are few and far between in this region, so your best bet is to dine at the various guesthouses or inns. Most offer good food at reasonable prices. Organized trips usually provide food, and if you decide to camp, there are small grocery stores in each town where you can buy the basics.

Local cuisine includes hot and spicy jerk chicken, pork, or beef; Jamaican patties, fluffy pastries stuffed with chicken, beef, peas, and potatoes; and the roti, an Indian wrap stuffed with potato and curried goat, chicken, shrimp, or beef, similar to a burrito. "Dip and fall back" is a spicy, salty stew served with green bananas and cornmeal dumplings.

Blue Mountain Inn, Gordon Town, serves great Continental cuisine on beautiful slopes.

Gap Cafe, in Hollywell, just north of Newcastle, offers great local atmosphere at 1,300 meters. Closed Mondays; offers lunch and afternoon snacks only.

Mount Edge Guesthouse, just south of Tree Tops, has two rooms and good local cuisine.

Tree Tops, tel 876/974-5831, south of Newcastle. This small inn serves good local food.

Getting to Blue Mountains and John Crow Mountains National Park

Bus service into the mountains is nonexistent, so if you decide to stay in the Blue Mountains your best bet is to fly into Kingston and take a taxi or rental car to your hotel. Highway B1 runs north out of Kingston through the Blue Mountains to Buff Bay, on the north coast just west of Port Antonio. Feeder roads off the B1, most fairly well signed, will take you to all the areas mentioned. Whether you stay on the north shore or in the mountains, the B1 is the main artery through the mountains. Most mountain hotels will make transfer arrangements if you let them know in advance (some hotels offer free transfers and shuttles into Kingston while others charge). If you elect to stay on the north shore you have a choice: fly into Kingston and take a taxi or drive over the mountains, using the B1, to the north coast, or fly into Montego Bay and take a bus, taxi, or drive to Port Antonio along the good coastal road, a combination of A1, A3, and A4. The coastal road is well signed and the drive will take a leisurely three hours.

Air Jamaica offers daily Kingston–Port Antonio and Montego Bay–Port Antonio flights for about $100 round trip.

Rental cars are best if you plan to visit other areas of the island.

Expect to pay $350 per week plus insurance. All the major cities have agencies, but it would probably be easier to rent at the airport you fly into. All the major North American agencies (Avis, Budget, Hertz, etc.) have outlets at the Kingston and Montego Bay airports.

COCKPIT COUNTRY

The Cockpit region is a large limestone plateau encompassing sizable portions of three parishes: the southern half of Trelawny parish, the eastern third of St. James parish, and the northern edge of St. Elizabeth parish. It is Jamaica's answer to the karst regions of Puerto Rico and Cuba, though not as spectacular. The 1,000-square-kilometer region is honeycombed with caves, sinkholes, and conical hummocks, and gets its name from the deep depressions, or "cockpits," between hummocks. It offers numerous opportunities for hiking, bird watching, and spelunking.

The ruggedness of the region provided excellent cover for the Maroons who had bases scattered throughout the area. It was one of the last strongholds for the Maroons, and many a British patrol was ambushed here. The southwest portion of the region was so treacherous that paranoid British soldiers dubbed it "the District of Look Behind." On older Maroon maps of the same area, it was affectionately referred to as "Me No Sen, You No Come" (roughly translated as "if we have not sent for you, you'd better stay away"). The names of towns and villages in the region—such as Quick Step, Wait-A-Bit, Barbecue Bottom, Kinloss, and Rest And Be Thankful—also reflect the area's Maroon history. Many of the region's inhabitants are descendants of the Maroons and still retain a certain autonomy to this day.

The fringes of the Cockpit have been cleared for agriculture and charcoal production, but the interior is still very much unexplored. Locals, believing the area is haunted by the ghosts of those who died during the wars, seldom venture into the interior. Some roads and four-wheel-drive tracks crisscross the region, as does a series of unmarked trails. Most of them lead to small vegetable or *ganja* plots. In 1994 a foreign journalist hiking alone in the area was murdered, probably because he stumbled onto a growing operation and was mistaken for a drug enforcement agent. Remember the saying "Me No Sen, You No Come" and always use a local guide.

Because of the area's superstitions and its remoteness, most of the Cockpit interior is pristine and still covered in primary vegetation. The rich mineral soils and 350-centimeter annual rainfall support a wide variety of plants, many of which are endemic to this region only. Soil conditions determine plant varieties, so the more fertile valleys support a tall canopy, with 30-meter-high mahogany and blue mahoe trees, while the drier, porous hummock slopes support cacti and thorny scrubs such as the aptly named scratchbush, which leaves you itching for days. Wear long pants.

Almost all of Jamaica's 27 endemic bird species are found in this region, including black- and yellow-billed parrots, parakeets, rare Jamaican blackbirds, Jamaican todies, and endangered golden swallows. Mongoose, feral pigs, 22 bat varieties, the odd yellow boa, and swallow-tailed butterflies can also be seen in the valleys.

For more information on visiting Cockpit Country, contact the Touring Society of Jamaica, c/o Strawberry Hill Hotel, Irish Town, Jamaica, tel 876/944-8400, fax 876/968-6779 or 876/944-8408.

Things to See and Do in Cockpit Country

The easiest and most rewarding trail through Cockpit Country is the 17-kilometer (10 hours one way) **Windsor-to-Troy trail**. Starting at Windsor in the north, it skirts the Windsor cave system and winds its way south, through the heart of the karst region, to Troy. Stop at the seldom-visited **Windsor Caves** just south of Sherwood Content at the end of the paved road. Two rasta-looking guides, Franklyn "Doc" Taylor and his brother, Martell, hang out at the brightly painted rum shop at the end of

Jamaica's rugged Cockpit Country

the paved road. For an additional fee they will also take you to two other nearby caves: **Rat Bat Cave** and the **Royal Flat Chamber Cave.** They are also available to guide you to Troy. After a storm or during the rainy season, you can hear the Martha Brea River roaring through the cave about 100 meters below ground. Don't miss the cloud of bats leaving the cave at dusk.

The area is honeycombed with more than 250 charted caves. Spelunking is becoming more popular in Cockpit Country, and the region is a favorite haunt of the Jamaican Caving Club, which publishes the excellent caving guide *Underground Jamaica*, by Alan Fincham. Many of the caves are not marked on maps, but are accessible with help from local guides or the Jamaican Caving Club (see "Outfitters and Guides," below). Some of the cave openings are located at the bottom of sinkholes and rappelling is necessary to descend to the entrance. A few guides offer fully equipped spelunking; the Jamaican Caving Club hosts weekly trips to caves in the Cockpit.

Just two kilometers north of **Albert Town,** or three kilometers south of Ulster Spring, along the B5 on the eastern edge of Cockpit, the Quashi River cascades over a series of drops then plunges 40 meters into the **Quashi River Sink**, a large (40 meters deep) sinkhole complete with waterfall and swimming hole. The swimming hole, which can be reached by a not-so-easy trail down the crumbling south side of the sinkhole, is a great place for a refreshing swim under the falls. From here the river disappears into a limestone cave and resurfaces 16 kilometers to the north. The cave is accessible for about three kilometers, but footing is very slippery. Guides are available in Albert Town, and there are usually one or two hanging around the trailhead, which is marked by the side of the road. They charge about $15.

South of Albert Town near Wait-A-Bit is the village of Christiana, where you will find **Blue Hole River** and waterfall, and **Gourie Cave**. This location is similar to the Quashi River Sink but not as spectacular. The river tumbles over a ledge only 10 meters high and falls into a shallow pool more suitable for wading than swimming. The well-trodden trail to the river and cave starts on the highway; guides are available in Albert Town or at the trailhead. The cave was an old Maroon hideout, but seems to be primarily used today for sheltering sheep and goats. Two species of bats frequent the cave in large numbers, and their droppings combined with those of the other animals may be a bit much for some.

These caves form part of the longest cave system in Jamaica. It has not yet been charted or confirmed, but dye markers dropped into the cave's underground stream have shown up in Oxford, almost 16 kilometers to the west.

Outfitters and Guides in Cockpit Country
You must take a guide for trips through Cockpit Country.

Brian Zane, Albert Town, tel 876/990-6034, is a good choice for caving. He has all the equipment for rappelling and knows his caves.

Helitours Ltd., 120 Main St., Montego Bay, tel 876/979-8290 or 876/974-2265, offers one-hour narrated helicopter tours of Cockpit Country. Rates start at $95.

Jamaican Caving Club, tel 876/927-6661 or 876/927-2728, hosts weekly spelunking trips and can provide names of local guides.

Poseidon Divers, Gloucester Avenue at Reading Reef Club, Box 152, Reading, Jamaica, tel 876/952-3624 or 800/880-5224, fax 876/952-3079, offers diving and snorkeling in the Montego Bay Marine Sanctuary. One tank dive runs $50, and snorkeling costs $15 per hour.

Resort Divers & Watersports, LOJ Shopping Complex, Montego Bay, tel 876/952-4285 or 800/317-7310, fax 876/952-4288, has two locations along the north shore and offers deep-sea fishing, snorkeling, diving, sailing, and glass-bottom boat tours.

Robert Sutton, Mandeville, tel 876/963-8569, is the best bird man on the island and organizes hiking trips in the Cockpit and Great Morass regions.

Trelawny Adventure Guides, Albert Town, tel 876/919-6992 or 876/990-6034, is a great choice for the Albert Town area.

In addition, Peter Bentley's **Sense Adventures** as well as the **Jamaican Alternative Tourism, Camping and Hiking Association** and the **Touring Society of Jamaica** offer all sorts of trips and information on the Cockpit (see "Outfitters and Guides near Blue Mountain and John Crow National Park," above).

Where to Stay in Cockpit Country
The Cockpit is easily accessible from north shore towns such as Montego Bay, at the region's northwestern boundary, or Ocho Rios. The latter is more central for those planning to see both Cockpit Country and the Blue Mountains.

Coral Cliff Hotel, 165 Gloucester Ave., Box 253, Montego Bay, Jamaica, tel 876/952-4130, fax 876/952-6532, has 32 cozy rooms overlooking MoBay, air conditioning, pool, and good restaurant. Rates $60 to $80.

Hibiscus Lodge, 83–87 Main St., Box 52, Ocho Rios, Jamaica, tel 876/974-2676, fax 876/974-1874. This well-appointed 26-room hotel, on a cliff overlooking the ocean around Ocho Rios, is a good, centrally located property for those planning to visit both the Cockpit and Blue Mountains. Rates $93 to $105.

Sundance Resort, 1 Kent Ave., Box 467, Montego Bay, Jamaica, tel 876/952-4370, fax 876/952-6591, email: sundance@cwjamaica.com, is a comfortable 65-room property a block from the beach that includes air conditioning, pool, and restaurant. Rates $65 to $80.

Where to Eat in Cockpit Country

There are very few places to eat within Cockpit Country so packing food is a must. The opposite is true along the north shore from Montego Bay to Ocho Rios.

Lyle's Intensified Inn, 36 Barnett, MoBay, tel 876/952-4980, serves great Jamaican snacks such as rotis and patties.

Margaritaville, on Gloucester just south of the Casa Blanca Hotel, tel 876/952-4777, is a great place to watch the sunset and enjoy Continental cuisine.

PJ's Saloon & Restaurant, north end of Gloucester Avenue, MoBay, serves tasty jerk pork and chicken and offers live reggae music nightly.

TJ's Snack & Pastries, at the north end of Albert Town, will do in a pinch, offering Jamaican favorites such as patties, rotis, jerk pieces, and sweet breads.

Getting to Cockpit Country

Due to its isolation, the Cockpit is best covered from Montego Bay, on the western edge, or Ocho Rios, on the east. Few, if any, buses run into the sparsely populated area, but taxis will drop you off for a hefty price (justified, they say, because of the beating their cars take on Cockpit roads). Your best bet is an organized tour from one of the operators mentioned in "Outfitters and Guides," above. Most of them will pick you up at your hotel for an additional price.

A four-wheel-drive vehicle is by far the best option, and the roads are not that difficult to navigate. There are always people working in the fields who can give you directions. Expect to pay $60 per day or $350 per week plus insurance. You will find few gas stations in the interior, so make sure your tank is full before heading out.

From Montego Bay drive east on the road to Wakefield and follow the signs to Windsor and Albert Town. The road to Wakefield connects to a number of side roads that take you to other villages. From Ocho Rios head west along the coast road to Duncan, then south to Clarks Town and Albert Town. The maps distributed by the local tourism department are good enough for driving through the area, but you may want to get a more detailed map for hiking.

BLACK RIVER AND GREAT MORASS

The 71-kilometer-long Black River, which runs from Balaclava, on the southern edge of Cockpit Country, south to the town of Black River, on the southern coast, is the island's second longest (the Río Minho in central Jamaica is 93 kilometers long). The river takes it name from the black color of its waters. Actually, it is the river bottom, lined with black peat moss, that makes the clear water appear black.

In the eighteenth and nineteenth centuries, the Black River basin was the center of Jamaica's famous logwood industry. The logs, cut in the interior, were floated down the Broad and Black Rivers to the port, where they were shipped overseas. They were an important source of Prussian-blue dye in the garment industries of Europe and the United States.

In all, five large rivers meet here. The swampy, savanna-like area they form as they meander from the Cockpit plateau towards the coast is called the Great Morass. The Lacovia Gorge, which cuts between the Santa Cruz and Don Figuerero Mountains in the north, divides the Great Morass into the Upper and Lower Morass.

The area is one of Jamaica's most important and complex ecosystems, and presently a battleground for environmentalists (local and foreign) and developers (mostly foreign multinationals). Developers want to bulldoze the mangroves, fill the delta, and erect huge concrete resorts along the coast. Most locals don't want anything to do with a Montego Bay- or Negril-style mass tourism resort area, and a number of local groups have organized to fight for a lower impact approach. The Black River & Great Morass Environmental Defense Fund, along with a number of U.S. conservation groups, are pressuring the government to declare the entire area a national park.

The delta supports 12-meter-high red mangroves that give way to white mangrove and ferns further upriver. Upstream past the mangroves are large tracts of sedge savannah and green rivers of wild cane and wild ginger. Sawgrass and bull thatch (its branches and leaves are used to thatch roofs and to make baskets, hats, and placemats) dominate the savannah. Further upriver the open marsh vegetation gives way to marsh forest, with large tracts of blue mahoe, boarwood, and logwood, introduced in the early 1700s from South America.

The morass is vital to the survival of the island's remaining 300 wild American crocodiles and 100 West Indian manatees. It is also home to more than 100 species of birds, including the cinnamon-colored jacan, West Indian whistling duck, purple gallinule, and red-footed coot. The waters of the Morass also nurture important stocks of marine life, such as shrimp, snook, tarpon, and mullet.

The crocs can be seen early in the morning as they bask in the sun, replacing body heat lost during the cool nights. Manatees are very rare, but can be seen munching water hyacinth near the banks of the Black River. The best way to explore the morass and Black River is by flat-bottomed boat charter.

For more information on visiting the Black River area, contact the Jamaica Tourist Board, 1 High St., Black River, tel 876/965-2074.

Things to See and Do in the Black River Area

The main attraction in the Black River region is exploring the backwaters of the river and the Great Morass. This is best accomplished by flat-bottomed boat or, for the more adventurous, dugout canoe. Most boat trips leave from the dock in town and head up the main river, about a two-hour tour. Special side trips deeper into the Morass via smaller tributaries are also easily arranged. As you head upriver the river narrows, and in some places the huge aerial roots of the black mangroves form tunnels through which smaller boats can pass. Scattered along the river's edge, protruding through the reeds and hyacinth hugging the shoreline, are the tops of conical or funnel-shaped bamboo baskets, used for trapping shrimp and crabs. The traps are tended by local fishermen in dugout canoes. Most of the island's remaining crocs are found in this area, but

© Dannielle Hayes/Jamaican Tourist Board

Exploring the Black River

Crocodile on the Black River

many are now fairly tame because boat captains feed them. Still, it is an exciting trip.

One of the other places worth seeing is **Y.S. Falls**, a series of cascades just as spectacular as Dunn's River Falls near Ocho Rios. It is a great spot for a picnic or swim (don't worry; the crocs seldom venture this far upriver). In the rainy season when the water is higher, a couple boat operators offer inflatable raft rides over the multi-level cascades. It is a short, exciting Class III white-water ride and not dangerous.

Straddling the main coast road, three kilometers west of Black River, is the small (1,200-hectare) **Font Hill Wildlife Sanctuary**. As yet, it does not have official government sanctuary status because the land is actually owned by the Jamaican Petroleum Corporation. A few short trails lead to the beach and a few small ponds, where you may be lucky enough to spot a croc. If you run into one of the wardens patrolling the park, he will take you to see a croc for a small fee.

Outfitters and Guides in the Black River Area

A number of small and large operators run informative boat trips up the river as well as through the delta and morass. They know what they are doing and have fed some of the animals, so don't be surprised if a four-meter-long croc swims up to your boat for a snack.

Independent guides who will take you upriver in dugout canoes or small row boats hang out around the bridge in town. You can also ask the tourist office to recommend someone. These trips run from $10 to $15.

South Coast Safaris, 1 Crane Rd., Black River, Box 129, Mandeville, Jamaica, tel 876/965-2513, fax 876/965-2986, offers four daily trips upriver into the morass for $15. Longer trips that include Y.S. Falls and lunch run $26. The company provides transfers from Montego Bay for $65 return plus the river trip.

St. Bess Attractions, below the tourist office, Black River, tel 876/965-2374, fax 876/965-2229, offers similar trips upriver. They also rent boats with oarsman for independent exploring.

Where to Stay in the Black River Area

Ashton Great House, three kilometers north of town, Box 104, Luana, Black River, Jamaica, tel and fax 876/965-2036, is a cozy inn on 90 hectares overlooking Black River. Rates $30 to $50.

Bridge House Inn, 14 Crane Rd., Black River, Jamaica, tel 876/965-2631, has 14 air-conditioned rooms with bar, TV lounge, and great Jamaican cooking. Rates $30 to $35.

Port of Call Hotel, 136 Crane Rd., Black River, Jamaica, tel 876/9652360, fax 876/965-2410, has 19 basic rooms, some with air conditioning. Amenities include a pool, Jacuzzi, and restaurant. Rates $30 to $65.

Waterloo Guest House, 44 High St., Black River, Jamaica, tel 876/965-2278, is a good example of the older style homes typical of the late 1800s. It claims to be the first house in Black River to get electricity, in 1900. It has 22 air-conditioned rooms and a restaurant popular with the locals. Rates $30 to $45.

Where to Eat in the Black River Area

All the small inns and guesthouses have good inexpensive restaurants. On weekends the place to eat is **Ashton Great House** for their jerk pit barbecue ($15).

Bayside Jerk & BBQ Centre, 17 High St., Black River, serves great local jerk and seafood dishes.

Turn's Café Lounge, at the corner of High and North Streets, Black River, is open 24 hours.

Getting to the Black River Area

Because Black River is on the main Kingston–Negril–Montego Bay road, buses run regularly. From Kingston airport buses run to Negril all day. From Montego Bay airport there is regular bus service to Negril, where you can transfer to one heading to Kingston. Ask at your hotel which buses to take. A number of tour operators running the river trips provide transfers from hotels in Montego Bay or Kingston to Black River.

Rental cars are recommended as the coastal roads are easy to drive.

JAMAICA SPECIFICS

Getting There
Most major North American carriers offer daily flights between North American cities and both of Jamaica's airports. Flying into Kingston is recommended for those wishing to cover the southern side of the island and the Blue Mountains. Montego Bay is best for Cockpit Country and north shore destinations.

Getting Around
Buses tend to run along the main coastal roads, but service into the interior is very patchy. **Air Jamaica** has connector flights to most major cities on the island for around $100 return.

Rental cars are the best way to get around the island, and all the major agencies are represented.

Taxis are another option, but use the ones approved by JUTA (Jamaican Union of Travellers Association). Their rates between cities are posted at hotels and airports. Freelance taxis may offer better deals, but extreme care should be taken when using them. Theft and fare arguments are common among these operators.

Camping in Jamaica
With few exceptions Jamaica's camping network is very much in its infancy and no official sites exist. It is unsafe to camp in non-designated camping spots around the island. Your best bet is to contact the **Jamaican Alternative Tourism, Camping and Hiking Association**, Box 216, Kingston 7, Jamaica, tel 876/927-0357 or 2097, or **SENSE Adventures** (same address and numbers). The **Touring Society of Jamaica**, c/o Strawberry Hill Hotel, Irish Town, Jamaica, tel 876/944-8400, or in U.S.A. 800/OUTPOST, fax 876/944-8408, is another excellent source.

Tourist Information
The Jamaican Tourist Board (JTB) operates local offices at the airports in Kingston and Montego Bay and in Port Antonio, Black River, Negril, and Ocho Rios.

JTB (Kingston), 2 St. Lucia Ave., Box 360, Kingston 5, Jamaica, tel 876 929-9200, fax 876/929-9375. At the airport, tel 876/924-8024, fax 876/924-8673

JTB (Montego Bay), Cornwall Beach, Box 67, Montego Bay, Jamaica, tel 876/952-4425, fax 876/952-3587. At the airport, tel 876/952-3009, fax 876/952-2462

JTB (Black River), Hendriks Building, 2 High St., Black River P.O., St. Elizabeth, Jamaica, tel 876/965-2074, fax 876/965-2076

East Coast U.S.A., 801 Second Ave., 20th floor, New York, NY 10017, tel 212/856-9727, fax 212/856-9730

West Coast U.S.A., 3440 Wilshire Blvd., Suite 805, Los Angeles, CA 90010, tel 213/384-1123, fax 213/384-1780

Canada, 1 Eglinton Ave. E., Suite 616, Toronto, Ont. M4P 3A1, tel 416/482-7850, fax 416/482-1730

Web site: www.jamaicatravel.com
Email: jamaicatrv@aol.com

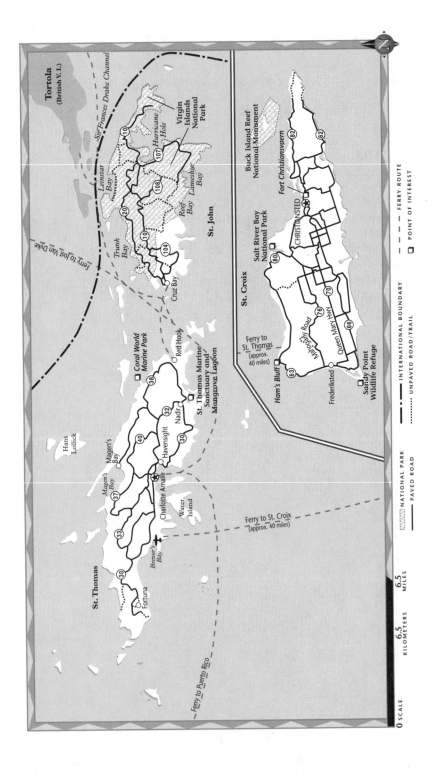

Snorkelers discover undersea treasures near St. Croix.

▲ White-sand beaches beckon on Bonaire.

▼ A straw basket takes shape in Trinidad.

▼ Curaçao's architecture reflects Dutch heritage.

▲ Ixora flower

▲ Caribbean schoolgirls await the bell.

▼ Sandy Island—an example of a coral island off Grenada

▲ One of Dominica's many idyllic bays

▼ Colorful floats abound at Carnival in St. Vincent.

▲ Local fruits and vegetables offered at an Aruba street market

▼ Sea kayaking off the U.S. Virgin Islands

El Yunque National Forest, Puerto Rico

▲ The Viñales Valley, Cuba

▼ Squirrel fish swim in RMS *Rhone* National Marine Park, Tortola.

Celebrating Carnival in St. Vincent

U.S. VIRGIN ISLANDS

9

ST. THOMAS, ST. JOHN, AND ST. CROIX

About 80 kilometers off the eastern tip of Puerto Rico lies a group of 70 or so islands, islets, and cays that make up the U.S. Virgin Islands. There are three main islands in the group: St. Thomas, 87 square kilometers; the largest, St. Croix, 220 square kilometers, about 65 kilometers south of St. Thomas; and the smallest of the three, St. John, 42 square kilometers and about 6 kilometers east of St. Thomas. Although the islands comprise a territory of the United States, the culture is more West Indian than American, and most people exhibit characteristic Caribbean warmth.

The islands are volcanic, but their mountain ranges do not rise high enough to trap the moisture-laden trades. As a result the islands receive less than 100 centimeters of rain annually and support only arid flora such as thorny woodland, mangroves, and a few pockets of tropical deciduous. This type of flora supports some 200 species of birds, but only a few mammals, such as mongoose and bats, and a few species of land-based reptiles, mostly lizards.

What they lack on land the islands more than make up for in marine life. The seas off the coast teem with marine life, including all the major sea turtles (which nest on the remote islands), humpback whales (this is their southern breeding grounds), and a variety of corals and fish. The islands are a mecca for sailors, divers, and fishermen.

To preserve dwindling habitats, the government has established a number of protected reserves and national parks. Almost the entire island of St. John is now the Virgin Islands National Park, and the waters around Buck Island, off the coast of St. Croix, have been designated the Buck Island Reef National Monument, the only one of its kind in the United States. Anchor damage to coral reefs is a major concern. Conservation groups and the Park Service are combating this problem by installing permanent moorings for pleasure craft. Many States-side conservation groups are active in the islands.

Most adventure and nature activities revolve around the sea—diving, snorkeling, fishing, kayaking, sailing—but visitors also enjoy excellent hiking, mountain biking, and horseback riding. This chapter will focus on St. John and St. Croix, as these two islands offer the most interesting nature adventure opportunities. As visitors to the U.S. Virgin Islands will most likely fly into Charlotte Amalie, St. Thomas, that city is also covered briefly.

U.S. Virgin Islands History

Columbus, who landed in these islands on November 14, 1493, was so impressed by their numbers and beauty that he immediately named them the "Virgins" after the legend of St. Ursula and the 11,000 virgins (see sidebar in next chapter, the British Virgin Islands). By 1733 the Danes had acquired the western three main Virgin Islands from the French and British while leaving the others under British rule. By 1860, with the sugar industry and inter-island trade both in decline, the islands had become a financial burden to Denmark so they put the Danish islands up for sale.

Following almost 50 years of negotiations, in 1917 the Americans, eager to protect the eastern approach to the Panama Canal, purchased the islands for a cool $25 million. They were put under the U.S. Navy's full control until 1927, when islanders were granted full American citizenship. This paved the way for full constitutional rule in 1931. Since 1968, Virgin Islanders have elected their own governor, legislature, and non-voting House Representative every four years.

CHARLOTTE AMALIE, ST. THOMAS

There are few natural sites on St. Thomas, but it will most likely be your port of entry and a stopover on your way to the other islands. The island's main town, Charlotte Amalie, is the capital of the Virgin Islands and the busiest cruise ship port in the Caribbean. In 1724 it was designated a free port (meaning duty-free) and began to attract such pirates as Captain Kidd, Blackbeard, and the wily privateer Sir Francis Drake. In many ways it still has that ambience and is one of the more popular duty-free ports in the Caribbean. Much of the island has been developed and, to make matters worse, sees an influx of more than one million tourists annually. Despite the congestion, there are a few things worth seeing during your stopover.

Things to See and Do in Charlotte Amalie

A short walk north from the waterfront in Charlotte Amalie is the **Cathedral of St. Peter and St. Paul** (built in 1848) with decorative pastel ceilings painted by two Belgian men of the cloth, Father Leo Servais and Brother Ildephonus. Further east, up **Synagogue Hill**, is the **St. Thomas Synagogue** (B'racha V'Shalom U'Gemiliut-hasadim). Complete with traditional sand-covered floor, it was erected in 1833 by the Sephardic Jewish community and ranks as the second oldest synagogue in the Western Hemisphere; the oldest is in Curaçao. East of the synagogue at the foot of Government Hill is the **Frederik Lutheran Church**, built in 1826. Inside are white wooden pews, a solid mahogany alter, and nineteenth-century chandeliers.

Two blocks south of the hill is **Fort Christian**, which gets its name from King Christian V of Denmark. Built in 1672, it is the island's oldest building and a U.S. National Landmark. Its dungeons house the **Virgin Islands Museum** featuring Arawak and Carib artifacts and paintings from the seventeenth and eighteenth centuries.

On the north shore is a sweeping arc called **Magen's Bay** and two kilometers of white-sand beach the *National Geographic* ranked as one of the 10 best beaches in the world. Four kilometers east is Coki Point and a great underwater observatory and aquarium called **Coral World**, the world's largest reef aquarium. Visitors descend eight meters into the undersea observatory to view a large variety of tropical fish in their natural reef habitat.

St. Thomas Marine Sanctuary and Mangrove Lagoon, on the south coast five kilometers from town, is an ideal spot to see a marine habitat up close. You can join a kayak tour or rent one and explore independently. **Virgin Islands EcoTours** (see "Outfitters and Guides on St. John," below) rents kayaks as well as snorkeling, windsurfing, and other water-sport equipment. They also offer half-day guided kayak tours of the lagoon.

Where to Stay in Charlotte Amalie

Admiral's Inn, Box 6162, St. Thomas, VI, 00803, tel 800/544-0493 or 340/774-1376. A short walk along the waterfront will take you to this inn with 16 air-conditioned rooms complete with TVs and verandahs. A pool, two restaurants (complimentary breakfast provided), and an excursion desk round out the offering. Rates $79 and up.

Danish Chalet Inn, Solberg Road, Charlotte Amalie, Box 4319, St. Thomas, VI, 00803, tel 800/635-1531 or 340/774-5764, fax 340/777-4886. Breakfast is complimentary in this intimate 13-room guesthouse just one kilometer north of the city. Most of the rooms have air conditioning and great views and there is a one-dollar honor bar and open-air Jacuzzi. Rates $65 and up.

Island View Guest House, Box 1903, St. Thomas, VI, 00803, tel 800/524-2023 or 340/774-4270, fax 340/774-6167. In the hills just north of town, this place has 15 rooms, some with air conditioning and shared baths. Other amenities include complimentary breakfast, pool, Laundromat, and great views. Rates $50 and up.

Where to Eat in Charlotte Amalie

Bumpa's, right on the waterfront, tel 340/776-5674. This small deli specializes in vegetarian breakfast and lunch.

Cuzzin's Caribbean Restaurant and Bar, 7 Back St., tel 340/774-4711. Set in a 200-year-old building this popular local eatery features local dishes such as conch creole.

Gladys' Cafe, Royal Dane Mall, tel. 340/774-6604. This small westside eatery serves Continental treats such as crêpes, omelettes, and quiche, and local specialties as saltfish and dumplings. Breakfast and lunch.

ST. JOHN

Six kilometers or a 20-minute ferry ride east of St. Thomas is St. John, one of those special places in the Caribbean. With only 42 square kilometers and 3,400 inhabitants, it is at the opposite end of the spectrum from St. Thomas. The first thing you notice as you step off the ferry in **Cruz Bay**, the main village on St. John, is the absence of hustle-bustle. The second thing you notice is the slopes surrounding the town. These slopes are covered, not by buildings, as in St. Thomas, but by plush 20-meter-high forests.

Two-thirds of the island has been designated the **Virgin Island National Park**, established in 1956 by Laurence Rockefeller. Much of the surrounding waters, marshes, and reefs are also part of the national park. A few resorts dot the island, but St. John is really for those seeking a more natural experience. The only way to explore the island is on foot.

VIRGIN ISLANDS NATIONAL PARK

It may be the smallest "natural area" in the U.S. park system, but it offers an array of natural experiences for those interested in exploring its boundaries. Comprising almost the entire island and offshore coral reefs, the park is part of an original parcel of land donated to the federal government by Laurence Rockefeller in 1956. In 1962 an additional section of the island was purchased by the federal government, and the total area became the nation's 29th national park.

Since then the National Park Service has established more than 20 marked trails and dozens of permanent mooring sites. In 1976 the park was designated a biosphere reserve by the United Nations, and in 1986 the Virgin Islands Biosphere Research Center was completed. Although some 1.2 million visitors visit the park annually, because of its size and design it nevertheless offers a true natural experience.

Most of the original forests were cleared decades ago; today's secondary growth ranges from moist semi-deciduous on the northwest slopes to scrub and thorny woodland on the east of the island. There are mangrove forests at Leinstar Bay, Hurricane Hole, and Lameshur Bay. More than 160 bird species have been documented in the park, including the green-throated Carib, bananaquit, and American oystercatcher. There are few mammals.

Snorkeling off St. John in the U.S. Virgin Islands

Besides hiking trails there are marked underwater trails in Trunk Bay as well as a number of great snorkeling sites just offshore but still within the park boundaries. In the several archaeological sites throughout the park you can search middens (ancient garbage sites) for Taínos tools and pottery. You are required to document all findings and turn them over to the Park Service before you leave the park.

Entrance to the park is officially free, but donations are accepted. For more information, contact the National Park Service center, a five-minute walk left of the ferry dock in Cruz Bay. The center is open daily 8:00 to 4:30, tel 340/776-6201.

Things to See and Do in Virgin Islands National Park

In all, 21 marked hiking trails crisscross the park and offer a variety of difficulty from easy to strenuous and from 30 minutes to 3 hours. Most trails follow the island's rugged topography, and you will experience large elevation swings over short distances. Since a number of trials cross each other, you can combine more than one to extend your hike.

Rangers provide daily organized hikes on a number of trails, but all are well marked and can be traversed independently using the National Park Service map. The **Reef Bay Trail**, by far the most interesting, is punctuated by interpretive signs about the flora and fauna. The trailhead is located eight kilometers east of Cruz Bay on Centerline Road near a stone barrier. From the barrier you descend a flight of steps to the trailhead marker.

About 30 minutes into the hike you will come to the first of two eighteenth-century sugar plantation ruins, the Jossie Gut Sugar Estate. Forty minutes further down the trail, you will see a turnoff for the **Petroglyph Trail**, which leads down to a small waterfall and pool where you will find rocks with ancient drawings. This rare freshwater supply on an otherwise dry island is a great place to view such wildlife as feral donkeys, small deer, bats, and dozens of birds that come here to drink.

The National Park Service center in Cruz Bay provides free detailed maps of the park and its trails.

The area is a paradise for shallow water diving and snorkeling. In Trunk Bay, orange markers guide snorkelers through two underwater trails. As you navigate the trail you are greeted by a host of friendly fish, which helps divert attention from a reef that shows signs of damage from irresponsible human contact with the coral. Another way to experience the beautiful reefs is to join one of the around-the-island snorkeling trips. These six-hour guided trips visit less crowded, more inaccessible reefs that are in excellent condition. For a totally different experience, head to Trunk Bay and try "snuba," a cross between snorkeling and scuba. You breathe through a long tube connected to a flotation device on the surface, which allows you to stay down as long as you want. (For more information on snuba, call 340/693-8063.)

Kayaking through the calm shallow waters off tiny offshore islets and the quiet mangrove backwaters is becoming very popular. You can rent kayaks for the day and explore alone or you can join an organized tour on trips up to six days. Many of the longer trips include a visit to the nearby British Virgin Islands group, two kilometers east.

OUTFITTERS AND GUIDES ON ST. JOHN

Arawak Expeditions, Box 853, Cruz Bay, St. John, VI, 00831, tel 800/238-8687, fax 340/693-8312, www.webtreks.com/Arawak, email: Arawak@worldnet.att.net. Offers guided half- and full-day kayak adventures as well as four- and five-day itineraries. Trips range from $40 to $800 depending on length. They can also arrange kayak rentals and guides.

Coral Bay, at Estate Carolina, tel 340/693-6850, offers everything from diving to sea kayaking rentals and excursions. They even rent windsurfers and mountain bikes, and provide free maps for snorkeling and getting around the island. They can also arrange powerboat rentals, fishing trips, and sailing charters. This is one-stop shopping for all your watersport needs.

Miss Lucy, Cruz Bay, tel 340/776-6804. This enterprising woman provides tailor-made hiking tours to every corner of the island and its offshore reefs.

Sadie Sea, National Park Service office, tel 340/690-4651 or 693-6572, offers six-hour guided round-the-island snorkeling trips for $40 every Wednesday and three-hour trips other days. They can also arrange deep-sea fishing trips. Check at the office for details.

Virgin Islands EcoTours, 2 Estate Nadir, St. Thomas, tel 340/777-2155. This small operation offers kayak trips to many areas in the islands including the Mangrove Lagoon.

Virgin Islands National Park, in Cruz Bay, tel 340/776-6201, offers ranger-led hiking tours but can also provide information on local guides.

WHERE TO STAY ON ST. JOHN

St. John is noted for cozy local lodgings, but be prepared to fork out the bucks.

Cruz Inn, across from the library in Cruz Bay, Box 566, St. John, VI, 00831, tel 800/666-7688 or 340/776-8688, fax 340/693-8590. This quaint 19-room guesthouse offers comfortable air-conditioned rooms with shared bath, and includes breakfast. Rates $50 to $75.

The Inn at Tamarind Court, Southside Road, Cruz Bay, Box 350,

Pissarro's Caribbean

Camille Pissarro was among the most influential Impressionists in the 1800s. Most people don't realize that he was born, in 1830, in a small Spanish Sephardic Jewish community in Charlotte Amalie. At the age of 14, he left the island to study business in Paris and returned a year later to help his merchant father run the family business on what is now Main Street. He lived upstairs of what is now the Tropical Perfume Shop. But his heart was not in the family business, and he spent every minute of his spare time painting. Realizing that his son would never become a merchant, his father sent him back to Paris in 1855 to study with the masters. In 1859 he held his first exhibition at the Salon in Paris.

Pissarro died at the age of 73 at his home in Eragny, just north of Paris. Today his paintings grace the walls of many of Europe's major museums. He was described as "godlike" by many of his students, including such luminaries as Vincent van Gogh, Paul Gauguin, and Paul Cézanne.

Pissarro's parents are buried in Savan, the Jewish cemetery on the low peninsula just west of Charlotte Amalie.

St. John, VI, 00831, tel 800/221-1637 or 340/776-6378, fax 340/776-6722. This basic inn offers 17 comfortable rooms with fan and shared baths. Breakfast is included in rate and served in an intimate courtyard, which also contains a popular local bar. A small restaurant, Etta's, serves up tasty local dishes. Rates $40 to $75.

CAMPING ON ST. JOHN

Cinnamon Bay Campground, Box 720, Cruz Bay, St. John, VI, 00830, tel 800/539-9998 or 340/776-6330, fax 340/776-6458. Set in the wooded slopes of Cinnamon Bay are 10 bare sites, 40 tented sites (permanent tents on wooden platforms), and 40 somewhat ugly open-air cot-

Maho Bay

tages. Amenities include four bathhouses with toilets, cold water showers, and a snack bar. Rates: bare sites $15, tented sites $40, cottages $50. Book six months in advance.

Maho Bay Campground, Box 310, Cruz Bay, St. John, VI, 00830, tel 800/392-9004 or 340/776-6226, fax 340/776-6504. Designed with environmental conservation in mind, this 114-site campground offers many amenities. Accommodations are in canvas cottages erected on wooden decks. Each has separate dining and cooking areas, propane stoves, and ice chests. Units on the hillside further from the beach tend to be cooler. A small commissary serves meals and stocks a few groceries. Rates $60 to $95. Book at least six months in advance.

WHERE TO EAT ON ST. JOHN
Since most accommodations include breakfast in the room rate, few places other than hotels and inns serve that meal. Most eateries open for lunch and dinner.

The Fish Trap, King Street, Cruz Bay, tel 340/693-9994. Next to the Raintree Inn, this place serves great seafood lunches and dinners at reasonable prices.

The Lime Inn, Lemon Tree mall, Cruz Bay, tel 340/776-6425, serves international cuisine with an all-you-can-eat shrimp dinner on Wednesday nights. It's a great local hangout.

Vie's Snack Shack, on East End Bay, St. John, tel 340/693-5033. This is the "only" place to eat on the east side of the island (near Coral Bay). Vie serves the best local food on the island. Specialties include spicy homemade island beef patties, garlic chicken and fish cakes (often called "Johnny cakes"), and, best of all, conch fritters. Alas, it's open only from 11:00 a.m. to 4:00 p.m.

ST. CROIX

The largest of the U.S. Virgin Islands, St. Croix lies 65 kilometers south of the other islands and strikes a comfortable balance between the serenity of St. John and the bustle of St. Thomas. It is relatively flat compared to the others and supports more agriculture, though tourism is the major industry. From the air 100 stone towers, the ruins of Dutch-built windmills used for grinding cane, dot the rolling hillsides and the grid pattern of the cane fields resembles a patchwork quilt.

The island's capital, **Christiansted**, is a picturesque town on the shore of a sprawling harbor on the north-central coast. The buildings in the four square blocks surrounding **D. Hamilton Jackson Park**, along the waterfront, have been designated a U.S. National Historic Site. South across the park is the **Old Customs House**, completed in 1750, and **Fort Christiansvaern**, built between 1738 and 1749, on the foundations of an old French fort destroyed in 1645.

Route 76, better known as **Mahogany Road**, runs west along the spine of the coastal range between Blue Mountain, at 334 meters the island's highest peak, and **Frederiksted**, on the west coast. Founded in 1750, Frederiksted is the island's second largest town. Mahogany Road snakes through the heart of St. Croix's miniature rain forest, where the canopy reaches 30 meters. Along the main road you will find a number of dirt roads and trails that lead into the forest. As you head west, watch for a sign that says "**St. Croix LEAP**" (Life Experience Achievement Program), an environmental program that utilizes forest wood to produce local wood art. There is a small gift shop and wood mill.

The **Sandy Point Wildlife Refuge**, on the southwestern tip of the island, is only open to the public on weekends a few months of the year and is one of the island's great birding locations. Least terns, white-tailed tropic birds, and American oystercatchers nest here. The refuge contains a large stretch of white-sand beach that is a regular nesting site for the great leatherback turtle as well as the green and hawksbill turtles. From March to June each year these behemoths of the deep come ashore to lay their eggs. The BBC filmed a leatherback turtle documentary here in 1996. Earthwatch has set up a monitoring program for the leatherbacks and is always looking for volunteers. If you would like to help, inquire at the St. Croix Environmental Association, 340/773-1989.

SALT RIVER BAY NATIONAL PARK

A small (370-hectare) tropical estuary on the central north coast just northwest of Christiansted, Salt River Bay National Park contains the largest remaining mangrove forest in the Virgin Islands. It was made a National Historic Park and Ecological Preserve in 1993 and will soon become a World Heritage Site and National Marine Sanctuary. Salt River Bay is believed to be the landing site of Columbus, whose 1493 log entries describe the bay and the hostilities encountered here. The park also contains the site of a sacred A.D. 350 Arawak Indian ball court (probably the reason the natives were hostile when he landed). The court was lined with large petroglyph-incised stones that now reside in the Copenhagen museum. Except for the 50-meter trail from the parking lot to the ball court, there are no trails in this mangrove swamp–dominated park.

On the southeast corner of the estuary at Triton Bay is the 4.8-hectare mangrove preserve where the Nature Conservancy monitors growth cycles of the white, black, and red mangroves. In total, more than 20 hectares of mangrove provide prime nesting habitat for some 100 bird species, including the endangered peregrine falcon, roseate tern, least tern, and brown pelican.

Just offshore and also part of the park is the acclaimed **Salt River Drop-off** dive site. A drop-off, or underwater cliff, is a place where the seabed drops steeply. At the Salt River Drop-off, divers descend the ledge to view the vertical coral gardens. The nutrient-rich waters flowing out of the river estuary and mangrove swamp support an abundance of small marine life like shrimp and crab larvae and small fish fry that in turn attract larger species such as grouper, snapper, amberjack, and sea turtles. These rich waters wash over the drop-off providing food for a wide variety of soft corals including sea fans, measuring three meters across, and brightly colored sea anemone. The richness of the marine life in this area prompted the construction of the underwater laboratory **Aquarius**, near the Salt River Drop-off, where scientists study the ecosystem of the bay.

On the west side of the bay is the **Salt River Marina**, where you can hire a boat for two-hour excursions into the mangroves led by guides well versed in the flora and fauna. The boat stops at each of the four types of

The white-sand beaches on Buck Island

mangrove so visitors can see the differences. Guides explain the life cycle of the mangrove, from how they reproduce and grow to how they support an abundance of marine life. Also in the marina is the **Anchor Dive Center**, which offers tours and dives along the drop-off.

For more information on visiting the park, contact the St. Croix Tourist Office, Box 4538, VI, 00822, tel 340/773-0495, fax 340/778-9259. St. Croix Environmental Association, tel 340/773-2989, fax 340/773-7545.

BUCK ISLAND REEF NATIONAL MONUMENT

This small volcanic outcropping and the reefs that surround it are only one kilometer long and the only underwater national monument in the United States. Uninhabited since the mid-1700s, it was given monument status in 1961. On the island, three kilometers off the coast of St. Croix and open to the public only from 8:00 to 5:00 each day, visitors will find a two-kilometer trail that loops around the tiny island, a small salt pond fringed with black mangroves, an observation tower with great views of St. Croix, and two blinding white-sand beaches on the west and southwest coasts. About 40 species of birds call the island home, including the mighty frigate bird and brown pelican. There are some 60 varieties of plants but no large shade trees—except, that is, for the poisonous manchineel trees along the west coast. Identifiable by their green crabapple-like fruit, these trees are found just above the high water line and can reach heights of 10 meters. They have shiny dark green elliptical leaves that are folded at mid-rib and often appear droopy. Don't be tempted by the shade of the manchineel tree.

The real action, however, takes place just offshore amid the surrounding reefs where the National Park Service maintains a 230-meter underwater nature trail complete with interpretive plaques describing the fish and coral along the trail. There are two reef systems: a shallow inner reef where you will find the trail and a deeper barrier reef 200 meters offshore. More than 300 species of fish inhabit the reef, including the foureye butterfly fish, blue and queen angels, and parrotfish. There are as many varieties of coral, including some of the largest elkhorn coral formations in the world.

Access is strictly limited to private operators licensed by the National Park Service, which maintains a few moorings in the park. All excursions depart from Kings Wharf in Christiansted, and the four licensed operators supply snorkeling gear. Since visits are limited, it is a good idea to book ahead.

For more information on visiting the monument, contact the St. Croix Tourist Office, Box 4538, Christiansted, VI, 00822, tel 340/773-0495, fax 340/778-9259, or the St. Croix Environmental Association, tel 340/773-2989, fax 340/773-7545.

OUTFITTERS AND GUIDES ON ST. CROIX

Anchor Dive Center, Salt River National Park, tel 800/532-3483 or 340/778-1522, offers diving trips in the Salt River Canyon and guided boat tours through the park.

Milemark Charters, 59 Kings Wharf, Christiansted, St. Croix, VI, 00820, tel 800/524-2012 or 340/773-2628, books day trips to Buck Island and supplies snorkeling gear. Rates $25 to $40.

Paul and Jill's Stables, Box 695, Frederiksted, St. Croix, VI, 00841, tel 340/772-2880, offers half-day horseback treks through the rain forest. Rates $50.

St. Croix Bike and Tours, 5035 Cotton Valley, St. Croix, VI, 00820, tel 340/772-2343. By bike is a great way to see the island. The company offers a variety of mountain bike and/or hiking tours of the island. You can hire one of their guides or rent a bike and go it alone.

St. Croix Environmental Association, Arawak Building, Suite 3, Gallows Bay, St. Croix, VI, 00820, tel 340/773-1989. This group has a list of guides who can take you all over the island. They will customize a trip or you can join one of their regular tours of the Salt River Bay National Historical Park or the rain forest. Rates: $20 adults, $12 children.

WHERE TO STAY ON ST. CROIX

Cactus Inn, 48 King St., Christiansted, St. Croix, VI, 00820, tel 340/692-9331. This comfortable inn has eight no-frills rooms complete with air conditioning, TV, and private bath. Rates $40 to $50.

Hilty House Inn, 2 Hermon Hill, Box 26077, Gallows Bay, St. Croix, VI, 00824, tel 340/773-2594, fax 340/773-2594. This elegant six-room plantation house has a large great room and pool. Rooms are grand with private baths but no air conditioning. Rates include continental breakfast. Rates $75 and up.

Pink Fancy Hotel, 27 Prince St., Christiansted, St. Croix, VI, 00820, tel 800/524-2045 or 340/773-8460, fax 340/773-6448. This charming inn, located in the center of town in a historic 1780 building, has 13 clean and simple rooms with air conditioning and kitchenette. Complimentary breakfast, a small pool, and a beautiful garden with bar complete the amenities. Rates $75 and up.

CAMPING ON ST. CROIX

Boy Scout Camp, Box 1353, Frederiksted, St. Croix, VI, 00840, tel 340/773-1733. On the south side, east of Camp Arawak, this is the better choice with bare sites, electrical outlets, showers, restrooms, and tent rentals. Rates $10.

Camp Arawak, Box 129, Christiansted, St. Croix, VI, 00820, tel 340/773-3944. About eight kilometers southeast of the capital, this camp rents bare sites and has pit toilets and running water. Canoe and snorkeling rentals are available. Rates $8.

WHERE TO EAT ON ST. CROIX

Alley Galley, 1100 Strand, Christiansted, opens at 7:30 a.m. and serves light meals (salads and sandwiches) all day and two-dollar piña coladas all night.

Brady's, 15 Queen St., Christiansted, serves three meals a day offering such West Indian treats as roti, saltfish and other fish cakes ("Johnny cakes"), fried plantain, pumpkin fritters, and *tannia* soup (*tannia* is a potato-like vegetable). Great lunches.

Le St. Tropez, 67 King St., Frederiksted, tel 340/772-3000. Serves familiar French favorites like quiche, roast duck, and frog legs. Lunch and dinner. Make reservations for dinner.

Top Hat, 52 Company St., Christiansted, tel 340/773-2346. The only Danish restaurant on the island serves such tasty dishes as homemade pork sausages, stewed red cabbage, Flikadeller (a type of meatball), and duck à la Danish (crisply broiled and served with sautéed apples). Open only for dinner. Reservations required.

U.S. VIRGIN ISLAND SPECIFICS

Getting to St. John and St. Croix

To St. John: St. John has no airport, so you must get there by boat or ferry from St. Thomas (also from Tortola in the BVIs). Ferries run between Red Hook, St. Thomas, and Cruz Bay, on the hour from eight in the morning to midnight (the 20-minute trip costs three dollars) and between Charlotte Amalie and Cruz Bay every two hours (the 45-minute trip costs seven dollars). Taxis, rental cars, and mountain bikes are available and can get you anywhere on St. John. The park boundary starts one kilometer north of Cruz Bay on Highway 20.

To St. Croix: American Eagle and LIAT have daily flights to St. Croix from St. Thomas, and most major carriers arrive daily direct from North American cities or through St. Thomas. The more adventurous should try Virgin Hydrofoil Services Inc., tel 340/776-7417, fax 340/776-7416, between downtown Charlotte Amalie and Christiansted. The trip takes just over an hour and costs a
little less than airfare.

Getting Around

The islands are small and taxis are convenient, but the best way to get around is by rental car or jeep. Expect to pay about $60 a day (gas is $1.50 per gallon). Hitchhiking is a safe and acceptable way to travel.

ABC Car Rentals, Box 10844, St. Thomas, VI, 00801, tel 800/524-2080 or 340/776-1222, fax 340/775-4369.

Olympic Car Rental, 1103 Richmond, Christiansted, St. Croix, VI, 00820, tel 800/344-5776 or 340/773-8000, fax 340/773-6870. Good fleet including four-wheel-drive vehicles.

St. John Car Rental, Box 566, Cruz Bay, St. John, VI, 00831, tel and fax 340/776-6103. Good fleet including four-wheel-drive vehicles.

Tourist Information

St. Croix, Box 4538, Christiansted, VI, 00822, tel 340/773-0495, fax 340/778-9259

St. John, Box 200, Cruz Bay, VI, 00830, tel. 340/776-6450

St. Thomas, Box 6400, Charlotte Amalie, VI, 00804, tel 340/774-8784, fax 340/774-4390

U.S.A.: 1270 Avenue of the Americas, Suite 2108, New York, NY, 10020, tel 212/332-2222, fax 212/332-2223

Canada: 3300 Bloor St. W., Ste. 3120, Centre Tower, Toronto, Ontario, M8X 2X3, tel 416/233-1414, Web site: www.usvi.net.

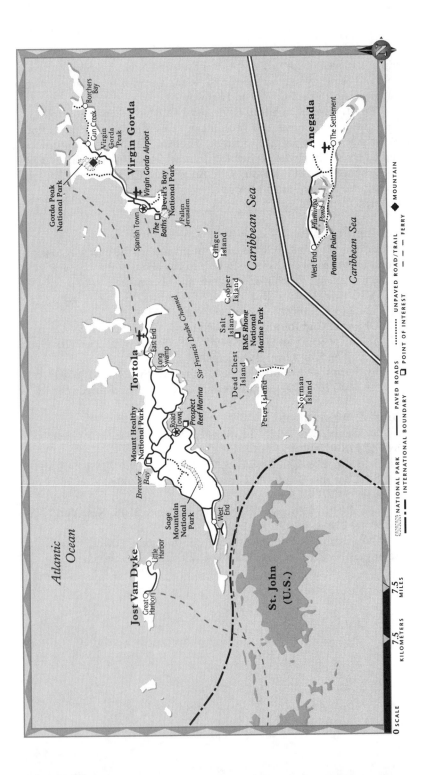

BRITISH VIRGIN ISLANDS

10

TORTOLA, VIRGIN GORDA, AND ANEGADA

Located just two kilometers east of the U.S. Virgin Islands, this archipelago of about 60 small islands, cays, and rocks comprises just under 155 square kilometers. Some 18,737 islanders, all British subjects, live on 12 of the islands, mostly on Tortola, Anegada, and Virgin Gorda (which are covered in this chapter as the islands offering the best opportunities for outdoor adventure), and Jost Van Dyke. The islands straddle the eight-kilometer-wide Sir Francis Drake Channel, probably the safest and most important corridor between the Atlantic Ocean and Caribbean Sea. As such, the BVIs have been a haven for seafarers for centuries and are the premier yachting destination in the Caribbean.

Tourism, which now accounts for 50 percent of the BVIs' GNP, took off in the 1970s. Today almost 300,000 visitors, mainly yachting types, pump almost $20 million into the BVI economy to give it the second highest standard of living in the Caribbean.

The flora and fauna of these islands are very similar to those of the U.S. Virgin Islands, but they are famous for their 16 native varieties of orchids and the hummingbirds that pollinate them. The BVIs are also home to the endangered two-meter-long rock iguana and the rare Anegada iguana. Over the years, much of the forest was cleared for agriculture and timber, but since the 1960s the government, along with the National Parks Trust, has initiated massive reforestation programs in all the national parks. The trust, which presently manages 11 sites, has also established a flamingo colony and bird sanctuary on Anegada and installed some 250 permanent moorings to protect the fragile reefs from further deterioration. The trust plans to add 12 more sites within the next two decades.

Although there is good hiking, cycling, and bird watching on four of the islands, the main focus in the BVIs is the sea. With more than 300 wrecks, miles of white-sand beaches fringed by shallow reefs, and humpback whales, the BVIs are an ideal destination for those seeking natural adventures such as deep-sea fishing, snorkeling, sea kayaking, diving, whale watching, and sailing.

British Virgin Islands History

Columbus sailed past the islands in 1493 on his second voyage and named all the islands (including the USVIs) "the Virgins." But the islands were too small and mountainous to capture anyone's attention until the Spanish found copper on Virgin Gorda in the early 1500s. It remained virtually unsettled and home to many buccaneers until the Dutch, with buccaneer protection, established a permanent settlement on Tortola in 1648. The French captured the islands in 1668 and the British took them away in 1672 and started colonizing. By 1720 the islands were governed by a British lieutenant governor and, with Anguilla, St. Kitts, and Nevis, became the Leeward Islands colony in 1816. They were given separate colony status in 1872 and today are a self-governed Dependent Territory of Great Britain (one of the four remaining British colonies in the Caribbean).

TORTOLA

Tortola is the largest island in the group, 55 square kilometers, with a population of 15,388; its capital city, **Road Town**, is also the capital of the BVIs. The island gets its name from the Spanish word meaning "turtle dove," an obvious moniker given the number of *zenaida* doves on the island. Unlike neighboring St. Thomas, Tortola is quiet and uncrowded, but a recent building spree in Road Town has detracted from its charm.

Tortola is home to the largest charter (boats with captains) and bareboat (captain yourself boats) fleets in the Caribbean: more than 400 boats handle almost 200,000 seafarers annually. There is not much to see here except for hotels and marinas, a few century-old buildings, a two-hectare botanical garden in Road Town, and several great beaches along the north coast. Of some interest to visitors are the two national parks:

Mount Healthy National Park, a forested half-hectare plot containing old sugar plantation ruins, and **Sage Mountain National Park**.

SAGE MOUNTAIN NATIONAL PARK

The land that defines this tiny, 37-hectare park around Sage Mountain was donated to the people of the BVIs by Laurence Rockefeller in 1964, with the understanding that it be protected. Rockefeller also donated land on other islands and helped create the BVI National Park Trust to manage the lands. The park is located along the western third of the island's volcanic backbone and contains the island's highest point, Sage Mountain, which at 542 meters is also the tallest point in all the Virgin Islands. Although it does not receive enough rainfall to be technically classified as rain forest, the park supports rain forest varieties such as orchids, six-meter-high fern trees, West Indian mahogany, and white cedar, the BVIs' national tree. An extensive reforestation program has been in place for 25 years to rebuild stands of native vegetation that were cleared decades ago.

The National Trust maintains three trails that wind through the park; you can easily walk them all in under four hours. Sage Mountain

The view from Sage Mountain (Long Bay on the right, St. John on the left)

Road leads up from the main Ridge Road to a parking lot with great 360-degree views. The well-marked **Main Trail** leads up to the **Rain Forest, Mahogany Forest,** and **Henry Adams Loop Trails**. Fifteen minutes up from the trailhead the Mahogany Forest and Rain Forest Trails intersect the Main Trail. From here the Mahogany Trail rises steeply to the summit of Sage Mountain. An observation tower at the summit affords spectacular views of both the BVIs and the USVIs. The Rain Forest Trail runs west from the intersection through great stands of rain forest. About 300 meters along the trail is a sign pointing to the shorter Henry Adams Loop Trail. This short but eventful trail cuts through some of the original old-growth forest, where you will find huge trees like the 30-meter-tall bullet-wood, which has a trunk 1.5 meters in diameter. Gates at the start of each trail keep the bovine population at bay, so please remember to close them behind you.

Large iguanas, pearly-eyed thrashers, Antillean crested humming-birds, and American kestrels are common in the park. Mountain guava trees with white blossoms are scattered throughout the park. Their green crabapple-sized fruit turns yellowish when ripe and provides a tasty treat for curious hikers. Signs along the trails identify nearby vegetation and fauna.

There is no fee for visiting the park. For more information, contact the BVI Tourist Board, P.O. Box 134, Waterfront St., Road Town, tel 284/494-3134. The National Parks Trust, P.O. Box 860, Fishlock Road, Road Town, tel 284/494-3904. (The National Park Trust plans on opening new trails within the next two years, so check with them for the latest information.)

RMS *RHONE* NATIONAL MARINE PARK

To the southeast of Road Town, between Salt and Peter Islands, is a 324-hectare marine park in which lies the wreck of the 2,738-ton RMS *Rhone*. Since being featured in the movie *The Deep*, the huge iron-hulled steamship has become one of the hottest dives in the Caribbean.

Rumor has it that the 94-meter-long RMS *Rhone*, a British mail packet ship, only two years old, was anchored outside Great Harbour on near-by Peter Island in 1867 when a fierce storm blew up. The ship was taking on passengers and provisions for a return trip to England when the hurricane-like storm blew in out of the east. The captain judged that the ship was in a vulnerable location and decided to head for a more sheltered anchorage.

As the crew was raising the anchor, the chain broke and the anchor sunk to the bottom. No longer able to anchor safely, the captain did the only thing he could: he gave the order to head for open water to try to ride out the storm. Before rounding Black Rock Point on Salt Island, just half a kilometer from open water, the gale winds forced the ship onto the rocks. The ship immediately split in two and went to the bottom, taking most of the crew and passengers with it.

The thickly coral-encrusted wreck now lies in 6 to 24 meters of crystal clear water, making it accessible to both divers and snorkelers. The larger bow section lies on its starboard side in about 20 meters of water while the upright stern lies only 6 meters below the surface. Scattered around the two sections is a variety of ship parts including the old boilers, propellers, engines, winches, and gear boxes.

Visitors to the wreck are quickly surrounded by large schools of curious grunts and the massive but friendly wreck mascot, a 140-kilogram jewfish, a variety of grouper. Divers and snorkelers alike have been able to pet this tame creature, but as yet no one has given him a name that sticks. In the shallow water west of the stern section are two large coral caves where the more adventurous explorers can experience an even wider variety of marine life.

The park also includes a scraggy outcropping of land aptly named Dead Chest Island because of its resemblance to a coffin (or dead man's chest). Rumor has it that the notorious pirate Blackbeard marooned 15 of his mutinous crew here with only the shirt on their backs and a bottle of rum. Many believe the tale inspired the lyrics, "Fifteen men on a dead man's chest, yo, ho, ho, and a bottle of rum." Besides legends, the island is also home to a variety of seabirds including the bridled tern and tropic bird. The island is arid and supports a wide selection of cacti and mangrove.

A number of charter boats, outside of Road Town, offer daily excursions to the RMS *Rhone* and Dead Chest Island.

For more information, contact the British Virgin Islands Tourist Board, P.O. Box 134, Waterfront Street, Road Town, tel 284/494-3134, or the National Parks Trust, P.O. Box 860, Fishlock Road, Road Town, tel 284/494-3904.

OUTFITTERS AND GUIDES ON TORTOLA

There are dozens of companies offering half-day, full-day, and longer excursions and charters to great diving and snorkeling spots. You can ask at the tourist office or just go to the docks in Road Town and make your selection.

Arawak Expeditions, Box 853, Cruz Bay, St. John, USVI 00831, tel 800/238-8687, fax 340/693-8312, Web site: www.webtreks.com/ Arawak, email: Arawak@worldnet.att.net. This is a U.S. Virgin Island outfitter that also runs kayak excursions in the BVIs.

Baskin' in the Sun, Box 108, Road Town, Tortola, BVI, tel 284/494-2858 or 800/650-2084, email: baskindive@aol.com, Web site: www.dive-baskin.com, offers the only five-star PADI operation on the island. They also offer "resort dives," dives for those without certification, and go to the RMS *Rhone*.

Caribbean Images Tours, Prospect Reef Marina, tel 284/494-1147, is one of the best snorkeling outfitters in the British Virgin Islands and everyone knows them. They go to the RMS *Rhone*. Phone them or ask at your hotel.

HIHO, Prospect Reef Marina, tel 284/494-8304, fax 284/494-0003, Web site: www.hiho-bvi.com, email: racebvi@caribsurf.com, rents kayaks and windsurfers, and provides instruction.

Last Stop Sports Bike Rentals, Box 3208, Road Town, Tortola, BVI, tel 284/494-0564, fax 284/494-0593, offers hiking, biking, and combination tours to Sage Mountain National Park. They also rent bikes and provide guides.

Miss Robbie Charter, Box 243, Road Town, Tortola, BVI, tel 284/494-4200, fax 284/494-4870, offers half- and full-day fishing and can arrange whale-watching charters.

National Park Trust, Ministry of Natural Resources, Box 860, Road Town, Tortola, BVIs, tel 284/4949-3904, manages parks and provides a list of qualified marine and land guides.

Rainbow Visions Photography, Box 680, Road Town, Tortola, BVI, tel 284/494-2749, fax 284/494-6390, email: rainbow@caribsurf.com, rents cameras and gives underwater photography lessons so you can capture all the great sights of the region.

Shadow's Stables, Box 60, Road Town, Tortola, BVI, tel 284/494-2262, offers trail rides to Sage Mountain as well as to Cane Garden Bay beach.

WHERE TO STAY ON TORTOLA

A & L Inn, Box 403, Road Town, Tortola, BVI, tel 284/494-6343, fax 284/494-6656, offers 14 air-conditioned rooms with phones, TVs, and private baths two blocks from the sea in the center of town. Small cafe and maid service. Rates $65 to $75.

Fort Burt Hotel, Box 3380, Road Town, Tortola, BVI, tel 284/494-2587, fax 284/494-2002. This very intimate eight-room property built around a 300-year-old Dutch fort is perched on a hill overlooking Road Town. It has great harbor views, private baths, air conditioning, and balconies as well as a small restaurant and pool. Rates $60 to $190.

Hotel Castle Maria, Box 206, Road Town, Tortola, BVI, tel 284/494-2553, fax 284/494-2111. This delightful old 30-room mansion, overlooking Road Harbour, is peaceful and quiet. Rooms have air conditioning, private baths, kitchenettes, and balconies. Amenities include a secluded pool, beautiful landscaped gardens, and friendly restaurant. Rates $60 to $120.

Way Side Inn Guest House, Box 258, Road Town, Tortola, BVI, tel 284/494-3606. This intimate property in the heart of Road Town has 20 basic rooms, no air conditioning, and shared bathrooms. Rates $35 to $45.

CAMPING ON TORTOLA

Brewer's Bay Campsite, Box 185, Road Town, Tortola, BVI, tel 284/494-3463, offers babysitting, beach bar, restaurant, and showers on a beautiful secluded beach with great snorkeling. Rates: bare sites $8, tented sites $35.

WHERE TO EAT ON TORTOLA

Beach Club Terrace, Bougher's Bay Beach Club, tel 284/494-2272, is a great place for West Indian cuisine like ox-tail soup and saltfish cakes. It serves three meals daily.

C & F Restaurant, Purcell Estate, Road Town, 284/494-4941, is a popular spot for both locals and visitors, serving a variety of West Indian delicacies such as curried lobster. Dinner only.

Marlene's Delicious Designs, near the Cutlass Building, Road Town. Marlene's serves tasty pastries, patties, excellent rotis, and desserts for lunch.

Pusser's Pub and the Outpost, near Village Cay Marina, tel 284/494-4199. This is probably the most famous local hot spot in the British Virgin Islands, serving great sandwiches, pizza, beer, and people watching.

Rays of Hope, Port Purcell, offers nutritious vegetarian lunches, take-out, and a fabulous juice bar with local concoctions.

VIRGIN GORDA

Thirteen kilometers east of Tortola is Virgin Gorda, by far the most popular of the BVIs. Viewing the island from offshore, Columbus thought its profile resembled a hefty woman lying on her back, so he named the island "fat virgin." Gorda Peak, at 417 meters, forms the "belly" of the fat virgin and dominates the island's landscape. The northeast half of the island is mountainous while the southeast is flat, and all land above 300 meters is considered part of the island's national park system.

Most of the 2,834 inhabitants of this small, 22-square-kilometer island live in or around the settlement of **Spanish Town**, the capital. Remarkably, most are still friendly despite being inundated with more than 100,000 visitors annually, most of them cruise ship passengers. Spanish Town was actually the capital of the BVIs until it was transferred to Road Town in 1741. The main tourist attraction on Virgin Gorda is **The Baths**, a pristine white-sand beach strewn with gigantic granite boulders, some the size of houses. Since many cruise lines have added The Baths to their itineraries, the beach can get grossly overcrowded during peak cruise season, December through March.

GORDA PEAK NATIONAL PARK

Located just off the main North Sound Road, about seven kilometers from Spanish Town, is Gorda Peak and its surrounding 107 hectares of park land. Established in 1974 to protect the remaining stands of indigenous forest and to preserve the watershed, the park was part of a parcel of land that Laurence Rockefeller donated to the government in the 1960s and includes all land above 330 meters elevation.

The National Trust maintains two groomed trails, but other unofficial trails also crisscross the mountain and park. A sign, on the northwest side of the North Sound Road, about five kilometers from Spanish Town, marks the trailhead for the main summit trail. The second trail branches off this main trail and takes a different approach to the summit. If you elect to hike the unofficial trailheads, it is best to inquiry locally at Olde Yarde Inn, which has the best trail maps of the park.

Red paint-dabbed rocks and tree trunks mark the trails while picnic areas and observation points offer ideal resting spots. A large gray wooden observation tower, tucked in between two even larger granite boulders, provides spectacular views of the surrounding countryside, North Sound, the Dog Islands, and on clear days, Mount Sage on Tortola.

Most of the island is covered in scrub woodland and cactus, but extensive reforestation over the last 20 years has transformed the park into lush forests similar to those on Tortola. Huge philodendrons and lacy ferns grow in the shadows of the tall mahogany, silk cotton, and white cedar trees. A wide variety of ground orchids, red palicoureas, and a sprinkling of flamboyant adds a little color to the green forest. Hummingbirds, thrashers, martins, and mockingbirds, seem to follow hikers throughout the park while the seldom seen, but often heard, iguanas rustle through the underbrush.

Park entrance is free. For more information contact BVI Tourist Board, P.O. Box 134, Waterfront Street, Road Town, tel 284/494-3134, or the National Parks Trust, P.O. Box 860, Fishlock Road, Road Town, tel 284/494-3904.

THE BATHS AND DEVIL'S BAY NATIONAL PARK

Along a palm-fringed beach on the southwest coast, about one kilometer south of Spanish Town, visitors will find the most famous sites in the BVIs: The Baths and Devil's Bay National Park. The 37-hectare park resembles a scene from a sci-fi movie, with massive round house-sized granite boulders—throwbacks to the Tertiary period 70 million years ago—strewn along the beach. Though their origin is still a mystery, some geologists feel they were formed by lava flowing up through cracks in the ocean floor. Over millions of years the sea floor rose and the exposed boulders were sculptured by the wind and sea until they

Snorkeling at The Baths on Virgin Gorda

acquired their present shape. Another group of geologists theorize that the boulders—which are very similar to those found in the Carolinas— were brought down to the Caribbean within the glaciers of the last ice age. When the ice flows receded they left the granite boulders behind. However, this does not explain the fact that this is the only place in the Caribbean where these formations are found.

The huge round rocks form a labyrinth of caverns and passages through which you can swim and walk. Sunlight filtering down through the cracks provides ample light for adventurers to find numerous shimmering, crystal-clear, saltwater grottoes ideal for bathing—hence the name "The Baths." A trail on the south side of the beach leads through the massive boulders to a secluded pink coral–sand beach and the 23-hectare Devil's Bay National Park. The one-kilometer trail winds its way along the shore through a magnificent cactus forest where you will find six-meter-high organ pipe and beachball-sized barrel cactus. Crested hummingbirds, sparrow hawks (the locals call them *killi-killi*), and ground lizards accompany you along the trail. At the south end of the beach another trail leads to Stoney Bay, at the southern tip of the island, where there are great views of Fallen Jerusalem and the other nearby islands. The best time to visit The Baths is in the morning, before the cruise ship tourists come in at around 11 a.m., or after around 3 p.m.,

Legend of the 11,000 Virgins

On November 14, 1493, Columbus sailed through a group of islands so beautiful and plentiful he named them "the Virgins." His choice of names was prompted by the legend of the 11,000 virgins. Legend has it that in A.D. 235 Britain was being threatened by the pagans advancing across Europe. One of the advancing pagan princes, hearing of the British king's beautiful virgin daughter, Ursula, requested her hand in marriage in exchange for sparing the king's life and Britain. Ursula, who had dedicated her life to sainthood, agreed to the arrangement on one condition: that 11,000 beautiful virgins would be her companions for three years, after which time she would marry the pagan prince. The prince agreed and Britain was spared.

During the next three years Ursula transformed the 11,000 virgins into an army of Amazons dedicated to fighting the pagans. What Ursula did not know was that the prince had sent spies to watch over his future bride and they soon discovered the plot. When the prince heard of the plot, he was so outraged he sent an army to capture Ursula and destroy her army of virgins. According to legend, the battle took place near Cologne in A.D. 238 and Ursula and her army of virgins fought to their deaths. Soon after the battle Ursula was granted sainthood and, although the virgins were defeated, their incredible beauty and dedication lived on in memory.

when they have returned to their ship. If you find yourself there when a cruise ship comes in, head for Devil's Bay.

Park entrance is free. For more information, contact the BVI Tourist Board, P.O. Box 134, Waterfront Street, Road Town, tel 284/494-3134, or the National Parks Trust, P.O. Box 860, Fishlock Road, Road Town, tel 284/494-3904.

OUTFITTERS AND GUIDES ON VIRGIN GORDA
It is probably best to stay on Tortola and plan a day outing to Virgin Gorda. Many of the operators mentioned for Tortola offer day excursions to Virgin Gorda. It is easy to go over in the morning, hike Gorda Peak, visit The Baths, and return in the late afternoon.

Andy's Jeep and Taxi Rental, The Valley, tel 284/495-5511, fax 284/495-5162, rents four-wheel-drive vehicles and scooters, and offers guided tours of the island.

Dive BVI Ltd., Box 1040, Yacht Harbour, Virgin Gorda, BVI, tel 284/495-5513, fax 284/495-5347, operates diving and snorkeling excursions out of the yacht harbor.

WHERE TO STAY ON VIRGIN GORDA
Aside from the inns listed below, your choices on Virgin Gorda are limited to large, exclusive hotels such as the 98-room Little Dix's Bay Resort, at $375 to $600 per day, or the 95-room Bitter End Yatch Club & Resort, at $390 to $550 per day. You can also stay on Tortola and day-trip to Virgin Gorda.

Olde Yarde Inn, Box 26, Spanish Town, Virgin Gorda, BVI, tel 284/495-5544, fax 284/495-5986. Located near the yacht harbor, this clean inn has 14 basic rooms with pool, Jacuzzi, and small restaurant. Rates $85 to $200.

Wheel House Hotel, Box 66, Spanish Town, Virgin Gorda, BVI, tel 284/495-5230. This conveniently located inn has 12 basic, clean rooms with air conditioning and breakfast included. Rates at the Wheel House run $85 to $200.

CAMPING ON VIRGIN GORDA
There are no campgrounds on Virgin Gorda. For environmental reasons, camping of any kind is prohibited.

WHERE TO EAT ON VIRGIN GORDA
The restaurants at the Olde Yarde Inn and Wheel House Hotel both serve good, inexpensive meals in informal settings.

Mad Dog, at The Baths, serves tasty sandwiches and drinks for lunch.

Top of the Baths Restaurant, tel 284/495-5497, serves three meals a day and is a popular spot with the yachting crowd and day visitors from Tortola. It also has great views over the bay and a freshwater pool for customers.

ANEGADA

Located 24 kilometers northeast of Tortola, Anegada is the BVIs' second largest island, at 39 square kilometers, but its highest point is only 8.5 meters above sea level and in some places it is only one kilometer wide. Unlike its sister islands, which are volcanic outcroppings, Anegada is actually a coral atoll formed when the seabed rose about 25 millions years ago. The island, which resembles a Pacific atoll, is completely surrounded by treacherous shallow-water reefs. Each year strong easterlies from Atlantic storms push water over the western half of the island, refilling the salt ponds and aerating the marshes. Little wonder the Spanish named it Anegada, which roughly translates as "flooded."

Most of the island's 188 inhabitants live at **The Settlement**, sharing their precarious perch with some 2,000 wild goats and donkeys. Rumor has it that the animals swam ashore from some of the many ships that floundered off the island's treacherous coasts. It is estimated that more than 300 wrecks dot the island's reefs and 150 have already been charted. Some of the noted wrecks are the *Paramatta*, a British steamship that hit Horseshoe Reef in 1853, and the 32-cannon British warship RMS *Astrea*, which sank in 1808. Tragic though these wrecks were, they place Anegada in the top five best diving and snorkeling spots in the Caribbean.

The locals consider the entire island a national park, even though there is no such formal designation. Residents aim to keep it as close to natural as possible. Thanks to the concerted efforts of the National Parks Trust and local Anegadans, plans to develop mega-hotels, resorts, and marinas have been stalled. Locals and the National Parks Trust cited the need to preserve the flamingo sanctuary and habitat for the endangered Anegada rock iguana, of which only 400 remain. The iguanas, reaching two meters in length and weighing up to nine kilograms, are found nowhere else in the Caribbean. The National Parks Trust has recently implemented an iguana relocation program on Guana Island to establish a second breeding colony.

According to historical records thousands of flamingos once roamed the British Virgin Islands, but poaching, loss of habitat, and nature eradicated the flocks by the early 1900s. In 1992 the National Parks Trust spearheaded an effort to reestablish a breeding colony on the island and 20 birds, from the Bermuda Aquarium and Natural History Museum and Zoo, were introduced back into the flamingo ponds. In 1995 four chicks hatched and the 36-bird flock now flourishes within the 445-hectare sanctuary.

Hikers, naturalists, snorkelers, and divers will find exceptional natural experiences on Anegada and should place it high on their list when in the BVIs.

THINGS TO SEE AND DO ON ANEGADA

The translucent waters of **Loblolly Bay** on the island's northeast coast offer some of the best snorkeling in the Caribbean. Here, three rows of fringing reefs, each slightly deeper than the other, protect the beach from the ravages of the Atlantic and provide habitat for abundant marine life. The deepest section of reef is seven meters, and you never have to wander farther than 100 meters offshore to explore the beautiful reefs. Snorkeling equipment can be rented from the beach bar.

For divers, **Horse Shoe Reef** has a great selection of coral gardens at depths of 10 to 20 meters. The forests of giant elkhorn and brain coral are frequented by giant grouper, blue parrot, large trigger fish, and sea turtles. A few coral-encrusted ship wrecks also dot the area, but are not that easy to find without a guide.

Flamingo Pond and **Red Pond**, on the western half of the island, provide ideal habitat for the island's small but growing population of flamingos and rock iguanas. The ponds are the remains of old salt pans used to produce salt back in the 1800s. Most of the area is protected and a trail, paralleling the road that circles the ponds, offers an easy two-hour hike through the scrub forest surrounding the ponds. The main trail, and its branch trails, is easy to follow and is kept clear by the many wild goats and donkeys traversing from one watering hole to another. The flamingos usually alternate daily feedings between the two ponds, so if you miss them at one site just head to the other. Campsite and hotel operators can provide all the information you need to explore the island, and most can arrange guided trips.

Just 15 kilometers long and 5 wide, Anegada is small and flat enough to walk from one end to the other in less than three hours. Most of the places mentioned are within easy walking distance from any of the campsites or hotels. A taxi is only a radio call away, and most drivers can direct you to all the best spots.

For fishermen, the coastline from **White Point**, in the southwest, to **West End Point** (the western tip) provides some of the best shallow-water sports fishing in the Caribbean. Along this coast the one-meter-deep water extends a kilometer offshore providing ideal habitat for such prized sport fish as permit, bonefish, tarpon, and snook. Most of the fishing guides on Anegada have a catch and release policy.

Arawak Expeditions offers kayak trips around the island and throughout the rest of the BVIs. Arrangements can be made to join one of their paddling trips (see "Outfitters and Guides," below). Their five-day BVI kayaking trip usually starts at Pomato Point on Anegada's southwest coast. From there they sail or paddle with the wind and current through the islands to Tortola or St. John in the USVIs.

Pomato Point on Anegada

OUTFITTERS AND GUIDES ON ANEGADA

Few operators run out of Anegada, but many outfitters and guides based in Tortola or Virgin Gorda run excursions to the island on an as-needed basis.

Anegada Reef Hotel, Anegada, BVI, tel 284/495-8002, fax 284/495-9362 (see below). The hotel offers deep-sea fishing excursions, rental bikes, and water-sport equipment.

Arawak Expeditions, Box 853, Cruz Bay, St. John, USVI 00831, tel 800/238-8687, fax 340/693-8312, Web site: www.webtreks.com/Arawak, email: Arawak@worldnet.att.net. This is a U.S. Virgin Island outfitter that also runs kayak excursions in the BVIs.

Garfield Faulkner will guide you to some of the best catch and release bonefishing in the Caribbean. Just ask at the Anegada Reef Hotel; he has no phone.

Tony's Taxi, tel 284/495-8027, offers guided tours of the island.

WHERE TO STAY ON ANEGADA

Anegada Reef Hotel, Anegada, BVI, tel 284/495-8002, fax 284/495-9362. Close to good beaches, this is the larger of only two hotels on the island, offering 16 basic rooms with air conditioning and hot plate for a coffee pot. They also provide one-stop shopping to rent jeeps, bikes, and fishing gear, and lead deep-sea fishing and bonefishing excursions. They also offer taxi service. Rates $130 to $250.

Ocean Range Hotel, The Settlement, Anegada, BVI, tel 284/495-8017. Very basic accommodations in town away from the nice beaches. Rates $65 to $85.

CAMPING ON ANEGADA

The accommodation of choice on Anegada is camping. Of the five campgrounds in the BVIs, three are found on Anegada, and all are situated on beaches only steps away from the island's magnificent blue water and great snorkeling reefs. Tucked beneath coconut palms or huge stands of seagrapes, the campsites are well equipped and offer comfortable, private surroundings. In contrast to the scorching daytime heat, nights are cool, and you will be lulled into a deep sleep by the caressing breeze and rhythmic sound of the waves lapping the beach.

Anegada Beach Campground, Box 2710, Anegada, BVI, tel 284/495-9466. Near Anegada Reef Hotel, this campground offers guided tours, windsurfing, snorkeling, fishing, beach bar, and restaurant. Rates: $5 bare sites, $25 prepared sites with 8-foot by 10-foot tents.

Mac's Place Camping, Anegada, BVI, tel 284/495-8020, offers only prepared sites with 8-foot by 10-foot tents, showers, toilets, BBQ grilles, and dining area. Rates $15 to $25.

Neptune's Campground, Box 2711, Anegada, BVI, tel 284/495-9439, only has prepared sites with tents, mattresses, linens, showers, beach bar, and restaurant. Rates $15 to $25.

WHERE TO EAT ON ANEGADA

The hotel and campground restaurants are the best places to eat on the island.

Cow Wreck Beach Bar & Grille, located on the great snorkeling beach in Cow Wreck Bay, serves up delicious Anegada seafood favorites.

Pomato Point Beach Restaurant, on Pomato Beach in Anegada, tel 284/495-8038, serves three tasty meals daily including a champagne breakfast on Saturdays.

BRITISH VIRGIN ISLANDS SPECIFICS

Getting There

There are no direct flights to the British Virgin Islands from outside the Caribbean. International visitors must fly into either St. Thomas or San

Juan, Puerto Rico, and take a commuter flight to Tortola. American Eagle and Leeward Island Air Transport (LIAT), offer daily flights from both St. Thomas and San Juan. A slower but far more exciting way to get to the BVIs is to take one of the many ferries from St. Thomas. Most modes of transport to Tortola will mean staying overnight in either San Juan, Puerto Rico, or St. Thomas.

Getting to Tortola: From St. Thomas or San Juan, Puerto Rico, take an American Eagle or Leeward Island Air Transport (LIAT) flight to Tortola. Most connecting flight schedules will probably necessitate overnighting in one of those locations. You can also take one of Smith's Ferry Services daily ferries, tel 284/494-4430, fax 284/495-4495, from Charlotte Amalie (St. Thomas, U.S. Virgin Islands) to Road Town, Tortola.

Getting to Virgin Gorda: Four companies offer regular (four trips per day) ferry service between Tortola and Virgin Gorda. A few small charter air companies also offer return flights from Tortola and some flights from St. Thomas, USVI: **Atlantic Air BVI**, tel 284/495-2000, flies daily between Virgin Gorda and Tortola; **Carib Air**, tel 284/495-5905 or 800/981-0212, flies daily between St. Thomas, USVI, and Virgin Gorda; and **Speedy's**, The Valley, Virgin Gorda, tel 284/495-5240, offers scheduled ferry service between Road Town and The Valley, but also offers a $30 trip that includes ferry trip, lunch at the Bath & Turtle restaurant, and transportation to and from The Baths.

Getting to Anegada: The only way to get to Anegada if you don't come on a chartered boat is by air. **Gorda Aero Services**, Beef Island Airport, Tortola, BVI, tel 284/495-2271, offers return trips to Anegada Monday, Wednesday, Friday, and Sunday.

Getting Around

The principal mode of transportation around the islands is charter boat. Two ferry services also offer daily sailings to at least five of the islands, and a few charter airlines offer flights to Anegada and Virgin Gorda. As for getting around on a particular island, you're best off renting a small car or scooter on the larger islands and bikes on the smaller ones. Expect to pay about $60 per day plus $2 per gallon of gas. Bikes rent for about $30 a day.

ABC Car Rentals, Anegada Beach Club, BVI, tel 284/495-9466, offers pick-up and drop-off at the airport. Rents four-wheel-drive vehicles.

International Car Rentals, Road Town, Tortola, BVI, tel 284/494-2516, fax 284/494-4715, rents small passenger cars and jeeps.

Last Stop Sports Bike Rentals, Box 3208, Road Town, Tortola, BVI, tel 284/494-0564, fax 284/494-0593, rents bikes and provides guided tours.

Speedy's Car Rental, The Valley, Virgin Gorda, BVI, tel 284/495-5235, fax 284/495-5240, rents passenger cars and four-wheel-drive vehicles.

Tourist Information
The British Virgin Islands Tourist Board has several offices:

Tortola, Box 134, Road Town, Tortola, BVI, tel 284/494-3134, fax 284/494-3866

East Coast U.S.A., 370 Lexington Ave., New York, NY, 10017, tel 800/835-8530 or 212/696-0400, fax 212/949-8254

West Coast U.S.A., 1804 Union St., San Francisco, CA, 94123, tel 800/835-8530 or 415/775-0344, fax 415/775-2554

Web site: www.bviwelcome.com

Email: bvitourb@mail.caribsurf.com

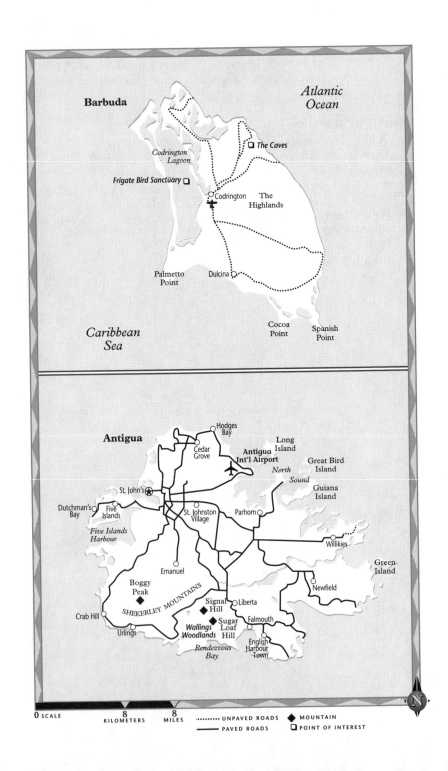

Barbuda

Atlantic Ocean

Codrington Lagoon

□ *The Caves*

Frigate Bird Sanctuary □

⊕ Codrington
✈

The Highlands

Palmetto Point

Dulcina ○

Caribbean Sea

Cocoa Point

Spanish Point

Antigua

Hodges Bay ○

Cedar Grove ○

Long Island

Antigua Int'l Airport ✈

Great Bird Island

North Sound

St. John's ✪

Dutchman's Bay ○

Five Islands ○

Five Islands Harbour

St. Johnston Village ○

Parhom ○

Guiana Island

Willikies ○

Green Island

Emanuel ○

Boggy Peak ◆

SHEKERLEY MOUNTAINS

Signal Hill ◆

Liberta ○

Newfield ○

Crab Hill ○

Sugar Loaf Hill ◆

Falmouth

Wallings Woodlands

Urlings ○

Rendezvous Bay

English Harbour Town

N

| 0 SCALE | 8 | 8 | ·········· UNPAVED ROADS | ◆ MOUNTAIN |
| | KILOMETERS | MILES | ——— PAVED ROADS | □ POINT OF INTEREST |

LEEWARD ISLANDS 11

ANTIGUA AND BARBUDA, ST. KITTS AND NEVIS

It is still a mystery to many historians and a bit of a joke to most sailors, how islands closer to the wind (the northeast trades) were dubbed Leewards, while those further to the lee were called Windwards, but stranger things have happened in the Caribbean. The six main islands that make up the Leewards are Anguilla, Antigua and Barbuda, St. Kitts and Nevis, and Montserrat. Antigua, at 280 square kilometers, is the largest in the group while Anguilla, at 90 square kilometers, is the smallest. Clustered together in the northern part of the Lesser Antilles, between Guadeloupe in the south and the BVIs in the north, the Leewards have volcanic origins, except for Anguilla and Barbuda, which are coral islands. The volcano on Montserrat has been erupting for almost two years. Most of the island's inhabitants have been evacuated and the capital city remains buried under almost two meters of ash. Montserrat and Anguilla will be mentioned only briefly in the following sections.

Columbus arrived on the Leewards in 1493, but only Antigua and St. Kitts were large enough to grow sugar cane and therefore attract European settlement. The islands changed hands a few times over the centuries, but the British have dominated the Leewards since making Antigua their naval headquarters in the Caribbean in 1750. Anguilla and Montserrat are still British colonies, but the twin island nations of St. Kitts and Nevis, and Antigua and Barbuda gained independence in the 1980s.

ANTIGUA AND BARBUDA

Located 480 kilometers southeast of Puerto Rico in the middle of the other Leewards, Antigua is not blessed with the rainfall and lush tropical beauty of some of its neighbors, but what it lacks in greenery it makes up for in white-sand beaches, 365 in all. Antiguans have a saying: "You can't get bored when you have a different beach to go to every day of the year." With a population of 78,000, volcanic Antigua is 23 kilometers long and 17 kilometers wide. The highest point is in the southwest corner, where Boggy Peak rises to a staggering 400 meters. From the air Antigua resembles a large amoeba with a bump at its southwest corner. It has a very serrated coastline with many bays and inlets. Scattered offshore along most of its east coast are dozens of small islands. The capital of Antigua is St. John's.

Barbuda is a flat 160-square-kilometer coral island lying 43 kilometers northeast of Antigua. Its highest point is only 38 meters and its 1,600 inhabitants share the island with about 5,000 frigate birds. The sparsely populated island of Barbuda is almost entirely protected and covered in dry woodlands. The island is famous as a hideaway for burnt-out jetsetters wishing to get away from it all. Princess Diana spent two weeks here after she and Charles split up. Codrington is the main town on Barbuda.

Most of the island of Antigua was clearcut for sugar cane centuries ago, and present-day Antiguans still suffer from that misdeed. With little ground cover to hold moisture, rain water (only about 110 centimeters annually) runs off quickly and the island stays brownish-green most of the year. Only the Shekerley Mountains in the southwest receive enough rainfall to sustain anything remotely resembling a tropical forest. Over the last 20 years attempts have been made to conserve water and coax the land into productivity. The construction of large water catchments, reservoirs, and irrigation systems have brought the grasslands back to the slopes of the southern highlands.

The absence of large rain forests, the presence of sunshine some 300 days a year, and 365 fantastic beaches propelled Antigua down the mass tourism path. Large coastal resorts were built and tourism soared. Everything was going great until Hurricane Luis hit the island in 1995, severely damaging most of the larger coastal resorts and throwing them into an economic tailspin. Although much of the damage has been repaired, the storm prompted the government to seriously consider diversification. Since many of the smaller inland properties, and most of the rain forests, fared better in the storm, the government decided to explore ecotourism and has taken steps to build awareness and concern for the remaining natural resources.

The Forestry Unit has constructed a network of nature trails through most of the remaining forests, and the National Parks Authority has published maps of the hiking trails. The remaining woodlands have not yet been designated national parks or forest reserves, but some areas of historical value such as Indian Town and Nelson's Dockyard are now national parks. Forest and marine ecosystems on offshore islands have been designated as wildlife sanctuaries. Barbuda's Codrington Lagoon, the largest frigate bird colony in the Caribbean, and Great Bird Island, off Antigua's east coast, with the largest red-billed tropic bird colony in the Leewards, are now both protected. The jagged coastline creates an ideal setting for mangrove forests and their backwater swamps, tidal flats, and brackish ponds.

Despite this somewhat bleak picture, the country still manages to support more than 170 species of birds and about 50 higher tree species. And what it lacks in land-based activities, it makes up for with marine activities such as fishing, snorkeling, sailing, and diving. Having said that, visitors can nevertheless enjoy good hiking, mountain biking, and horseback riding on the main islands.

Antigua History

In 1493 Columbus sighted Antigua and named it Santa Maria de la Antigua, after a statue of the Virgin Mary in Seville's Catholic Cathedral. As Antigua receives the least precipitation of any eastern Caribbean island, early settlers had to contend not only with a lack of fresh water, but with fierce Carib resistance as well. The Caribs usually attacked in dugout canoes called *periagoes*. To thwart the Caribs, the Antiguan government in 1693 enacted Law No. 88, entitled "An Act to encourage the destroying of the Indians and taking of their *periagoes*."

Needless to say, the act was very successful and by 1750 the Caribs were eliminated. From 1650 to 1834 the island thrived, with as many as 160 sugar plantations and just as many forts. It soon became Britain's naval headquarters in the Lesser Antilles and home to Britain's greatest naval hero, Admiral Horatio Nelson. In 1967 Antigua became the first eastern Caribbean country to win independent statehood from Britain; it gained full independence in 1981.

WALLINGS WOODLANDS, ANTIGUA

Wallings Woodlands, on the northern slopes of Signal Hill on the south side of Antigua, has been a protected area since 1912 when legislation made it illegal to cut the last trees on the island. The funny thing is that Antiguans have been protecting a secondary forest all these years. The original forest was cleared of trees two centuries before, when timber was in high demand for the building and repair of ships and forts. The second-growth forest includes some 30 higher tree and shrub species, some reaching 20 meters, such as the mahogany, alongside 10-meter-high organ pipe cactus.

To capitalize on the highland rainfall, paved irrigation ditches have been constructed along the slopes to catch rainwater and channel it down to the Wallings Reservoir. From here the water travels through a series of irrigation pipes to provide water for the grasslands and farms on the lower slopes.

Among the many birds found in the 240-hectare woodlands are the Antillean euphonia, thrashers, trembler, and yellow-throated vireo. In the winter months American redstart, northern thrush, and parulas are abundant. Around the reservoir, a number of pigeon and dove species, such as the white-crowned pigeon, bridled and ruddy quail-dove, and *zenaida* dove, are common.

The Forest Unit has blazed trails through the woodlands, but most are short hikes of an hour or less. The two-hour trail from Signal Hill, in the woodlands, to secluded Rendezvous Bay on the south coast is quite beautiful and not a strenuous walk. With its spectacular palm-fringed white-sand beach and beautiful coral gardens, the bay is great for beach-combing and snorkeling. You can get to the bay only by boat or on foot.

Numerous other trails are identified on the maps and in the guides published by the National Park Authority.

For more information, contact Visitor Information, Historical and Archaeological Society, Box 103, St. John's, Antigua, WI, fax 268/462-1469, email: museum@candw.ag.

OTHER THINGS TO SEE AND DO ON ANTIGUA

Tropical vegetation, similar to rain forest, can be found on the higher slopes of **Boggy Peak**, the island's highest point (400 meters), to the west of the woodlands. The peak's heavy rainfall supports huge silk-cotton and locust (called "stinking breath") as well as a variety of epiphytes, ferns, and lianas. Purple-throated Caribs and the odd scarlet tanager can be seen along the short trail, from the parking lot to the peak. The peak offers excellent island panoramas.

Great Bird Island, off the northeast coast, has large colonies of red-billed tropic birds, sooty terns, and brown noddies. This island is home to the country's only snake, actually a limbless lizard called a blindworm. Fringing the island are protected reefs great for snorkeling. To visit Great Bird Island, book a trip with a local operator (see "Outfitters and Guides," below). They will arrange comfortable transportation and overnight camping, a knowledgeable guide, food, and refreshments. You can also take a charter boat out of Crabbs Slipway & Marina in Parham Harbour (268/463-2113), but you'll pay almost the same amount just for the ride over and back (with no extra frills).

Two kilometers north of Great Bird Island is **Long Island**, home to one of the Caribbean's most exclusive private resorts, Jumby Bay. Most of the island is dry woodlands of loblolly, Norfolk pine, and lantana, but the Forest Unit has blazed nature and bike trails through the woodlands.

On the protected south coast is **Nelson's Dockyard National Park**, containing the ruins of the 200-year-old naval installation named after Horatio Nelson. A short nature trail leads up from the barracks to Shirley Heights offering great views of the southern coast.

CODRINGTON LAGOON, BARBUDA

Named after one of the first families to settle on the island, the Codrington Lagoon covers the western half of the island (approximately 4,000 hectares) with an opening to the sea along the north shore.

The Frigate Bird Sanctuary is located in the north-central section of the lagoon, accessible only by boat. Local boatmen take visitors from the jetty, in the small settlement of Codrington, out to the center of the lagoon. The birds nest in the tops of small dry shrubs and mangroves throughout the lagoon, and appear totally indifferent to humans. Visitors can get very close to these birds without startling them.

The sanctuary is home to the Caribbean's largest colony of frigate birds, *Fregata magnificens*, as well as 170 other species including brown pelican, ibis, cormorant, and kingfisher.

The best time to visit the frigate bird colony is from September to January, when more than 5,000 birds gather here to mate and rear their young. Male birds, with two-meter wingspans, glide around the colony with their crimson throat pouches inflated to the size of small beach balls. A few imported white-tailed deer and boar have been released on the island for hunting.

There is no charge for visiting the lagoon. For more information, contact the Historical and Archaeological Society, Box 103, St. John's, Antigua, WI, fax 268/462-1469, email: museum@candw.ag.

Frigate-bird colony on Barbuda

© Antigua Department of Tourism

OTHER THINGS TO SEE AND DO ON BARBUDA

Barbuda's limestone geology has produced a number of caves in the highlands region of the island, about six kilometers northeast of Codrington.
The **Darby Sink Cave** is a large sinkhole with an underground spring
that feeds a lush variety of trees, ferns, and lianas. The vegetation here is
totally incongruous with the dry shrub above. The **Dark Cave**, north of
the Darby Cave, is 90 meters long and 20 meters wide and contains a
number of freshwater pools. The pools support a rare species of blind
shrimp found nowhere else in the world. Near the entrance of the cave are
the ruins of an A.D. 800 Arawak settlement. To get to the caves from
Codrington, you can walk the dirt road, take a taxi, or drive a rental car.
The road to the caves is marked (and you can hardly get lost on an island
that's 6 miles wide and 15 miles long!). You do not need a guide, but you
may want to carry a flashlight.

The shallow waters and reefs surrounding Barbuda are the final resting
place for more than 80 charted ship wrecks. Marine reserves established in
1972 protect much of the coastal reefs and wreck sites around the island.

On the southern tip of the island between Spanish Point and Coco
Point is Gravenor Bay, an ideal snorkeling bay. The reefs that line the four-
kilometer-long bay lie close to shore and in less than seven meters of water.
The bay is sheltered from the Atlantic and the water visibility is about 30
meters. Goat and Cobb Reefs, off the northern tip of the island, are littered
with ship wrecks while the reef off the southern tip, the three-kilometer-
long and one-kilometer-wide Palaster Reef, has magnificent coral gardens
and marine life. It is one of the protected reefs along the Barbuda coast.

The shallow waters and reefs also provide ideal habitat for bonefish,
tarpon, and snapper, and the lagoon is a popular fishing spot.

To arrange diving or fishing trips, contact one of the local operators
(see "Outfitters and Guides on Antigua and Barbuda," below). They will
take care of everything for you.

OUTFITTERS AND GUIDES ON ANTIGUA AND BARBUDA

Ecotourism is not yet well developed on these islands, so your best bet is
to contact the **Environmental Awareness Group**, Box 103, St. John's,
Antigua, WI, tel 268/462-6236. It shares space with the Historical and
Archaeological Society and can provide information on all the activities
available.

Bo-Tours, Box 2323, St. John's, Antigua, WI, offers many tours
around the island and can arrange visits to offshore islands.

Historical and Archaeological Society, Box 103, St. John's,
Antigua, WI, fax 268/462-1469, email: museum@candw.ag, offers guided

hikes and trail guides and can arrange activities on offshore islands. If they don't offer it, they will direct you to those that do.

Kiskidee Travel and Tours, St. John's, Antigua, WI, tel and fax 268/462-4802, can organize combination sailing, snorkeling, and camping trips to offshore islands. Rates run around $160 per night for camping trips and include everything. At present, they are the only government-licensed operator offering camping.

Spring Hill Riding Club, Falmouth, 268/460-1333, offers half- and full-day riding trips through the rain forest.

Second only to the BVIs, Antigua and Barbuda have dozens of dive operators and fishing and sailing charters. You can rent equipment at every hotel or beach bar/dive shop along most of the beaches on Antigua. However, if you plan to day-trip to the offshore islands, your best bet is to join an organized trip with an outfitter.

Dive Runaway, Box 1603, St. John's, Antigua, WI, tel 268/462-2626, fax 268/462-3484. This is Antigua's best diving and snorkeling facility. They rent equipment and can direct you to choice sites.

Obsession, Catamaran Marina, Falmouth, Antigua, WI, tel 268/460-1036 or 1503, fax 268/460-1506, is one of the best deep-sea fishing outfits in the country.

WHERE TO STAY ON ANTIGUA AND BARBUDA

Given Antigua's trend toward mass tourism, most of the hotels on Antigua and Barbuda are large, all-inclusive, and usually pricey, but a couple of less expensive places offer good value.

Admiral's Inn, Nelson's Dockyard, English Harbour, Box 713, St. John's, Antigua, WI, tel 268/460-1027/1153, fax 268/460-1534. This inn, in a 200-year-old brick building, offers 15 comfortable rooms with air conditioning and baths. It is a bit overpriced but has great atmosphere. There is a good restaurant on the premises. Rates $94 to $124.

Catamaran Hotel, Falmouth Harbour, Box 985, Falmouth, Antigua, WI, tel 268/462-3174, fax 268/462-3496, features 16 basic rooms with air conditioning and private bath and offers diving, snorkeling, and fishing trips. Rates $65 to $80.

Lord Nelson Beach Hotel, Dutchman's Bay, Box 155, St. John's, Antigua, WI, tel 268/462-3094, fax 268/462-0751. This very basic but comfortable 16-room inn has ceiling fans and private baths. Rates $70 to $80.

CAMPING ON ANTIGUA AND BARBUDA

Camping is not permitted on any of the Leeward Islands except for short periods and with a licensed outfitter. **Kiskidee Travel and Tours** (listed above) is the only operator offering camping.

The Gibraltar of the West Indies

Perched on a hill high above the northern coast of St. Kitts is the massive 15-hectare fortress of Brimstone Hill, aptly named "the Gibraltar of the West Indies." The fortress, which played a pivotal role in the battle for control of the Leewards, has unobstructed views of Montserrat, Sint Eustatius, St. Barthélémy, Nevis, Saba, and St. Martin and gets its name from the lingering odor of sulfur constantly emanating from nearby Mount Liamuiga.

In 1689 the French forced the British from the island, but the British returned a year later and cornered the French at Fort Charles, on the coast below Brimstone Hill. Under the command of Sir Timothy Thornhill, the British hauled a few cannons up Brimstone Hill and bombarded the French until they surrendered. Realizing the strategic importance of the hill, the British decided in 1690 to construct the behemoth fort to dissuade the French from returning. For the next hundred years 2,000 slaves worked every day to construct five bastions with walls two to four meters thick, and to position 50 cannons.

Of the original five bastions, three have been fully restored, including the Prince of Wales Bastion, completed in 1973. The old barracks and officers quarters contain interesting displays of artifacts and paintings related to the fort's construction. Still visible, etched into the inside walls of the barracks, are the names and dates of those who fought and died here long ago, powerful and silent reminders of the island's violent past.

WHERE TO EAT ON ANTIGUA AND BARBUDA

Brother B's, Long Street and Soul Alley, St. John's, Antigua, WI, tel 268/462-0616, serves tasty West Indian meals and seafood six days a week. Breakfast, lunch, and dinner.

Cafe Club, Church Street and Corn Alley, St. John's, Antigua, WI, tel 268/462-4766, offers French atmosphere and cuisine in an eighteenth-century building. Jazz plays every night. Dinner only.

Calypso, Upper Radcliffe Street, St. John's, Antigua, WI, tel 268/462-1965, serves great West Indian and seafood dishes. Lunch and dinner.

ANTIGUA AND BARBUDA SPECIFICS

Getting There
Antigua is serviced daily by most North American airlines including American Airlines, Air Canada, and BWIA, with direct flights from major North American cities. It is also the hub island for Leeward Island Air Transport (LIAT). LIAT offers two daily flights from Antigua to Barbuda for about $50. With only two very expensive hotels worthy of an overnight, it is best to stay on Antigua and day-trip across to Barbuda.

Getting Around
Your best bet on Antigua is to rent a car. All the big guys are here, including **Avis, Hertz, National, Dollar**, and **Budget**. As on other islands, it is best to stick with them for reliable vehicles. **Jonas Rent-A-Car**, Box 1831, St. John's, Antigua, tel 268/462-3760, is probably the best local outfit. All of them have booths at the airport but will deliver a car to your hotel.

Because the island is small, taxis are good for certain single-destination drop-offs and pick-ups. Negotiate first and pay only half when dropped off and the other half when picked up. Minibuses link the major villages and are cheap but unpredictable.

Sun Cycles, Nelson's Drive, Hodges Bay, tel 268/461-0324, rents 18-speed mountain bikes by the day or week and will deliver and pick up.

Caribrep, North Street, Box 530, St. John's, Antigua, WI, tel 268/462-0818 or 3884, can arrange a day trip to Barbuda that includes return flight, lunch, a trip to the sanctuary and a beach for about $130.

On Barbuda your best bet is to grab one of the taxis that meet the plane. They are very enterprising and can arrange just about any trip you want. Everything is negotiable.

Tourist Information
Your first stop should be the tourism office at the airport. For more information on Antigua:

St. John's: Antigua and Barbuda Department of Tourism, Long and Thames Streets, P.O. Box 363, St. John's, Antigua, WI, tel 268/462-0480 or 0029, fax 268/462-2483

Antigua and Barbuda Department of Tourism, 610 Fifth Ave.,

Suite 311, New York, NY 10020, tel 212/541-4117 or 800/268/4227, fax 212/757-1607

Antigua and Barbuda Department of Tourism and Trade, 60 St. Claire Ave. E., Suite 304, Toronto, Ont., Canada M4T 1N5, tel 416/961-3085, fax 416/961-7218

Web site: www.interknowledge.com/antigua-barbuda
Email: info@antigua-barbuda.org

ST. KITTS AND NEVIS

Nestled in the northern Leeward Islands, between the Virgin Islands and Antigua, the twin-island nation of St. Kitts and Nevis resembles a large exclamation mark on a map of the Caribbean. St. Kitts, the stroke of the exclamation mark, is a long narrow volcanic island, about 37 kilometers long and 8 kilometers wide, occupying about 176 square kilometers. Nevis, its small circular sister, is only 11 kilometers in diameter and occupies about 93 square kilometers. In all about 45,000 people live on both islands, 36,000 of them on St. Kitts. Both have high dormant volcanoes: Mount Liamuiga (1,155 meters) on St. Kitts and Nevis Peak (985 meters) on Nevis. The capital of St. Kitts is **Basseterre**, of Nevis, **Charlestown**.

St. Kitts and Nevis are presently stuck somewhere between mass tourism and ecotourism. A few large, all-inclusive beach resorts dot the big island, but both islands have dozens of small, intimate inns tucked into the lush forested hillsides and are actively promoting them along with the rain forest. As yet, few visitors explore the virgin rain forests and extensive offshore reefs, a rewarding experience for those who do. Although the forests are protected by legislation governing the cutting of trees, and dive operators enforce strict marine etiquette, there are still no traditional national parks, forest reserves, or marine sanctuaries.

National parks, like those on Antigua, tend to be historical rather than natural. For example, Brimstone Hill Fortress National Park is the site of one of the largest forts in the Caribbean. However, environmental awareness is growing. The island recently proclaimed the second week of January "Annual Environmental Awareness Week," and it appears that ecotourism is gaining more acceptance.

The island's high elevations induce the trade winds to provide adequate moisture to sustain a number of vegetation zones including tropical rain forest, secondary forest, and elfin woodlands. Mangroves line much of the undeveloped coastline while the dryer rain shadow areas on the lee of the island provide ideal conditions for dry woodlands. Candlewood,

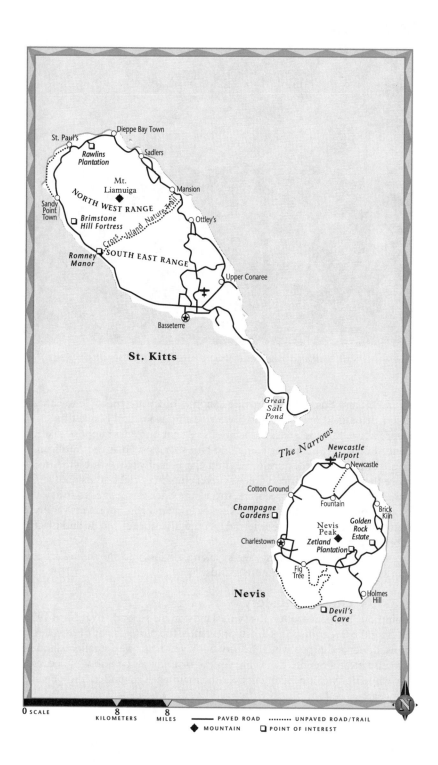

St. Kitts

Dieppe Bay Town
St. Paul's
Rawlins
Plantation
Sadlers
Mt.
Liamuiga
Mansion
NORTH WEST RANGE
Sandy
Point
Town
Brimstone
Hill Fortress
Cross Island Nature Trail
Ottley's
Romney
Manor
SOUTH EAST RANGE
Upper Conaree
Basseterre

Great
Salt
Pond

The Narrows

Newcastle
Airport
Newcastle
Cotton Ground
Fountain
Champagne
Gardens
Brick
Kiln
Nevis
Peak
Golden
Rock
Estate
Charlestown
Zetland
Plantation
Fig
Tree
Holmes
Hill
Nevis
Devil's
Cave

0 SCALE   8   8
        KILOMETERS   MILES   ——— PAVED ROAD ········ UNPAVED ROAD/TRAIL
                                        ◆ MOUNTAIN ☐ POINT OF INTEREST

N

Mt. Liamuiga overlooks the sugar cane harvest on St. Kitts.

gommier, and Spanish oak provide canopies of 25 meters while the characteristic tangled mass of cloud forests or elfin woodland blanket the slopes above 700 meters. These various vegetation zones support an abundance of wildlife, including some 120 bird species such as the Antillean crested hummingbird, purple-throated Carib, and yellow warbler. Also, more than 100,000 African green (vervet) monkeys call both islands home. With no natural predators, these cute but destructive (to fruit crops) primates have flourished. Nevis is known for its abundant variety of butterflies including the southern daggertail, flambeau, yellow and black zebra, and painted lady.

Mountain biking, hiking, sea kayaking, diving, and snorkeling are the most popular activities on these islands.

St. Kitts and Nevis History

Columbus happened upon the two islands on his second voyage in 1493, naming the larger one St. Christopher, after the patron saint of travelers or himself, depending on which history book you read. The smaller island he named Nuestra Señora de las Nieves ("Our Lady of the Snow"), because the white fluffy clouds hanging over the main peak reminded him of a snowcap.

Control of the islands passed back and forth between the French and English until the Treaty of Versailles, in 1783, when the islands were ceded to Britain. The two islands and Anguilla formed a single British federation, governed from St. Kitts, until the Anguillan rebellion in 1967 forced Britain to break up the federation. St. Kitts and Nevis opted for independent statehood while Anguilla elected to stay under British rule. On September 19, 1983, St. Kitts and Nevis became fully independent, and recent elections on Nevis hint that the two will most likely split in the near future. The name of the island was always officially St. Christopher, but was so often referred to as St. Kitts that the government changed its name to St. Kitts in 1988.

MOUNT LIAMUIGA, ST. KITTS

Until 1983 St. Kitts' highest peak was known as Mount Misery for the hardship that followed its eruptions. Its name was later changed to Liamuiga, the Carib word for "fertile isle." The peak, located in the North West Mountain Range, dominates the northern part of the island. The area surrounding the base of the peak comprises much of the island's sugar plantations, and cultivated fields stretch up to the 400-meter level before giving way to the rain forest. From here 20-meter canopies of candlewood, mahogany, and gommier dominate the forest while the space below the canopy is thickly packed with heliconias, ferns, wild orchids, and philodendrons.

Some of the damage from Hurricane Hugo's 300-kilometer-per-hour winds in 1989 is still evident, but the loss of some trees has enabled light to penetrate the canopy and fuel ground vegetation. These natural clearings also offer fantastic—and previously obscured—views out over the island. The high canopy forest gradually thins out around 800 meters elevation, where it is replaced with the shorter, more stunted cloud or elfin forest plants, which can withstand strong winds and cooler temperatures.

The three-hour hike up the peak can be strenuous in places. The trailhead starts at the end of the road through the Belmont Estate, on the northern end of the island near Dieppe Bay Town, but a more convenient approach to the trail is through Rawlings Plantation Inn, where an easy 2-kilometer trail leads to the main ascent trail. The main trail winds its way through the rain forest, where you will see purple-throated Caribs and Antillean crested hummingbirds darting back and forth across the path, all the while being serenaded by the incessant loud bleeping of the West Indian tree frog (*eleuthradactylus johnstonei*). It's a wonder how a frog less than two centimeters long can make such a loud noise. Curious African green monkeys, traveling in groups of 30 or more, are also common throughout the area. Brought to the island by French settlers as pets, the monkeys now outnumber their human neighbors two to one. The best

Brimstone Hill on St. Kitts

time to see them is early in the morning, when they leave the protection of the dense forest to feed in the wild plum trees growing along the trails.

Hugo's destruction is more evident at the north rim of the crater, about 330 meters below the highest point, and the path up to the summit has been badly damaged. Only experienced hikers should continue to the summit. The 120-meter-deep and kilometer-wide crater is covered with volcanic rocks, some vegetation, and the lingering smell of sulfur. On a clear day the panoramic views of St. Eustatius and Saba (Dutch Islands to the north) and Montserrat to the east, complete with its smoking volcano, are breathtaking.

For more information, contact Greg's Safaris, Box 65, Basseterre, St. Kitts, WI, tel 869/465-4121, fax 869/465-1057.

OTHER THINGS TO SEE AND DO IN ST. KITTS

On a spur of Mount Liamuiga, about two kilometers southwest of the summit, is the **Brimstone Hill Fortress,** by far one of the Caribbean's largest and most well-preserved forts. Spread over almost 20 hectares, it was begun by the French and completed by the British and became known as "the Gibraltar of the West Indies."

The **Cross Island Nature Trail** begins at the Wingfield estate, above the north-central leeward coast near Romney Manor, crosses the island between the North West and South East Mountains, and ends at the Molineux estate on the windward coast. The trail, also known as the "Nine Turn Gut," takes about six hours to traverse, but is only moderate in difficulty. It meanders through some private property, so it is important to hire a guide who knows the people.

The southeastern peninsula is much dryer than the rest of the island but has lots of saltwater marshland and half a dozen salt ponds. The **Great Salt Pond** is the largest and one of the best places on the island to see abundant birdlife. More than 30 species have been recorded in the area including Wilson's plover, whimbrel, black-tailed godwit, Lesser Antillean flycatcher, and black-whiskered vireo.

A new kayak route has been established along the southern coast of the island that takes in mangroves, beaches, and a couple good snorkeling locations including an eighteenth-century wreck. The four-hour trips are conducted by Turtle Tours (see "Outfitters and Guides," below).

The best snorkeling beaches lie along the southern and eastern coasts of the southern peninsula. **Banana Bay, Major's Bay Shitten Bay,** and **Frigate Bay** are all good snorkeling spots. All of the dive shops and beach resorts, including seven along Frigate Bay, rent snorkeling equipment. The best diving spots lie in 20 to 30 meters of water and require a boat to get there (see "Outfitters and Guides on St. Kitts and Nevis," below, for dive operators). **Nags Head** and **Monkey Reef**, off the southern peninsula, feature large schools of jacks and great reef formations. **Sandy Point Bay**, off the northeast coast, features giant basket sponges some three meters in diameter.

More than 200 wreck sites dot the island's coastline attracting divers from all over the world. Four larger, twentieth-century ships have been sunk to establish reefs and create intermediate dive sites. Off the central west coast are two of these ships that were sunk to provide dive sites. The 50-meter-long freighter *River Taw*, sunk in 1984, and the 30-meter-long **MV** *Talata*, sunk in 1985, both rest in about 20 meters of water. The *Taw* was rated one of the 20 best dives in the Caribbean by *Skin Diver* magazine.

NEVIS PEAK, NEVIS

Unlike its bigger sister, Nevis has taken an eco-approach to tourism. Less developed than St. Kitts, many of its hotels are small inns located on the slopes of Nevis Peak, in the center of the island, instead of large properties at water's edge. The island's only large resort, the Four Seasons Resort, has had little impact on the eco-culture of the island. The island's rugged topography and small size prevented clearcutting, and much of the interior remains dominated by primary rain forest.

An abandoned sugar mill on the Hamilton Estate in front of Nevis Peak

Nevis Peak, at 985 meters, last erupted in 1692, but rumblings have been felt as recently as 1950. Nevertheless, the mountain is considered safe despite the many *solfataras* (vents) spewing sulfurous fumes scattered throughout its slopes. The slopes are covered in lush tropical rain forests and the wildlife is even more abundant than on St. Kitts' volcano. Vervet monkeys and as many as 60 species of birds have been recorded here.

Two trails ascend the mountain: the Zetland and Hamilton Trails, named after the estates at which they begin. The six-kilometer **Hamilton Trail** takes about five hours. The more commonly used, and steeper, **Zetland Trail**, also called "The Trail," starts at the Zetland Plantation and winds its way through fields of cane and nutmeg trees before disappearing into the rain forest. It is the shorter (4.5 kilometers) and more difficult of the two trails, but gets you to the top quicker (four hours). The trail is especially difficult after a rain, and the last hundred meters or so are very steep and muddy—you literally have to grab hold of small trees and shrubs to pull yourself up. But the view from the top and the abundant flora and fauna along the way make the ordeal worthwhile. It is best to get to the summit early before the thicker clouds roll in. The climb can be done in conjunction with other trails and turned into an overnight camping trip arranged by a local guide.

Another great trail, the **Rainforest Trail** loops around the mountain at a lower elevation. It is much easier than the Zetland Trail and seldom leaves the rain forest. A must for birders and nature lovers, the six-kilometer trail starts at Stoney Hill, just above the Golden Rock estate on the southern slope of the mountain, and takes about four hours to traverse. The Golden Rock Plantation Inn on the Golden Rock Estate has maps and can arrange a guide. For more information, contact the Nevis Tourism Bureau, Charlestown, Nevis, WI, tel 869/469-1042, fax 869/469-1066.

OTHER THINGS TO SEE AND DO ON NEVIS
Charlestown, the capital, is one of the best preserved examples of the 17th and 18th century Caribbean in the Lesser Antilles. Of particular interest is the house where the great American statesman Alexander Hamilton was born in 1757. The house, located on the north end of town, dates back to the late 1600s and now houses the **Museum of Nevis History**. Inside are photographs of old Nevis and documents from Alexander Hamilton after he became the first Secretary Treasurer of the United States under George Washington.

A number of shorter trails crisscross the island and many intersect, so it's best to hire a guide for all your rain forest hikes. The Nevis Historical and Conservation Society publishes the *Hiking Guide to Nevis*, which covers six trails for independent hikers. It is available at the Museum of Nevis History in Alexander Hamilton's old house in Charleston.

The **Devil's Caves**, a group of underwater coral grottoes and old lava tubes off the southern tip of the island, and **Champagne Gardens**, named for its bubbles rising from a sulfur vent, make for interesting diving.

OUTFITTERS AND GUIDES ON ST. KITTS AND NEVIS
Most of the hotels arrange tours for any land or sea adventure.

Greg's Safaris, Box 65, Basseterre, St. Kitts, WI, tel 869/465-4121 or 5209, fax 869/465-1057, offers guided hiking and birding tours.

Kriss Tours, New Street, Basseterre, St. Kitts, WI, tel 869/465-4042, offers full- and half-day tours of major attractions.

Michael Herbert, Heb's Nature Tours, Rawlins Village, Gingerland, Nevis, WI, tel 869/469-2501, offers custom tours. You tell him what you want to do and he'll arrange it.

Pro-Divers, Box 174, Basseterre, St. Kitts, WI, tel 869/465-3223, fax 869/465-0625, provides all sorts of diving and snorkeling trips.

Scuba Safaris, Oualie Beach Club, Newcastle, Nevis, WI, tel 869/469-9518/9116, fax 869/469-9619, covers all the best diving and snorkeling spots around Nevis and can also arrange deep-sea fishing trips.

Sunrise Tours, Charlestown, Nevis, WI, tel 869/469-2758, provides a number of packaged hiking tours from two-hour walks to two-day hikes.

Sunshine Travel and Tours, Cayon Street, Basseterre, St. Kitts, WI, tel 869/465-2193, fax 869/465-7498. This operator arranges everything from hiking to horseback tours on both islands.

Turtle Tours, Basseterre, St. Kitts, WI, tel 869/465-3223, offers four-hour kayaking trips along the southern coast of St. Kitts. No previous kayaking experience needed; the guides will instruct.

Windsurfing Nevis, tel 869/469-9682 or 800/682-5431, rents mountain bikes, windsurfers, and kayaks, and organizes tours.

WHERE TO STAY ON ST. KITTS AND NEVIS

Most accommodations on the islands are not cheap, but many offer eco-adventure packages with rooms. Camping is not permitted except when overnighting on a trail with a licensed guide.

Gateway Inn, Box 1253, Frigate Bay, St. Kitts, WI, tel 869/465-7155, fax 869/465-9322, email: gateway@caribsurf.com, Web site: www.ubenetwork.com/gateway/index. This small, 10-room property just above the beach in Frigate Bay has no amenities other than fully equipped rooms. Rates $75 to $100.

Hurricane Cove Bungalows, Oualie Beach, Nevis, WI, 869/469-9462, offers 11 basic, fully equipped bungalows on the cliff above Oualie Beach. Pools are on site and snorkel gear is provided. Rates $80 to $100.

Ocean Terrace Inn (O.T.I.), Box 65, Basseterre, St. Kitts, WI, tel 869/465-2754 or 800/524-0512, fax 869/465-1057, email: tdcoti@caribsurf.com. This is the main eco-hotel on the island. It provides seven-day diving or land adventure packages including hotel, tours, beach, shuttle, and more. This is the headquarters for Greg's Safaris (see "Outfitters and Guides," above) and also has a dive shop. The inn has 60 basic air-conditioned rooms (some fully equipped), a pool, and a good restaurant and bar. Rates: $70 to $100 for rooms, week packages start at $600.

Oualie Beach Hotel, Oualie Beach, Nevis, WI, tel 869/469-9735 or 800/OUALIE 1, fax 869/469-9176, email: oualie@caribsurf.com, Web site: www.oualie.com. There are 22 comfortable rooms with air conditioning and fridge. Like O.T.I., they can arrange everything for you. There is a dive center on the property and they offer diving, kayaking, deep-sea fishing, and mountain biking. Rates $120 to $180.

WHERE TO EAT ON ST. KITTS AND NEVIS

Most of the good restaurants are located in the hotels and inns, but there are a few others with good food and service.

Ballahoo Restaurant, The Circus, Basseterre, St. Kitts, tel

869/465-4197, fax 869/465-7627, serves fine West Indian cuisine at reasonable prices. This is a popular hangout for eco-types.

Coconut Cafe, Timothy Beach, St. Kitts, tel 869/465-3020. One of the few places open for breakfast, lunch, and dinner, Coconut serves great West Indian meals and seafood.

Miss June's, Jones Bay, Nevis, tel 869/469-5330. People drive for miles to get some of Miss June's Caribbean-style home cooking. This place is small and reservations are a must.

Unella's By The Sea, Charlestown, Nevis, tel 869/469-5574. This intimate eatery serves down-home West Indian cooking.

ST. KITTS AND NEVIS SPECIFICS

Getting to St. Kitts and Nevis

St. Kitts is serviced mainly through San Juan or Antigua by American Airlines, BWIA, and Leeward Island Air Transport (LIAT). Weekly charter flights operate from Toronto, Chicago, Dallas, and Boston. Nevis is serviced from St. Kitts by LIAT and Carib Aviation. There are two daily, 45-minute ferry crossings between St. Kitts and Nevis, $8 round trip.

Getting Around St. Kitts and Nevis

Forget about the minibuses unless you are running heavily traveled routes such as those from town to beach. Taxis are dependable and reasonable, but a five-hour island tour will cost about $50 and you can't find one after 11:00 p.m. The best way to get around is by rental car, about $45 a day. **Avis** and **TDC** have booths at both airports.

Tourist Information

St. Kitts and Nevis Tourism Department, Box 132, Basseterre, St. Kitts, WI, tel 869/465-2620 or 4040, fax 869/465-8794

Nevis Bureau of Tourism, Main Street, Charlestown, Nevis, WI, tel 869/469-1041/5521, fax 869/469-1066

St. Kitts–Nevis Tourism Office, 414 E. 75th St., New York, NY, 10021, tel 212/535-1234 or 800/582-6208, fax 212/734-6511, email: info@stkitts-nevis.com

St. Kitts–Nevis Tourism Office, 365 Bay St., Suite 806, Toronto, Ont., Canada, M5H 2V1, tel 416/368-6707, fax 416/368-3934, email: skbnevcan@sympatico.ca

Web sites: www.interknowledge.com/stkitts-nevis/index.html; www.stkittsnevis.org/; and www.stkitts-nevis.com

Email: mintcande@caribsurf.com; nevtour@caribsurf.com

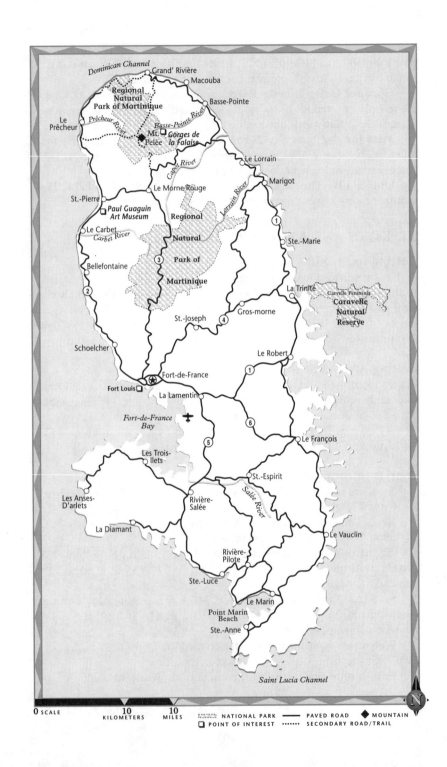

Dominican Channel

Grand' Rivière
Macouba
Basse-Pointe

Regional Natural Park of Martinique

Le Prêcheur

Prêcheur River
Basse-Pointe River

Mt. Pelée
Gorges de la Falaise

Capot River

Le Lorrain

Marigot

St.-Pierre

Le Morne-Rouge

□ *Paul Guaguin Art Museum*

Regional

Le Carbet
Carbet River

Natural

Ste.-Marie

③

Park of

Bellefontaine

②

Martinique

La Trinité

Carvelle Peninsula

Caravelle Natural Reserve

St.-Joseph

Gros-morne

④

Schoelcher

Le Robert

Fort-de-France

①

Fort Louis □

La Lamentin

Fort-de-France Bay

⑥

⑤

Le François

Les Trois-Ilets

St.-Espirit

Les Anses-D'arlets

Rivière-Salée

Salée River

La Diamant

Le Vauclin

Rivière-Pilote

Ste.-Luce

Le Marin

Point Marin Beach

Ste.-Anne

Saint Lucia Channel

N

0 SCALE   10   10
         KILOMETERS MILES

␂␂␂␂␂ NATIONAL PARK   ▬▬ PAVED ROAD   ◆ MOUNTAIN
□ POINT OF INTEREST   ••••••• SECONDARY ROAD/TRAIL

FRENCH ANTILLES

12

MARTINIQUE AND GUADELOUPE

The French Antilles constitute four main islands spread across 560 kilometers of the Caribbean Sea and occupy about 3,000 square kilometers of land mass. Martinique and Guadeloupe, the two larger islands, are sandwiched between Windward Islands while the two smaller islands of St. Martin and St. Barthélemy are tucked away in the Leewards.

This chapter will focus on Martinique and Guadeloupe, rugged volcanic islands with large expanses of tropical rain forests. St. Martin, which shares half of an island with its Dutch neighbor Sint Maarten, and St. Barts (short for St. Barthélemy) are flatter, dryer islands. About 800,000 people, mostly a mixture of African and French, live on the "French Sisters."

In 1974 the islands became two distinct regions of France and islanders were granted the same rights as those in the *métropole* (France). Martinique is one region while St. Barthélemy, St. Martin, and Guadeloupe (including its offshore islands) make up the second. Despite being surrounded by Dutch and British countries, the French Antilles have managed to maintain their French culture. French is the official language on all the islands, with some English spoken on St. Barts and St. Martin.

MARTINIQUE

Martinique is located in the Windward Island chain, 24 kilometers south of Dominica and 35 kilometers north of St. Lucia. It is the second largest

205

of the French islands, with an area of 1,100 square kilometers and a population of 380,000. It is a rugged volcanic island, like the others in this region of the Caribbean, and has two distinct mountain ranges. The northern range includes the island's highest peak, the famous Mount Pelée (1,397 meters), which erupted in 1902 killing 30,000 and almost wiping the coastal town of St. Pierre off the map. The southern range consists of low-lying rolling hills called *mornes* that average about 514 meters. Between these ranges is the plains area known as Plaine de Lamentin, where most of the island's industry and population are concentrated. French is the official language and few locals speak any English.

Martinique has few officially protected areas (after all, France has only 10 parks in their entire empire), but still ranks high in ecotourism. The northern range has always been a popular hiking spot and its rugged remoteness has precluded development. Much of the rest of the island was cleared for sugar cane and tobacco and remains under the plow. The island's remaining woodlands, about 17,000 hectares, are managed by the Office National des Forêts. No one may cut or deface the forests in any way, and the penalties for infraction are harsh by Caribbean standards. To boost awareness of the forest ecosystem and promote forest health, the Office National des Forêts constructed 31 hiking trails in the woods. It also designated the unique Caravelle Peninsula a nature reserve.

Despite losing much of its forests, Martinique still has a diverse variety of flora including such rain forest giants as large-leafed mahogany, *acomat boucau* (large-leafed chestnut), and white gommier. A few thickets of mangrove along the coast are still intact; the largest and most accessible of these are located along the Caravelle Peninsula. In all, about 2,800 species of plants have been identified in Martinique. Sadly, many of the bird species so common on neighboring islands are no longer seen on Martinique; the mongoose and deforestation have claimed many species. Two endemic species, the rufous-throated solitaire and Martinique oriole, can be seen on most rain forest trails, along with four varieties of hummingbirds and bananaquit. Shore birds and waders, such as the black-necked stilt, curlew, caiali, and woodcock, have fared much better and are common in mangrove swamps. The fer-de-lance pit viper is common in the dryer south and lowland plains. If you are bitten, you have two hours to get an antidote.

Hiking is the number one outdoor activity on the island, and diving, mountain biking, and kayaking are all growing in popularity. Most of the large resorts, along the south and southwest coasts, have dive shops renting snorkel gear and offering diving trips. Most of the best diving is along these coasts. Another great diving spot is **St. Pierre**, in the north, where

Napoleon's Joséphine

*A few miles south of Martinique's capital, Fort-de-France, lies
the peaceful little village of Trois-Ilets. The village is famous for
its Pagerie Estate, the birthplace of France's Empress Joséphine,
the wife of Napoleon Bonaparte. She was born on the small
sugar estate on June 23, 1763, and was christened Marie-Rose
Joséphine Tascher de la Pagerie.*

*Legend has it that while out for a walk, Joséphine and her
cousin, Aimée Dubuc de Rivery, met an old woman known for
her fortune-telling ability. After reading their palms, the old
women said that Joséphine would become an Empress and that
Aimée would become something more than an Empress. If the
legend is true, the old women was right on: Aimée became the
Sultana Validé, stepmother of Emperor Mahmoud II of Constan-
tinople, and Joséphine became Empress of France.*

*Joséphine wed Napoleon in 1796 after her first husband,
Alexandre Vicomte de Beauharnais, was beheaded during the
French Revolution. She reigned as Empress of France for five
short years (1804–1809) before Napoleon divorced her for not
bearing him an heir.*

*Some of the buildings of the old Pagerie Estate have been
restored and converted into La Musée de la Pagerie. The
museum contains a good selection of Joséphine's belongings,
including love letters written by Napoleon during their courtship.*

the big eruption of 1902 sent many ships to a watery grave. More than a
dozen wrecks litter the floor of the bay. Kayaking is best along the quiet
southern coastline of the **Caravelle Peninsula**.

Mountain biking is not permitted in the parks, but mountain bike
trips can be arranged (see "Outfitters and Guides," below). One of the
best of these is along the **Caravelle Peninsula**. VT Tilt rents mountain

The waterfront at Fort-de-France with Fort St. Louis in the background

bikes and offers guided bike trips through the rain forest (on roads not trails), along the southwest peninsula of Les Anses d'Arlets, and along the southern coast (see "Getting Around" for more on bike rental agencies).

Martinique History

Some historians believe that Columbus first sighted the island on November 3, 1493. He named it St. Martinino, after St. Martin. (Indians on neighboring islands called it *Madinina*, which meant "Land of Flowers.") On June 15, 1502, Columbus decided to explore the island he had seen years before (thus the confusion over the actual year he sighted it) and landed on the northwest coast near Carbet. His log entry proclaimed the island "the best, most fertile, sweetest and most charming land in the world." Two days later he ate his words and fled in a hail of Carib arrows.

The French settled the island in 1635, but the British took it away in 1762. By 1802 the French were back in control and made the island their Caribbean headquarters. St. Pierre was made the capital and remained the seat of French government in the Caribbean until its destruction in 1902 by fiery Mount Pelée. In 1974 Martinique was made a separate region of France with four seats in the French National Assembly.

FORT-DE-FRANCE

Founded in 1681, Fort-de-France did not become the capital until 1902, when Mount Pelée destroyed St. Pierre, the island's first capital. The city of 180,000 is on the north side of a large bay on the southwest coast. Guarding the bay is the impressive **Fort St. Louis**, which was built in 1639 and still functions as a French military base. Some tour groups are allowed to bring in visitors for limited tours of the fort; ask at the gates. In the center of town is the baroque structure called **Bibliothèque Schoelcher**, now the public library, which was originally built in Paris for the 1889 Paris Exposition, then dismantled and shipped here, where it was reassembled. A tour of the library is easy and interesting.

REGIONAL NATURAL PARK OF MARTINIQUE (PNRM)

The PNRM, a 17,000-hectare region in the north-central mountain range between Fort-de-France and Mount Pelée, is actually a collection of protected areas scattered all over the island. Almost 60 percent of the island's forests come under the jurisdiction of the national park system. The three main areas covered under the park are **Mount Pelée** and about 7,000 hectares of its surrounding forests; the **Pitons du Carbet** and its surrounding forests, which stretch from Balata Tourtet, just north of Fort-de-France in the south, to Le Morne Rouge in the north, about 9,000 hectares in all; and the **Réserve Naturelle de la Caravelle**, about 520 hectares. Plans are underway to officially include all the southern hill forests in the park system.

The Forest Department blazed and now maintains 31 trails of varying difficulty throughout the park system. Twenty-three of the trails crisscross the three main areas included in the park while eight trails wind through the southern hill region. These trails range from 30-minute walks to grueling nine-hour hikes. All the trails are marked—in French—so if you don't understand that language a guide is a must. The Forest Department offers guides and guided tours every day. They have also published a detailed guide of the trail system (again, in French). Most of the rain forest hikes are at elevations over 500 meters, and many trails follow the 1,100-meter ridges of the central and northern ranges.

What remains of the primary rain forests on Martinique is fantastic. Because of the diversity of flora at different elevations and the fact that most hikes cross a number of vegetation zones, there is never a dull moment. Huge hardwoods like mahogany, chestnut, trumpet, and gommier create 50-meter canopies that give way to smaller tree ferns, cedar, and pine at higher elevations. These higher elevations are a good place to see the shy rufous-throated solitaire and Lesser Antillean swift. The lucky few may catch a glimpse of a broad-winged hawk.

St. Pierre, with cloud-shrouded Mt. Pelée in the background

Two trails that offer exceptional experiences with nature are the **Mount Pelée** and the **Pitons de Carbet Trails**. The semicircular Carbet Trail runs along steep jagged ridges, some only a meter wide, between Piton Boucher and Piton Carbet in the north, Piton Lacroix in the west, and Piton de l'Alma in the east. Most of the trail is above 900 meters, but first ascent/descent passes through lush rain forest.

No trip to Martinique would be complete without climbing "The Mountain," Mount Pelée. The climb has been made easier by a new road that ascends the first 3.2 kilometers up the side of the mountain to a car park and restaurant. From here the hike takes only five hours, and the views on a clear day are absolutely fantastic. On a clear morning you can see Dominica, in the north, and St. Lucia, in the south, as well as a view of the length of the island. It is important to get to the summit early before it is overcome by mist. Also, stay on the trail at all times: Underground fumaroles with thin rock crusts and gaping cracks in the earth covered by vegetation are common. Anyone leaving the trail literally risks falling into trouble.

For more information on visiting the PNRM, contact Centre d'Information du Parc Naturel Régional de la Martinique, Maison de Tourisme vert, 9 Boulevard de Général de Gaulle, BP 437, 97205 Fort-de-France Cédex, tel 596/73-19-30.

OTHER THINGS TO SEE AND DO ON MARTINIQUE

One of the best-kept secrets on the island, probably because it is not shown on any tourist map, is **Gorges de la Falaise**. Situated on the lower slopes of Mount Pelée, on the north side of the village of Ajoupa-Bouillon, is a beat-up old sign that reads "Gorges de la Falaise-Narrow Passes." Follow the dirt road to the obvious trailhead at the edge of the cultivated field. A few local guides usually hang out there waiting for visitors to lead down to the gorge. They will point out, in French and broken English, most of the sights as you descend into the gorge. After a one-hour walk you will come to a beautiful 12-meter-high cascade that tumbles into an even more beautiful mountain pool.

Another must on your to do list is a walk along the trails of the **Caravelle Peninsula**, on the eastern side of the island. The peninsula is covered by dry evergreen forests and the coastline smothered in thick tropical mangrove and swampy backwaters. This is the spot for bird lovers to see the endemic Martinique oriole, yellow warbler, yellow-crowned night heron, ruddy turnstone, semipalmated plover, and many shore birds. Along the north shore are a number of small beach enclaves offering great swimming and snorkeling.

OUTFITTERS AND GUIDES ON MARTINIQUE

The Forest Department has done an excellent job marking and maintaining the trails, but you should still take a guide for the longer hikes. The government guides serve a five-year apprenticeship and can handle every emergency. Rates vary according to hike and number of people.

Caribtours, BP 292, 97286 Lamentin Cédex 2, Martinique, FWI, tel 596/50-93-60, fax 596/50-48-49. They claim if you give them 24 hours they can arrange any tour you want, including hiking, mountain biking, kayaking, canyoning, and snorkeling—or any combination of these.

Centre d'Information du Parc Naturel Régional de la Martinique, Maison de Tourisme vert, 9 Boulevard de Général de Gaulle, BP 437, 97205 Fort-de-France Cédex, tel 596/73-19-30, hosts guided tours to all areas of the island. Each week they post scheduled guided tours. The center also publishes a driving guide outlining a dozen self-drive tours around the island.

Les Kayaks du Roberts, in the town of Le Robert, just south of the Caravelle Peninsula, tel 596/65-33-89, fax 596/65-70-68, offers guided trips and possible kayak rentals.

Madinina, 89 rue Blénac, 97200, Fort-de-France, Martinique, FWI, tel 596/70-65-25, fax 596/73-09-53. This is another "we-arrange-anything" company. Expect to pay between $40 and $50 per tank dive and about $40 for a two-hour snorkel trip.

Planete Bleue, Marina de la Point du Bout, Trois-Ilets, Martinique, FWI, tel 596/66-08-79, fax 596/66-10-01. This operator is south of Fort-de-France on the west coast.

Tropicasub Plongee, Le Mouillage, BP 17, 97250, St. Pierre, Martinique, FWI, tel 596/78-38-03, fax 596/52-46-82. This PADI dive shop is on the northwest coast.

WHERE TO STAY ON MARTINIQUE

Martinique, like Guadeloupe, is not inexpensive. Even the most basic room costs an arm and a leg. The three hotels below, located next to each other and across from the central park (Place de la Savane), give the best value.

Impératrice, 15 Rue de la Liberté, 97200 Fort-de-France, Martinique, FWI, tel 596/63-06-82, fax 596/72-66-30. Boasts an attractive facade, 24 clean rooms with air conditioning, and a good restaurant. Rates $60 to $80.

Le Lafayette, 5 rue de la Liberté, 97200 Fort-de-France, Martinique, FWI, tel 596/73-80-50, fax 596/60-97-75. Look for the unmistakable blue-and-white awning facade. Inside you'll find 24 clean rooms with air conditioning and an on-site restaurant. Rates $60 to $70.

La Malamaison, 7 rue de la Liberté, 97200 Fort-de-France, Martinique, FWI, tel 596/63-90-85, fax 596/60-03-93. What this inn lacks in attractiveness it makes up for in friendly staff. It has 20 clean rooms with air conditioning and a restaurant. Rates $50 to $60.

CAMPING ON MARTINIQUE

Camping is permitted in all wild areas, but there are no formal sites. Fires are not permitted, and you must take plenty of water. Under no circumstance should you drink water from mountain streams: Bilharzia, a parasite that attacks the liver, is everywhere. Given that most campgrounds are always full, it's best to find a cozy hotel.

Another popular way to see the island and camp out (if you can find a spot) is to rent a camper or RV. **West-Indies Tours**, Le François, tel 596/54-50-71, is best but not cheap.

Point Marín Campground, on Point Marín Beach, Saint-Anne, tel 596/76-72-79, fax 596/76-97-82, has both tents and tent trailers to rent and 22 bare sites as well as showers and toilets. Rates $15 to $25.

Nid Tropical, Anse á l'Ane, 97229 Trois-Ilets, Martinique, FWI, tel 596/68-31-30, fax 596/68-47-43. This small, unattractive campground has bare sites and no amenities. Rates $14.

WHERE TO EAT ON MARTINIQUE

Even the smallest town or village has great restaurants, but expect to pay a bit more than you are use to for a good meal.

La Grand Voile, Pointe Simon, Fort-de-France, tel 596/70-29-29. This is one of the better eateries in town but a bit expensive. Serves delicious French seafood.

Le Planteur, across from the park, Fort-de-France, tel 596/63-17-45. The second-floor location with balcony means you get great French cuisine *and* views of the park and bay.

Marie-Sainte, 160 rue Victor-Hugo, Fort-de-France, tel 596/70-00-30. Quick, tasty local lunches. Popular with locals and visitors in the know.

MARTINIQUE SPECIFICS

Getting There
Martinique has an international airport but few direct flights from North America. Most North American visitors arrive via Puerto Rico, but BWIA does have a few weekly flights direct from New York.

Getting Around
The island has well-signed roads in good condition, and cheap rental cars ($40/day or $250/week). All the major rental car companies have booths at the airport and, most of their staff speak English.

Buses service the immediate suburbs of Fort-de-France while "collective taxis" serve the interior. A trip in one of them and you will realize why the locals call them "weed killers." They buzz up and down the mountain roads at breathtaking speeds and stop for passengers along the way.

For a real treat, try renting one of the popular scooters or automatic motorcycles from **Funny**, 80 Rue Ernest Deproge, Fort-de-France, tel 596/63-33-05, or **Discount**, Point du Bout, Trois-Ilets, tel 596/66-04-35. Expect to pay $25 to $40 depending on rental.

Many hotels rent mountain bikes. So do **Locasport**, Le Carbet, tel 596/78-01-48; **Volga Plage**, Schoelcher, tel 596/73-87-57; and **VT Tilt**, at Point du Bout in Trois-Ilets, tel 596/66-01-01.

Tourist Information
A helpful staff at the airport tourist booth should be your first stop.

Office Départemental du Tourisme de la Martinique, 2 Rue Ernest Deporge, BP 520, 97206 Fort-de-France Cédex, 596/63-79-60, fax 596/73-66-93

U.S.A., Martinique Promotion Bureau, 444 Madison Ave., 16th floor, New York, NY 10012, tel 212/838-7800, fax 212/838-7855, email: Martinique@nyo.com, Web site: www.nyo.com/Martinique

Canada, Office du Tourisme de la Martinique au Canada,

1981 Avenue McGill College, Suite 480, Montreal, Quebec, H3A 2W9, tel 514/844-8566, fax 514/844-8901
Web site: www.martinique.org

GUADELOUPE

Located at the northern end of the Windward Islands, about 100 kilometers north of Dominica, Guadeloupe is actually two islands, Basse-Terre on the west and Grande-Terre on the east. Joined by geological forces the islands resemble a giant butterfly and are divided by a narrow saltwater channel called Rivière-Salée. Guadeloupe also has three offshore islets. Covering 2,000 square kilometers, Guadeloupe is the largest of the French Antilles and has a population of 440,000. The island's highest point (and the highest point in the Lesser Antilles) is 1,467-meter La Soufrière volcano.

Although Guadeloupe developed mass tourism to handle the throngs of French visitors who vacationed here, most of it was confined to the flatter, less attractive Grande-Terre side of the island, where most of the island's white-sand beaches are found. The more rugged Basse-Terre side has black-sand beaches and dense forests with hillier coastlines. As the east side became crowded with tourists, locals escaped to the high mountains on the western side. Increased pressure on the rain forests forced the government to take protective measures; in 1989 it established the National Park of Guadeloupe. The park now protects large reserves of primary forest on Basse-Terre. The government also designated thousands of hectares of coastline and marine formations as protected areas. In all, more than 20 percent of Guadeloupe is now protected.

Besides the agouti and mongoose, Guadeloupe also has a large population of raccoons, believed to have come ashore from American ships that foundered off the coast in the late nineteenth century. Two iguana species, the green and the rare Caribbean, almost extinct on the main island, can be found on the small offshore islands. The fertile soil and high annual rainfall provide ideal conditions for hundreds of species of flora including 300 tree varieties, such as chestnut, *acomat*, mahogany, and bamboo. This abundant vegetation supports some 200 varieties of birds, including the *perdrix* (a large pigeon), the *zenaida* dove, and the rare Guadeloupe woodpecker.

Guadeloupe ranks high on the list of best hiking destinations in the Caribbean. At last count there were 40-odd trails on the Basse-Terre side of the island, 10 more on Grande-Terre, and a half dozen on the offshore islands. These trails vary in length from one hour to five days and cover

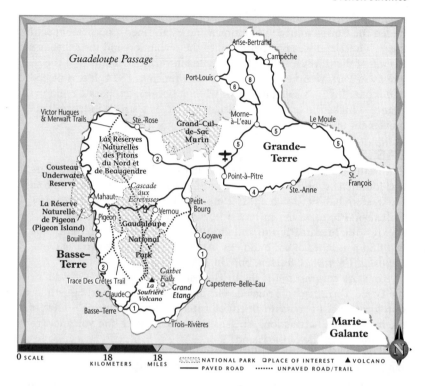

Guadeloupe Passage

Anse-Bertrand
Campêche
Port-Louis
Morne-à-L'eau
Le Moule
Victor Hugues & Merwart Trails
Ste.-Rose
Grand-Cul-de-Sac Marin
Grande-Terre
Las Réserves Naturelles des Pitons du Nord et de Beaugendre
Point-à-Pitre
St.-François
Cousteau Underwater Reserve
Cascade aux Écrevisses
Ste.-Anne
Mahaut
Petit-Bourg
La Réserve Naturelle de Pigeon (Pigeon Island)
Pigeon
Vernou
Guadeloupe
Bouillante
Goyave
National
Basse-Terre
Park
Carbet Falls
Trace Des Crêtes Trail
La Soufrière Volcano
Grand Étang
Capesterre-Belle-Eau
St.-Claude
Basse-Terre
Trois-Rivières
Marie-Galante

0 SCALE   18 KILOMETERS   18 MILES   NATIONAL PARK   PLACE OF INTEREST   ▲ VOLCANO   — PAVED ROAD   ······ UNPAVED ROAD/TRAIL

every attraction on the island, as well as all vegetation zones on the island and the diverse flora and fauna they support. Few islands in the Caribbean can boast the network of maintained trails or the ready availability of so many knowledgeable, multilingual guides as can Guadeloupe. These two factors allow visitors to safely explore almost the entire island, from coastal areas to mountainous regions above 1,200 meters. Dozens of spectacular natural sites such as dramatic waterfalls, bubbling hot springs, and an active volcano round out this hiker's mecca.

In addition to hiking, mountain biking, kayaking, snorkeling, and diving opportunities are also abundant. The island is the winter practice location for the French cycling team, so biking is also popular.

Guadeloupe History
The Carib name for the island was *Karukera*, which meant the "island of beautiful waters," but Columbus, who arrived in 1493, renamed it Santa Maria de Guadeloupe de Extremadura, which in turn was shortened by the French to Guadeloupe. First attempts at settlement were unsuccessful due mainly to the fierce Caribs, and it was not until 1635 that the French

forced the Caribs to flee to Dominica and established a permanent settlement. The island was prosperous until the revolution and the subsequent freeing of the slaves in 1794. It briefly fell into British hands, but the Treaty of Paris returned the island to the French in 1814. It was placed under Martinique's rule until 1974 when it became a separate region of France. Unlike the other French islands, there is a strong independence movement on Guadeloupe.

BASSE-TERRE

The island's capital, Basse-Terre, on the western slopes of La Soufrière, was founded around 1640 and is a good place to stay for those exploring the western half of the island. It is more laid-back than its counterpart, **Pointe-à-Pitre**, on the eastern side. Around the town's two main squares, the **Jardin Pichon** and the **Place de Champ d'Arbaud**, you will find a number of old buildings. At the south end of town lies the imposing **Fort St. Charles**, built in 1643.

In stark contrast to the flat dry limestone formations of Grande-Terre, the Basse-Terre region's rugged volcanic mountains support large tracts of rain forest and a good assortment of waterfalls and hot springs. Most of the main natural attractions, such as the national park and volcano, are located on this side of the island.

PARC NATIONAL DE LA GUADELOUPE

The national park, which covers almost 20 percent of the entire island and more than 50 percent of Basse-Terre, protects the heavily forested mountain range that traverses the full length of Basse-Terre. The range rises in the north around Piton de Ste.-Rose (at 360 meters) and gradually climbs to smoldering La Soufrière volcano in the south. Most of the western half of the island was evacuated in 1976 during the volcano's last eruption.

In 1992 the park was classified a World Biosphere Reserve by UNESCO because of the wealth of flora and fauna residing within its boundaries. These boundaries actually include three protected areas: the **Grand Cul-de-Sac**, consisting of 2,085 hectares of underwater reefs and 1,622 hectares of coastal mangrove swamp; **La Réserve Naturelle de Pigeon** (Pigeon Island), or Cousteau Underwater Reserve, as it is affectionately called; and **Les Réserves Naturelles des Pitons du Nord et de Beaugendre**, the rest of the mountain range.

The **Route de la Traversée** cuts through the heart of the park between the towns of Vernou and Mahaut. Off this highway are some of the park's main attractions as well as dozens of access points to 320 kilometers of trails. These trails, varying in length from a few minutes to a few hours, all penetrate deep into the forest that surrounds the road. Lining

A graveyard on Guadeloupe

the scenic route are rain forest giants such as gommier, white chestnut, mahogany, carapite, and sweetleaf. The trails and scenic lookouts offer great vantage points to see a number of bird species such as the stolid fly-catcher, Lesser Antillean pewee, ruddy quail-dove, and rare *le tapeur*, or Guadeloupe woodpecker.

The main road crests the main ridge near Morne Léger, where a short 90-minute hike takes you to the 615-meter peak and affords great views of the east coast. Farther west the road winds up through Les Deux Mamelles pass at 734 meters. This is the usual starting point for those hiking the **Trace des Crêtes Trail**. The 16-kilometer trail runs from Mamelles to Marigot on the southwest coast and should be attempted only by the very fit. From this trail a number of cross trails fan out into the western and eastern boundaries of the park.

The two longest and most difficult trails in the park are the **Victor Hugues** and **Merwart Trails**, both about 25 kilometers. These trails traverse the park north to south along its length and include many side trails to waterfalls and La Soufrière. There are actually four trails ascending the volcano, each varying in degree of difficulty.

The Caribbean has a number of active volcanoes, but few are as accessible and dramatic as Guadeloupe's 1,467-meter-high **La Soufrière**. Most of the trails ascending the mountain begin near Savane-à-Mulets (signs direct you to parking facilities). From the parking lot the main summit trail rises gently through an area destroyed by the last eruption, in 1976. About an hour along the main trail, hikers reach the marker for the **Circuit Trail**, which circles the volcano. Off this trail are dozens of shorter trails to specific attractions such as waterfalls, fumaroles, and bubbling mud pots. On the main trail the going gets progressively more difficult—steep and slippery—as you approach the summit, which is usually draped in a shroud of mist. Steam rises from the trail in a number of places. In fact, if you reach down and touch the ground, you will feel how warm it is. Don't be startled if you feel earth tremors while climbing; the area registers more than 200 annually. The trail continues along the crater lip, pass steaming fumaroles and small bubbling craters of mud. Just past the small concrete shelter, a short trail on the right takes hikers up the final 200 meters to the summit. The round trip from the parking lot will take about four hours, but many hikers opt to explore some of the many side trails, such as the 45-minute trail to the **Chutes du Galion**, a spectacular 40-meter waterfall.

For more information, contact Parc National de la Guadeloupe, Habitation Beausoleil, Montéran, Boite Postale 13, F 97120, St. Claude, Guadeloupe, FWI, tel 590/80-86-00, fax 590/80-05-46.

OTHER THINGS TO SEE AND DO ON GUADELOUPE

In the southeast corner of the national park, inland from St. Sauveur, is **Carbet Falls**, the tallest falls in the eastern Caribbean. The water, which originates at La Soufrière, cascades 240 meters over lava cliffs in three stages. The water at the top is 95 degrees Celsius and sulfurous but cools by the time it reaches the pool below—the only place on the water's route where it is safe to bathe. The falls rise out of the tropical forest and have no facilities. You can get to Carbet Falls by taking L'Echelle Trail off of the main Soufrière Trail. It takes two hours to get to the falls and back.

Near the falls is **Grand Etang**, a 20-hectare lake surrounded by wetlands. The thick stands of epiphytes, anthuriums, bromeliads, and ferns provide some of the best bird habitat on the island, and the trail around the lake is a very popular birding area. Because the area is very swampy, swimming is not recommended.

The best way to explore the Carbet Falls/Grand Etang area is to take the trail that circles the lake. The trail follows wet but solid ground through several vegetation zones. Along the trail are a number of small streams and a few smaller ponds where you can see turtles, frogs, and various birdlife. The best way to get to the lake trail is to take Highway D4 north from Trois-Rivières to L'Habituée. There you will find a parking lot marked "Grand Etang" and a trailhead at the far end. With moderate hiking, the trip up to the lake, around the lake trail, and back down to the parking lot will take about five hours.

A five-minute boat ride from Malendure Beach on the west coast is the **Pigeon Island Underwater Park,** more commonly referred to as "Cousteau Underwater Reserve," after the famous underwater explorer Jacques Cousteau. It was established in 1992 as part of the Parc National de la Guadeloupe to protect the area's reefs and marine life. The spectacular reefs around the island were favorite filming spots for the late Jacques Cousteau. Pigeon Island is actually two volcanic cones that joined and rose out of the Caribbean on the west coast of Guadeloupe. The tiny islands, covered in scrub and dry woodlands, are home to a variety of shore birds. There are two short trails on the island, and sturdy shoes are necessary to hike over the jagged volcanic rocks.

The waters surrounding the island are great for snorkeling and diving. The shallow reefs off the south and west coasts offer abundant marine life including great patches of tube sponges and clouds of damselfish and gray snappers. In the deeper waters off the north shore, the reef falls off to about 30 meters over a series of ledges. The area is rich in huge sea fans and two-meter-high tube sponges. Marine life in the park has exploded since all fishing was banned in 1992. Fishing boats and glass-bottomed boats make regular five-minute trips from Malendure Beach out to the island. Some supply snorkel equipment, and there is a water-sport outlet on Malendure beach that rents gear (see "Outfitters and Guides," below).

OUTFITTERS AND GUIDES ON GUADELOUPE

Although many of the trails are marked, most are in French so a French-speaking guide is a must. A guide is especially required for the longer trails where hikers can easily get lost on branch trails. A detailed trail guide outlining several itineraries is sold at the park headquarters just northeast of the capital. For more information, contact Parc National de la Guadeloupe, Habitation Beausoleil, Montéran, Boite Postale 13, F 97120, St. Claude, Guadeloupe, FWI, tel 590/80-86-00, fax 590/80-05-46.

There are many dive operators and water-sport/dive shops located along the coast and on all popular beaches, such as Malendure, and they all rent equipment. The best snorkeling, however, is to be found around Pigeon Island. You will need a boat to get there; inquire at Malendure Beach. Many of the people offering trips over to the island also rent gear.

Biking or touring on roads is popular, but mountain biking on trails is not permitted in many places. If you want to mountain bike, it is best to join an organized trip. Most hotels offer or can arrange mountain bike or bicycle rentals.

Fête des Cuisinières

*Each year in Pointe-à-Pitre, Guadaloupe, in the square
near Basilique de St Pierre et St Paul, dozens of women in
elaborate madras dresses and starched tête créole tur-
bans gather for a gigantic cookoff called the Fête des
Cuisinières, or Festival of the Female Cooks. After a short
service in the church they emerge and parade through the
crowded streets of Pointe-à-Pitre.*

*The 70-year-old celebration, which takes place each
August, is not only a grand cookoff competition but an
event honoring the culinary skills of Guadeloupe's women
chefs, who make up the majority of the island's restaura-
teurs. More than 600 guests are invited to sample the
African, French, and East Indian delicacies of dozens of
chefs. In attendance are members of the prestigious
Societé de Cuisinières (the island's chefs association), who
select the winners in a number of categories.*

*In a shimmering river of creole colors, the women
surge through the crowd to the school, where their cre-
ations will be judged. Colorful silk scarves called foulards,
draped with layers of gold chains, hang about their necks,
and around their waists hand-embroidered aprons bearing
their initials almost cover bright orange, red, and yellow
plaid madras billowing over layers of fancy lace cotton pet-
ticoats. In their arms are decorative wicker baskets containing their latest gastronomical delights.*

*At the school they mingle with the judges, who have
been waiting with eager anticipation. To a chorus of "oohs
and aahs," and amidst much hugging and kissing, the
judging begins.*

Alizés Leader Tours, Rue Thomas Edison, BP 2098, ZI de Jarry 97122, BAIE Mahault, tel 590/26-61-32, fax 590/26-62-29, offers one-day mountain bike trips as well as multi-day biking/hiking combos.

Emeraude Guadeloupe, Place de la Mairie, 97100, Basse-Terre, Guadeloupe, FWI, tel 590/81-98-28, fax 590/81-98-12, offers guided tours all over the island and can help with lodging.

Karucycle, Grande-Terre, tel 590/82-21-39, rents mountain bikes and bicycles.

Les Heures Saines, Rocher de Malendure, 97132 Pigeon, Guadeloupe, FWI, tel 590/98-86-63, fax 590/95-50-90, arranges snorkeling and diving trips to Pigeon Island Underwater Park.

Organisation des Guides de Montagne de la Caraïbe, Maison Forestière de Matouba, 97120 St. Claude, Guadeloupe, FWI, tel 590/80-05-79. This group has 12 government-trained guides who speak some English and can arrange trips of one to five days, including everything. Talk to them first.

Parfum d'Aventures, 13 Galerie dú Port Marina, 97118 Saint-Francois, Guadeloupe, FWI, tel 590/88-47-62, fax 590/88-47-91, offers kayaking, canyoning, and hiking trips.

Plaisir Plongée Caraïbe, Plage de Malendure, 97132 Pigeon, Guadeloupe, FWI, tel 590/98-82-43, fax 590/98-82-84, offers snorkeling and diving as well as bungalows.

WHERE TO STAY ON GUADELOUPE

There is no shortage of places to stay, but be prepared to pay a bit more for rooms.

Couleur Caraïbe, Bouillante, Guadeloupe, FWI, tel/fax 590/98-89-59. Located in the heart of the park just off the Route de la Traversée, this rustic inn has six clean, fully equipped bungalows tucked into the rain forest. There's a good restaurant on site. Rates $60 to $80.

Relais de la Grande Soufrière, St. Claude, Guadeloupe, FWI, tel/fax 590/80-01-27. This historic inn, dating back to 1859, is located on the lower western slopes of the volcano. The 22 rooms are elegant and the views from the pool deck great. Rates $50 to $85.

Relais du Houelmont, Basse-Terre, Guadeloupe, FWI, tel 590/81-95-72, fax 590/81-27-17. In the heart of Basse-Terre, this eight-room inn is very basic and clean, and there is a good restaurant on the property. Rates $55 to $65.

CAMPING ON GUADELOUPE

Camping is permitted in the park, but there are no equipped sites. You must use a hammock and cook on a portable campstove. No fires are allowed and you will have to pack in all your water and food. It's best to go with a tour if spending more than one day in the park; the outfitter will provide everything.

There is one fully equipped campground at **Les Sables d'Or**, Plage de Grande Anse, 97126 Deshaies, Guadeloupe, FWI, tel 590/28-44-60, which is usually very crowded with French tourists. The "camping car" or RV is another good choice (see "Getting Around Guadeloupe," below).

WHERE TO EAT ON GUADELOUPE
The French live to eat, so you won't have any difficulty finding a good meal. Most hotels and inns have good restaurants.

Chez Paul, 97190 St. Claude, Guadeloupe, FWI, tel 590/80-29-20, is probably the most popular eating spot on this side of the island. Specialties include chicken colombo (broiled chicken in curry sauce) and French cuisine.

La Touna, on the beach in Bouillante, tel 590/98-70-10. This is a good place to eat after visiting Pigeon Island. It serves mainly seafood, on a terrace overlooking the sea.

Ti-racoon, near zoo off the Route de la Traversée, tel 590/98-83-52. Stop here for excellent creole dishes in the heart of the rain forest.

GUADELOUPE SPECIFICS

Getting There
No direct flights from North America service the island except from Montreal, Canada. Most North American flights go through Puerto Rico. American Eagle has two daily flights from Puerto Rico. Another way is through Antigua, then on to Guadeloupe on Leeward Island Air Transport (LIAT).

The airport is on the east side of the island in Pointe-à-Pitre, but the drive to Basse-Terre takes about 45 minutes. Shuttle buses and taxis make frequent runs between the airport and Basse-Terre.

Getting Around
The roads in Guadeloupe are excellent, so renting a car is the best way to go. All the big rental agencies (**Avis**, **Hertz**, **Budget**, **Thrifty**) are located at the airport and the rates are competitive ($40 to $50 per day).

For those who want a different experience, campers are available for rent. These "camping cars," as the locals call them, are actually small vans with pullout beds and pop-tops. Most sleep four. **Alligator Vacances**, tel 590/26-72-71 or 23-17-52, fax 590/26-86-58, and

Antilles Locap Soleil, near airport, tel 590/90-95-72, are two companies offering campers.

For the more daring there are moped and motorcycle rentals at **Moto Guadeloupe,** tel 590/82-17-50, and **Vespa Sun,** tel 590/91-30-36. Mountain bikes can be rented at many hotels.

Tourist Information

Office du Tourisme de la Guadeloupe, 5 Square de la Banque, BP 422, 97163 Pointe-à-Pitre, Guadeloupe, FWI, tel 590/82-09-30 or 89-46-89, fax 590/83-89-22

Office du Tourisme de la Basse-Terre, Maison du Port, 97100 Basse-Terre, Guadeloupe, FWI, tel 590/81-24-83, fax 590/81-07-11

East Coast, U.S.A., Guadeloupe Tourism Office, 444 Madison Ave., New York, NY 10022, tel 212/838-7800, fax 212/838-7855

Canada, Guadeloupe Tourism Office, 1981 McGill College Ave., Montreal, Quebec H3A 2W9, tel 514/288-4264, fax 514/845-4868

Web sites: www.cieux.com/gdlp.html and www.guidecreole.com/english

Email: guidecreole@annuaire-guadeloupe.com

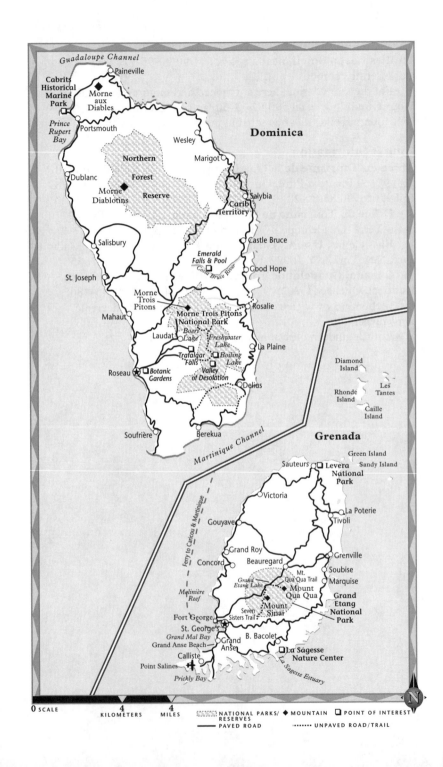

Guadaloupe Channel

Cabrits Historical Marine Park

Paineville

◆ Morne aux Diables

Prince Rupert Bay

Portsmouth

Wesley

Dominica

Dublanc

Marigot

Northern Forest Reserve

◆ Morne Diablotins

Salybia

Carib Territory

Salisbury

Castle Bruce

Emerald Falls & Pool

Good Hope

St. Joseph

Costa Bruce River

Morne Trois Pitons

Rosalie

◆ Morne Trois Pitons **National Park**

Mahaut

Boeri Lake

Freshwater Lake

Laudat

La Plaine

◆ Trafalgar Falls

◆ Boiling Lake

Roseau ◆ *Botanic Gardens*

Valley of Desolation

Delius

Soufrière

Berekua

Diamond Island

Les Tantes

Rhonde Island

Caille Island

Grenada

Martinique Channel

Green Island

Sauteurs ◆ **Levera National Park**

Sandy Island

Victoria

La Poterie

Tivoli

Ferry to Carriacou & Martinique

Gouyave

Grand Roy

Grenville

Concord

Beauregard

Soubise

Grand Etang Lake

Mt. Qua Qua Trail

Marquise

Melinière Reef

◆ Mount Qua Qua

Grand Etang National Park

◆ Mount Sinai

Fort George

Seven Sisters Trail

St. George's

B. Bacolet

Grand Mal Bay

Grand Anse Beach

Grand Anse

□ **La Sagesse Nature Center**

Calliste

Point Salines

La Sagesse Estuary

Prickly Bay

0 SCALE

4 KILOMETERS

4 MILES

▨▨▨ NATIONAL PARKS/ RESERVES

◆ MOUNTAIN

□ POINT OF INTEREST

— PAVED ROAD

•••••• UNPAVED ROAD/TRAIL

N

WINDWARD ISLANDS 13

DOMINICA, GRENADA, ST. LUCIA, AND ST. VINCENT AND THE GRENADINES

The four small Windward Island nations of Dominica, Grenada, St. Lucia, and St. Vincent and the Grenadines account for about 2,000 square kilometers. The southernmost island in the group, Grenada, is the smallest (350 square kilometers) while the northernmost island, Dominica, is the largest (751 square kilometers). St. Lucia (616 square kilometers) and St. Vincent and the Grenadines (390 square kilometers) are sandwiched in between. Although created millions of years ago, the Windwards are still very active with volcanoes, boiling lakes, and large fumaroles found on each island.

Although they are visible from each other, they were sighted by Columbus on different voyages. Dominica ("Sunday" island), in the north, was sighted in 1493; Grenada and St. Vincent, both in the south, in 1498; and for reasons still unknown, St. Lucia, in the middle of the group, not until 1502.

Spain's interest in Central American gold, the ruggedness of the islands, and fierce Caribs deterred early settlement. The islands remained virtually untouched until the late 1500s, when the French and British moved into the region to set up bases. Between 1500 and 1800 the islands changed hands frequently, until France ceded the islands to Britain in 1810.

Today all are independent nations, but the mixture of French, British, and Carib influences is quite evident in the language and culture of all Windward Islanders. Small communities of Black Caribs, people who are descendants of those who fought Columbus, the French, and the British can still be found on Dominica and St. Vincent.

DOMINICA

Located about 500 kilometers southeast of Puerto Rico between Guadeloupe and Martinique, Dominica is the most rugged island in the Lesser Antilles. The largest and least populated of the Windwards, about half of Dominica's 74,000 people lives in the capital, **Roseau**. The Caribs called Dominica *Wai'tukubuli*, meaning "tall is her body." Made up mainly of forests and mountains, the island supports five ecological zones, 365 rivers, three large freshwater lakes, and the highest mountain in the Lesser Antilles, Morne Diablotin, at 1,447 meters. Almost 30 percent of the island is now protected and the people aim to keep it that way. The island's coat of arms reads "*Après Bondi, c'est la ter*," creole for "After God, it is the land."

Dominica has some of the most interesting and best hiking in the Caribbean, but also offers other activities including kayaking, diving, snorkeling, and mountain biking. For environmental reasons, camping is not permitted on Dominica.

Dominica History

Columbus sighted the island on Sunday, November 3, 1493, and christened it Dominica, the Latin word for "the Lord's day." Spain had little interest in the island, but England and France fought over it for three centuries. The French finally ceded the island to the British in 1810. By 1967 it had gained independent statehood, and on November 3, 1978, it became an independent republic.

With no spectacular beaches, Dominicans realized years ago that their claim to fame would be the island's natural wonders. The first step to preserving these was to establish several national parks and reserves. Dominica was declared "the Nature Island" and its natural beauty promoted. The Central Forest Reserve was established in 1952, followed by the Morne Trois Pitons National Park in 1975, the Northern Forest Reserve in 1977, and the Cabrits National Marine Park in 1986. More than 50 percent of the island remains forested, providing habitat to more than 1,000 species of flowers, plants, and trees including the huge *chataignier* and gommier trees, as well as 79 varieties of orchids and 200 species of ferns. Many of the larger trees in the rain forest are between 300 and 350 years old. These forests also support 172 bird species, including two of the rarest parrots in the world: the Sisserou (Imperial Amazon) and Jacquot (red-necked Amazon), both endemic. The government and RARE, a Chicago-based tropical bird conservation group, are presently involved in a joint conservation program to save the parrots.

ROSEAU

Located on the southwest coast, the capital is ideal for forays into most of the island's interior. A few older buildings in town, such as the 1841 Romanesque **Roman Catholic Cathedral of the Assumption**, on Virgin Lane, and the 1775 **Fort Young**, now a hotel, are worth a look. The island's 16-hectare **Botanical Gardens**, established in 1890, contain more than 150 species of flora as well as a yellow school bus crushed under a giant baobab toppled by Hurricane David in 1979.

MORNE TROIS PITONS NATIONAL PARK

Named after the park's highest peak, located in its northern section, Morne Trois Pitons National Park was established in 1975 to protect a large sample of the island's flora and fauna. This 6,880-hectare park on the south-central part of the island contains five ecological zones, from dry woodland to elfin forests, and most of the flora and fauna species found on the island.

Vegetation in the park ranges from the 40-meter-high rain forest *chataignier* tree, with its immense system of buttressed roots, to the delicate .5-meter-high elfin woodland *kaklin*. Over the centuries some of the more accessible areas of the park have been logged, but most of the forest remains original old growth. In 1979 Hurricane David did extensive damage on the exposed southern slopes of the park, but much of that vegetation has made a comeback. Probably the most important tree in the forest is the 30-meter-high gommier, still used to make canoes and the principal nesting tree for the island's two endangered parrot species. Of the 79 orchid varieties found in the park, none can be considered showy except for the colorful bee and epidendrum orchids.

Like many oceanic islands, the park's habitat supports few mammals and reptiles but is packed with bird and insect species. The small rodent-like agouti (*hutia* on other islands), cave bat, and *manicou* (opossum) are common throughout the park, as is the mongoose. The giant eight-centimeter-long Hercules beetle, with a huge crab-claw-like mandible, and the extremely colorful seven-centimeter-long caterpillar of the Monarch butterfly are two of the more interesting insects common in the region.

Sightings of the two-meter-long *tête chien* (a boa) or two-meter-long green iguana are very rare, but there are still a few left in the drier woodland forests. Of particular interest are two frog species: the large,

20-centimeter-long *crapaud* and the 2-centimeter-long *gounougr*. The huge *crapaud*, called "mountain chicken" locally, is considered a local delicacy (frog legs) and as a result has been hunted nearly to extinction. However, government restrictions on hunting and captive breeding farms have contributed to the frog's comeback. The *gounouge*, a tiny tree frog, has one of the loudest calls in the forest. Its young hatch as complete frogs, the tadpole stage taking place in the egg.

The most common and vocal bird in the forest is the *siffleur montagne*, or mountain whistler. Its mournful four-note call is one of the few bird calls distinguishable in the canopy. Sightings of the island's two large Amazon parrots, the Jacquot and Sisserou, are very rare. RARE has implemented a conservation and anti-poaching program, but both species have probably reached non-sustaining levels. Best estimates put the Sisserou (*amazona imperialis)* at fewer than 100 individuals, and the Jacquot (*amazona arausiaca*) at fewer than 300. The pet and collector trade is the main contributor of the bird's demise.

Two dollars is charged for park entrance. For more information, contact the National Parks Office, Bath estate, Roseau, Commonwealth of Dominica, WI, tel 767/448-2401, or Dominican National Development Corporation, Division of Tourism, Valley Road, Box 293, Roseau, Commonwealth of Dominica, WI, tel 767/448-2045, fax 767/448-5840.

Most of the island's major natural land-based attractions are found within or near the park boundaries and can be explored from the mountain village of Laudat. Many of the trails leading to these attractions are difficult and only a few are marked, so a local guide is a must for most forays into the forest.

The most popular and difficult hike on the island is through the **Valley of Desolation** to **Boiling Lake**. This 10-hour return hike is without a doubt the most interesting in the entire Caribbean. The trail begins just south of Laudat, about six kilometers northeast of Roseau, and climbs steeply through verdant rain forest, up the slopes of Morne Nicholls and beyond, to an active volcanic valley where sulfur vents dispense their smelly and corrosive contents. Most of the valley's vegetation has been killed (hence the name "Desolation"), but the scenery is like nothing you have seen on this earth. Because underground fumaroles are common in the valley, stay on the trail or risk falling through the thin surface crust. At the north end of the valley is Boiling Lake, the second largest fumarole in the world. This bubbling mass of 100-degree Celsius mud and water was first discovered in 1875 by F. Watt and H. Nicholls (for whom the adjacent mountains are named).

Other interesting hikes include **Freshwater** and **Boeri Lakes**, and the **Middleham Rainforest Trails**. A three-kilometer dirt road heads

The Carib Territory

The Carib Indians started their northern migration up through the Windward Islands, from South America's Orinoco River Basin, around A.D. 600. Paddling 20-meter-long canoes, they reached Dominica around A.D. 1000 and numbered more than 5,000. By 1750, war and disease had reduced their numbers to fewer than 400, and they took refuge in the rugged northeastern part of the island. In 1903 the British Governor Hesketh Bell designated 1,500 hectares of the northeastern region of the island a Carib Reserve. In 1985 the word "reserve" was changed to "territory."

Today about 1,800 Carib descendants live in six villages in the territory, the largest being Salybia, where there is a church with a hollowed-out gommier canoe for an altar. Only a few of the elders are full-blooded Caribs with characteristic high cheekbones, oval eyes, copper-colored skin, and long, straight black hair. To keep the race alive, Carib men are allowed to marry outside the tribe but Carib women must marry Carib men.

Unlike their fierce forefathers, these Caribs are friendly, shy, and live uncomplicated lives. They have managed to survive against great odds and the old Carib pride still shines in their eyes. It is truly fitting that the Caribbean be named after such a proud people. A recently completed road through the territory allows visitors to see traditionally carved gommier canouas (canoes) and women delicately weaving traditional baskets, purses, and mats.

north from the mountain village of Laudat to Freshwater Lake. From here a rugged but short 2.5-kilometer trail leads northwest across steep ridges to teardrop-shaped Boeri Lake. Both lakes are situated about 850 meters above sea level, cover roughly three hectares, and are safe for swimming. The two-hour return hike to Boeri Lake can be done independently but is best explored with a guide from Laudat. Other trails out of Laudat—such as the Middleham Rainforest Trails, which lead to the spectacular 90-meter-high **Middleham Falls**, and the trail to the summit of Morne Trois Pitons—are difficult, take two to four hours, and require a guide. Spectacular **Emerald Falls and Pool**, on the northern border of the park just east of Pont Casse, and 30-meter high **Trafalgar Falls** (two kilometers south of Laudat) are located along well-marked trails of less than one hour, so a guide is not required. These trails offer good opportunities to see much of the island's flora and fauna.

The quiet waters of **Scotts Head/Soufrière Bay Marine Reserve**, located in the southwest corner of the island, is an ideal place to snorkel, dive, and kayak. Nature Island Dive (see "Outfitters and Guides in Dominica," below) offers kayak and snorkel rentals complete with itineraries for experienced independent kayakers or one-day guided kayak-snorkel trips complete with lessons. They also offer dives to fascinating spots like **Champagne Reef**, where hot gases escaping from undersea vents form walls of "champagne bubbles." Nature Island Dive has mountain bikes for rent and provides maps of local trails with each rental. They also have full-day guided bike trips through the **Layou Valley** and along the southeastern coast.

Lush Emerald Pool

NORTHERN FOREST RESERVE

Established in 1977, the Northern Forest Reserve supplements the Central Forest Reserve (the island's first) and protects the last remaining habitat of the endangered parrots. Totaling 8,900 hectares on the north-central part of the island, the park also contains the island's tallest peak, Morne Diablotin, at 1,447 meters. Managed logging still takes place in the reserve, but forestry officials select the areas and the trees to be logged. Some tree poaching still occurs. Much of the flora found here is similar to that in the national park, but the real attraction in the reserve is catching a glimpse of one of the rare parrots or the even rarer Diablotin, a black-capped petrel.

The parrot viewing areas are at the Syndicate estate, near the settlement of Dublanc, a coastal village just south of Portsmouth. From the settlement, trails lead into the foothills surrounding Morne Diablotin. The birds feed mainly at sunrise, so it's important to arrive at the viewing areas before dawn; most trips start around 4:00 a.m. The viewing area is a small clearing in the rain forest ringed by a number of gommier and silk-cotton trees. Before and after feeding, the parrots rest, groom, and socialize. Parrot viewing is usually done in combination with the four-hour hike up to Morne Diablotin peak. If you elect to climb the peak, it's best to go with an outfitter or guide, who also knows the best parrot viewing spots.

The southern boundary of the Northern Reserve forms the northern boundary of the Central Reserve and the 1,457-hectare Carib Indian Territory, where an estimated 3,000 Carib descendants still live. The northern boundary of the reserve is defined by the Indian River, which flows into Prince Rupert Bay on the northwest coast of the island. A number of fishermen offer boat rides up the mangrove- and bloodwood-lined river to the grasslands beyond. In places the mangrove and huge bloodwood form natural tunnels through which the river flows.

For more information, contact the National Parks Office, Bath estate, Roseau, Commonwealth of Dominica, WI, 767/448-2401, or the Dominican National Development Corporation, Division of Tourism, Valley Road, Box 293, Roseau, Commonwealth of Dominica, WI, tel 767/448-2045, fax 767/448-5840.

CABRITS HISTORICAL AND MARINE PARK

On the northern peninsula of Prince Rupert Bay and just outside the northwest boundary of the Northern Forest Reserve, the newly established 430-hectare Cabrits Historical and Marine Park protects Dominica's largest wetland and dry coastal forest. Most of the park, which is marine marsh, contains rare species of mangrove including the *bwa mang*, which reaches 35 meters in height. Within the park boundaries are two sections of coastal waters and reefs, and a number of seventeenth-century ship wrecks. The ruins of seventeenth-century Fort Shirley are part of the park. Kayaking along this coast is growing in popularity, as is mountain biking. Guided diving and snorkeling trips are also offered.

There are no paved trails, amenities, or visitors centers in the park. You can hike the many easy, flat, and short trails (none over an hour) along the peninsula, but you need a boat or kayak to explore the island's largest marsh. There are a couple dive operators in Portsmouth offering snorkel rentals, but for independent exploration your best bet is to rent from Nature Island Dive or sign up for one of their trips through the park (see "Outfitters and Guides in Dominica," below).

OUTFITTERS AND GUIDES IN DOMINICA

Dominica is a small island and a few operators can arrange any adventure. Any hotel can help you with arrangements and licensed guides.

Dominica Tours, Castle Comfort, Box 34, Roseau, Commonwealth of Dominica, WI, tel 767/448-2638 or 2639, fax 767/448-5680. Andrew Armour arranges island tours as well as hikes and photo safaris to all the good spots. Dominica Tours has a desk at Portsmouth Beach Hotel.

Ken's Hinterland Adventure Tours, 62 Hillsborough St., Box 1652, Roseau, Commonwealth of Dominica, WI, tel 767/448-4850, fax 767/448-8486, email: khatts@tod.dm, Web site: www.delphis.dm/khatts.htm. Ken George-Dill offers hiking, botany, and natural history tours to all the attractions and can take care of all your ground transportation needs, including airport transfers and rental cars.

Nature Island Dive, Box 2354, Roseau, Commonwealth of Dominica, WI, tel 767/449-8181, fax 767/449-8182, Web site: www.natureislanddive.dm. One-stop shopping for scuba diving, snorkeling, kayaking, whale-watching, mountain-biking, and hiking tours. They also rent mountain bikes, snorkel equipment, and kayaks by the hour or day.

Wilderness Adventure Tours, 81 Bath Rd., Roseau, Commonwealth of Dominica, WI, tel 767/448-2198, fax 767/448-3600, offers specialized hiking, photo, and naturalist tours.

WHERE TO STAY ON DOMINICA

Castaways Beach Hotel and Dive Center, Box 5, Roseau, Commonwealth of Dominica, WI, tel 767/449-6244/5, fax 767/449-6246, email: castaways@netrunner.net or castaways@mail.tod.dm, Web site: www.castaways.dm. This comfortable 26-room beachfront property specializes in water and land tours as well as whale watching. Rates $72 to $100.

Fort Young Hotel, Box 519, Roseau, Commonwealth of Dominica, WI, tel 767/448-5000, fax 767/448-5006, email: fortyoung@tod.dm. This is a more upscale, 33-room hotel built into the seventeenth-century ruins of Fort Young in the center of town. Rates $95 to $105.

Papillote Wilderness Retreat, Trafalgar, Box 2287, Roseau, Commonwealth of Dominica, WI, tel 767/448-2287, fax 767/448-2285, email: papillote@tod.dm. This basic eight-room guesthouse in the mountains above Roseau is only steps away from picturesque Trafalgar Falls. If you want a room in the rain forest, this is the place. Rates $60 to $75.

CAMPING IN DOMINICA
Camping is not permitted on the island.

WHERE TO EAT ON DOMINICA
Outside of Roseau, hotel dining is about the only option.

Callaloo, 66 King George V St., Roseau, Commonwealth of Dominica, WI, tel 767/448-3386, serves West Indian cuisine specializing in callaloo soup and mountain chicken.

Mango's Bar and Restaurant, Bay Street, Portsmouth, Commonwealth of Dominica, WI, tel 767/444-3099, offers colorful local cuisine with great Caribbean ambience.

Pearl's Cuisine, 50 King George V St., Roseau, Commonwealth of Dominica, WI, tel 767/448-8707, serves delicious local dishes.

DOMINICA SPECIFICS

Getting There
No direct international flights land in Dominica, but American Eagle, Air Guadeloupe, and LIAT have daily flights from Puerto Rico, Martinique, Barbados, and St. Lucia.

Getting Around
The best way to explore the island is to let someone else do the driving. Use one of the many tour operators and do combination tours (driving/sightseeing/hiking). Since roads are good, the next best way to see the island is by car. **Budget** and **Avis** both rent four-wheel-drive vehicles, as do a number of local agencies such as **Island Car Rental**, tel 767/448-2886, fax 767/448-0737, and **Valley Rent-a-Car**, tel 767/448-3233. Many tour operators also rent cars.

Tourist Information
Dominican National Development Corporation, Division of Tourism, Valley Road, Box 293, Roseau, Commonwealth of Dominica, WI, tel 767/448-2045, fax 767/448-5840

National Parks Office, Bath Estate, Roseau, Commonwealth of Dominica, WI, tel 767/448-2401

Forestry and Wildlife Division, Botanical Gardens, Roseau, Commonwealth of Dominica, WI, tel 767/448-2401

U.S.A., Dominica Tourist Office, 10 E. 21st St., New York, NY, 10010, tel 212/475-7542, fax 212/475-9728, email: Dominicany@msn.com

Web sites: www.delphis.dm/home.htm and www.caribbean-on-line.com/dm/dm.html

GRENADA

The smallest, second most populated, and definitely busiest of all the Windward Islands, Grenada nonetheless is a beautiful island with spectacular beaches. It is called "the spice island" because of its production of exotic spices such as nutmeg, clove, vanilla, cinnamon, and ginger.

With a population of 95,000, Grenada is about 160 kilometers west of Barbados and—together with the country's two other, smaller islands, Carriacou and Petit Martinique—occupies about 350 square kilometers.

Much of Grenada's forests have been cleared for agriculture and development, but officials took early action to protect what little was left, establishing Grand Etang Forest Reserve, the only one on the island. Legislation is being considered for the creation of other protected nature areas.

Although most of what stands today are second-growth forests of non-indigenous species, enough original forest remains on the steeper slopes to reestablish biodiversity. Among the 450 plant species found on the island, West Indian mahogany, gommier, balsa, and mountain cabbage palm are the most common. Small mona monkeys, native to West Africa and introduced by slaves as pets, now frolic throughout the island, as does the nine-banded armadillo, imported as a protein supplement for the slaves. More than 150 bird species call Grenada home, including the very rare Grenada dove, of which fewer than 100 remain.

Grenada offers interesting hiking and biking, but most of its appeal centers on the beach and sea, with diving, snorkeling, and sailing the most popular outdoor activities.

Grenada History

Columbus sighted the island in 1498, but did not land because of the fierce Caribs. The Caribs welcomed settlers and colonists with arrows until their final defeat in the late 1600s. During those two centuries, and the following 200 years, the island changed hands no fewer than six times. Finally, the 1783 Treaty of Versailles permanently ceded the island to the British, from which it gained independent statehood in 1967.

On February 7, 1974, Grenada became an independent nation and following elections in 1979, the New Jewel Movement (a left-wing party) took control of the island and declared itself the People's Revolutionary Government. After leaders started getting too friendly with Castro, the Americans decided to intervene. In 1983 the island gained international attention when a joint U.S.–Caribbean force invaded the island and restored democracy.

ST. GEORGE'S
Most excursions on Grenada can best be undertaken from the capital city, St. George's. Named after Britain's King George III, the capital is tucked away on the southwest coast in a bay many feel is the most picturesque in all the Caribbean. The bay is actually the rim of a collapsed extinct volcanic crater. Home to about 15,000 Grenadians, St. George's dates back to the late seventeenth century; many eighteenth- and nineteenth-century buildings still stand.

Guarding the entrance to the harbor is **Fort George**. Constructed in 1705, it has dozens of 300-year-old cannons, tunnels, and passageways to explore. On Tyrrel Street are **St. George's Methodist Church**, the oldest in the capital, built in 1820, and the **Roman Catholic Cathedral**, built in 1884 on the foundation of an earlier (1804) church. The church's tower (circa 1818), from the original church, commands the best views of the city. The 1.2-hectare **Botanical Gardens** displays more than 2,000 plant species from all over the Caribbean.

GRAND ETANG NATIONAL PARK
Established to protect the remaining watershed for the capital, the park occupies the southern half of the mountainous spine that dominates most of the island's interior. The highest peak on the island, Mount St. Catherine, at 840 meters, is found at the northern edge of the chain while Mount Sinai (702 meters) and Mount Qua Qua (723 meters) are in the park. The Forest Center, located on the highway from St. George's that cuts right through the park center, is a visitors center complete with maps, trail guides, and exhibits interpreting the park's flora and fauna. Park staff can help you plan your trip or find a guide. There are always teenage guides hanging around hoping someone will hire them. They are good, knowledgeable guides, and many have received training from the Forestry Department.

The park is named for Grand Etang (French for "big pond") Lake. Located at the center of the park, the lake is the flooded remains of an extinct volcanic crater. A few endemic plant species, such as the Grand Etang fern, and a number of tall canopy varieties like mahogany and gommier are found around the lake. The thick growth supports such mammals as the mona monkey, armadillo, and opossum, all still hunted for food. Birds in the park include the broad-winged hawk (*gree-gree*), bat falcon, Lesser Antillean tanager, and yellow-billed cuckoo.

A number of marked trails crisscross the park ranging from short, 30-minute jaunts like the **Lake Shoreline Trail** to the longer, more rigorous **Seven Sisters Trail**, which offers the best views of virgin forest and wildlife. This three-hour trail leads to a forest grotto of seven cascading waterfalls, each with its own bathing pool. The trailhead begins in a nutmeg plantation just south of the lake. The more difficult **Mount Qua Qua Trail**, signed with interpretive plaques, follows the ridge from the lake up to Qua Qua peak, where you'll be rewarded by fantastic views of the lake and the island's northeast coast. The popular park is crowded with visitors and locals alike on weekends.

There is no fee for visiting the park, but park map and trail guides cost two to five dollars. For more information, contact the Grand Etang Forest Center on the main highway that passes through the park.

THINGS TO SEE AND DO ON GRENADA

On the northeast peninsula is the tiny, 160-hectare **Levera National Park**, which includes two tiny offshore islands, a brackish lagoon, and two magnificent white-sand beaches—primary nesting sites for green and hawksbill turtles. Hawksbill are first on the scene, from May to September, while the greens nest from June to November. During high tide and on no-moon nights are the best times for viewing nesting and hatching. The black-necked stilt, common snipe, and Audubon's shearwater are common here, and the protected offshore reefs offer great diving and snorkeling. Due to its northeast exposure the area can get quite rough during the windy season, December to March.

Another great side trip is the tranquil **La Sagesse Estuary**, scheduled to become a national park. Located on the southeastern coast, it encompasses a great snorkeling reef, mangrove estuary, and three palm-fringed beaches surrounded by dry scrub and thorny woodlands. A small pond forms in the rainy season between the beach and woodland, providing ideal habitat for migrating as well as local shore birds. Caribbean coot, brown-crested flycatcher, and northern jacana are common in the area.

Most of the south and west coasts are fringed with great snorkeling and scuba diving reefs such as **Moliniére Reef** and **Grand Mal Bay**, both on the west coast. You'll need to rent equipment in one of the towns (see "Outfitters and Guides in Grenada," below). There are daily ferries/boats and flights to **Carriacou** and **Petit Martinique**, where the snorkeling and diving is also excellent. Boats depart from Carenage (St. George's) for the three- to four-hour trip to Hillsborough, Carriacou. Thirty-minute ferries from Hillsborough take you to Petit Martinique, or you can hire local fishermen around the docks to take you. No trip to the island is complete without spending a day on the three-kilometer-long **Grand Anse Beach**, one of the best beaches in the Caribbean; it is about two kilometers south of St. George's on the west side of the island. Also visit the **Belvidere Estate**, where you can see various spices being cultivated and processed. It is on the western side of the island about two kilometers inland from the coastal town of Gouyave, which is about 10 kilometers north of St. George's.

OUTFITTERS AND GUIDES ON GRENADA

You don't really need a guide to hike most of the trails, but to get the most out of the islands natural history, you should hire one.

Carriacou Silver Diving, Main Street, Hillsborough, Carriacou, Grenada, WI, tel and fax 473/443-7882, email: scubamax@ grenadines.net. If you plan to head over to the sister islands, this is the dive shop you want.

Henry's Safaris, tel 473/444-5313, fax 473/444-4847 or 4460. Denis Henry, an excellent guide with his own minibus, can show you everything on the island, and he can also arrange off-island and water tours.

Sanvics Scuba and Watersport Club, Renaissance Grenada Resort, Grand Anse Beach, Grenada, WI, tel 473/444-4753, fax 473/444-5227. Snorkeling, wreck diving, and trips to offshore islands are offered by this outfitter.

Sensational Tours, Box 813, St. George's, Grenada, WI, tel 473/444-1594 or 1842 or 2243, fax 473/444-1103, email: qkspice@ caribsurf.com, offers island, hiking, and bird-watching tours as well as rental vehicles.

Telford Bedeau, one kilometer south of Grenville in Soubise, tel 473/440-8163, is another great guide, but you will have to pick him up (he has no transportation).

WHERE TO STAY ON GRENADA

Blue Orchard Hotel and Restaurant, Box 857, St. George's, Grenada, WI, tel 473/444-0999, fax 473/444-1846. This small, 15-room inn opposite Grand Anse Beach has a great restaurant. Rates $50 to $90.

Cedars Inn, Box 73, True Blue, St. George's, Grenada, WI, tel 473/444-1404, fax 473/444-4652. In the hills above St. George's this quiet inn has 20 rooms with pool, air conditioning, tour desk, and good restaurant. Rates $60 to $80.

La Sagesse Nature Centre, Box 44, St. George's, Grenada, WI, tel and fax 473/444-6458. Located on the southeast coast about 30 minutes from St. George's, this is not really a nature center but a quaint eight-room inn situated on a great beach near La Sagesse Estuary. It provides information and rents snorkel equipment to guests. (If not staying at the center, it's best to bring your own equipment, but you can grab lunch and information here.) Rates $40 to $75.

CAMPING ON GRENADA
Camping is not permitted anywhere on the island except at Grand Etang National Park. For information, check at the Forest Center at the park.

WHERE TO EAT ON GRENADA
Most inns and hotels have good local cuisine, but there is little else outside St. George's.

Aquarium Beach Club and Restaurant, Point Salines near the airport, tel 473/444-1410. Located right on the beach, this eatery serves delightful local dishes.

Canboulay Restaurant, on Morne Rouge overlooking St. George's, tel 473/444-4401, offers great views and tasty local cuisine in an intimate atmosphere.

Cicely's, L'Anse aux Epines, near airport, tel 473/444-4334, serves great local dishes in picturesque Prickly Bay.

GRENADA SPECIFICS

Getting There
Many international and North American carriers have direct flights to Grenada from New York, Miami, Toronto, and Montreal. Regional carriers fly from Puerto Rico, Antigua, and Barbados.

Getting Around
The island is small and the roads are good, so the best way to get around is by rental car or tour guide. Many of the tour operators rent vehicles, but Avis and Hertz have outlets at the airport. For a good local company try **YandR Car Rentals Ltd.**, Lance aux Epines, Box 486, St. George's, Grenada, WI, tel 473/444-4448, fax 473/444-3639, email: yandr@ caribsurf.com. For bike rentals try **Ride Grenada**, tel 473/444-1157.

Taxis are expensive but plentiful, so try to negotiate fares. Minibuses run back and forth on all main roads entering and leaving St. George's, but they don't run on any schedule.

Tourist Information

Grenada Board of Tourism, Burns Point, Box 293, St. George's, Grenada, WI, tel 473/440-2279 or 2001 or 1346, fax 473/ 440-6637, email: gbt@caribsurf.com

U.S.A.: Grenada Tourism Office, 820 Second Ave., Suite 900D, New York, NY, 10017, tel 212/687-9554 or 800/927-9554, fax 212/573-9731

Canada: Grenada Consulate, 512 Duplex Ave., Toronto, Ont. M4R 2E3, tel 416/485-8724 or 800/267-7600, fax 416/485-8256

Web sites and email: Web site: www.interknowledge.com/grenada; email: grenada@panther.netmenia.co.uk

ST. LUCIA

Only 44 kilometers long and 23 kilometers wide, St. Lucia rises out of the Caribbean about 166 kilometers west of Barbados. The most populated of the Windwards, a third of its roughly 150,000 inhabitants lives in the capital, Castries. The island's rugged, lush tropical backbone (the central range tops 900 meters) gives way to wide coastal plains fringed with great white- and black-sand beaches. Probably the most distinguishable landmark in the Caribbean, Petit and Gros Pitons rise up on the southwest coast. The island's beauty and desirability earned it the nickname "Helen of the West," after Helen of Troy.

Agriculture and development during this century have taken their toll on the forests. Today only 11 percent of the remaining forests is primary, and only 13 percent of that is rain forest. Most of the remaining forests are now protected in a number of reserves; the government's recently established National Environmental Action Plan aims to designate more protected areas around the island. The government has also embarked on a joint conservation program with the U.S.-based conservation group RARE to save the endangered national bird, the St. Lucian parrot. Unlike the other Windwards, St. Lucia has established a number of marine management programs to protect the shorelines and reefs around the island.

Despite its reduced rain forest, the island boasts more than 500 species of plants and some 120 species of birds. All the big Caribbean trees, such as mahogany, blue mahoe, silk-cotton, and gommier, are

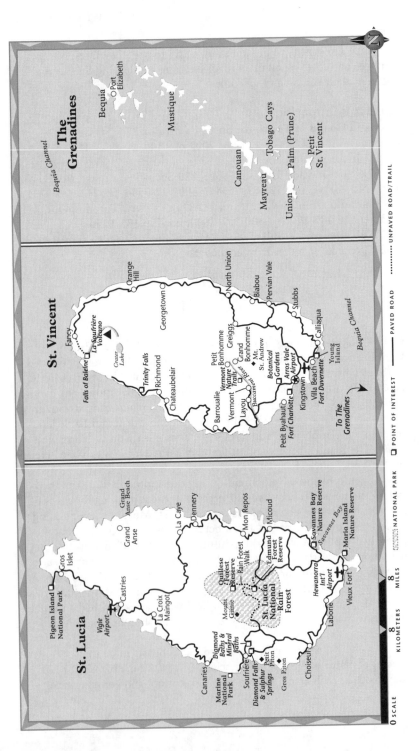

The Grenadines

Bequia Channel

Bequia
Port Elizabeth

Mustique

Canouan

Mayreau
Tobago Cays
Union
Palm (Prune)
Petit St. Vincent

St. Vincent

Fancy
La Soufrière Volcano
Falls of Baleine
Crater Lake
Trinity Falls
Richmond
Chateaubelair
Orange Hill
Georgetown
North Union
Biabou
Pervian Vale
Stubbs
Petit Bonhomme
Vermont Nature Trails
Greiggs
Grand Bonhomme
Mt. St. Andrew
Botanical Gardens
Barrouallie
Vermont
Layou
Buccament
Petit Byahaut
Fort Charlotte
Arros Vale Airport
Kingstown
Villa Beach
Fort Duvernette
Young Island
Calliaqua
Bequia Channel
To The Grenadines

St. Lucia

Pigeon Island National Park
Gros Islet
Castries
Vigie Airport
Grand Anse Beach
Grand Anse
La Caye
Dennery
La Croix Maingot
Mon Repos
Micoud
Quilesse Forest Reserve
Rain Forest Walk
Mount Gimie
Edmund Forest Reserve
St. Lucia National Rain Forest
Savannes Bay Nature Reserve
Savannes Bay
Maria Island Nature Reserve
Canaries
Marine National Park
Diamond Baths & Mineral Baths
Soufrière
Diamond Falls & Sulphur Springs
Petit Piton
Gros Piton
Choiseul
Laborie
Hewanorra Int'l Airport
Vieux Fort

SCALE

0   8
KILOMETERS   MILES

0   8
MILES

NATIONAL PARK   □ POINT OF INTEREST   —— PAVED ROAD   ·········· UNPAVED ROAD/TRAIL common, and an extensive reforestation program in some areas has led to healthy stands of Caribbean cedar and pine, used extensively in the island's furniture- and boat-building industries. Besides the endangered parrot (*amazona versicolor*), there are four other endemic birds: the rare Semper's warbler (only two sightings in 1998), St. Lucian black finch, St. Lucian peewee, and St. Lucian oriole. The island's most infamous character is the fer-de-lance, a poisonous pit viper the locals call "the serpent."

St. Lucia History

Between its discovery by Columbus in 1502 and permanent British rule in 1796, the island changed hands between the British and the French 14 times. The first settlement on the island was overseen by the French pirate Jambe de Bois, or "Wooden Leg," in 1595. The Dutch followed in 1600, the British in 1605, and the French in 1659. The British took final control in 1810, and the island remained under British rule until it was granted independent statehood in 1967 and full independence in 1979. Despite nearly 200 years of British rule, the island retains much of its French heritage; many islanders, especially in the interior, still speak a French creole.

CASTRIES

Named after France's Marquis de Castries, the capital is located on the northwest coast in another of the Caribbean's spectacular harbors. As a result of four major fires between 1796 and 1948, no historical buildings remain except the **Roman Catholic Cathedral of the Immaculate Conception**. Adjacent to **Columbus Square**, in the center of town, it was built in 1897 and managed to escape all four fires. It features a unique selection of biblical paintings in which all the characters are African. The island's desirability is also reflected in the number of forts and gun batteries surrounding Castries. Impressive **Fort Charlotte**, built in 1784 by the French, sits atop **Morne Fortune** ("Good Luck Hill") southeast of the town and has a commanding view of the harbor.

ST. LUCIA'S NATIONAL RAIN FOREST

Almost all of St. Lucia's rain forest is now protected in the National Rain Forest, a 7,700-hectare protected area in the south-central part of the island, and in the adjoining Edmund and Quilese Forest Reserves. The National Rain Forest also contains the island's highest peak, Mount Gimie (950 meters), a few great hiking trails, and habitat for the Jacquot parrot, the island's national bird.

Due to loss of habitat, many of St. Lucia's endemic birds are extremely rare. Sightings of such rarities as Semper's warbler, the St. Lucian oriole, the *fou-fou* (Antillean crested hummingbird), and the

Petit Piton in St. Lucia

white-breasted thrasher are all but impossible without the help of a local guide. The thrasher is found only in the Grand Anse region.

The biggest thrill for hikers in the rain forest is a sighting of Jacquot, the St. Lucian parrot (*amazona versicolor*). In 1979 there were fewer than 100 birds remaining in the wild, but a concerted effort by local and international conservation groups has returned the bird to a nearly sustainable population of 450. Logging of the bird's favorite nesting tree, the gommier, along with poaching for the international pet trade still pose serious threats to its full recovery. Since parrots mate for life, they are usually seen in pairs at dawn and dusk, when they come to the edge of the forest to feed on wild fruit trees. Those that miss seeing these beautiful birds in the wild can see them at the Forestry Department's parrot aviary and breeding center just north of Castries, in Union. At last count there were six parrots in the breeding program.

Among the Forestry Department's trails throughout the forest is the spectacular **Rain Forest Walk**, which winds its way across the center of the forest between the Quilesse and Edmund Forest Reserves. The trail skirts the eastern slopes of Mount Gimie, and from this elevation the pitons and the northern range are visible. East of Fond St. Jacques, the trail passes through an abandoned cocoa plantation where you can view parrots. The 11-kilometer hike takes four hours one way and is moderate to difficult in places. Because it is unmarked and joined by many branch trails, it is best done with a guide. You'll need to obtain a permit from the Forestry Department; guides and outfitters will handle this for you or you can get one in Mahaut or Fond St. Jacques. Though the hike can start or end in either Mahaut or Fond St. Jacques, many locals say it is easier to walk from Mahaut to Fond St. Jacques (east to west). For more information, contact the Forest and Lands Department, tel 758/452-3231.

OTHER THINGS TO SEE AND DO ON ST. LUCIA

In the hills east of the town of Soufrière are the **Sulfur Springs**, a series of open volcanic vents similar to those on Dominica. You can walk around them and, at times, look down into them. Just a few hundred meters away, **Diamond Falls** cascades 500 meters down the cliffs in a series of six cascades. The water from these falls passes through the hot springs before ending up below in quiet pools and the **Mineral Baths**. The baths were first developed by Louis XVI of France in 1784. You can bathe in these cooler waters. Just south of Soufrière are the twin pitons, each with trails to the top. The waters along the coast north of Soufrière are designated a marine national park.

To the southeast of the national forest are two other coastal reserves: the **Savannes Bay** and **Maria Island Nature Reserves**. The mangrove swamps and coral reefs of Savannes Bay are the best preserved of all those on the island. Just offshore, Maria Island is home to one of the rarest reptiles in the world, the nocturnal, or *couresse*, snake.

OUTFITTERS AND GUIDES ON ST. LUCIA

Permission to enter any of the protected areas must be given by the Forestry Department. Most guides will include a permit as part of their fee. The Forestry Department, tel 758/452-3231, offers guided tours in most of the reserves and parks, and also leads naturalist tours for those more interested in biology, ornithology, and entomology.

Explorer Adventures, Box 463, Castries, St. Lucia, WI, tel 758/450-8356, fax 758/450-8392, can provide transportation and guided tours to all attractions on the island.

Legacy Tours, Box 665, Castries, St. Lucia, WI, tel 758/452-0220, can arrange just about any tour you want.

Martial Simon, Bay Street, Soufrière, St. Lucia, WI, tel 758/454-7390, is the most reliable guide for trips through the rain forest.

Scuba St. Lucia, Rex St. Lucian Hotel, tel 758/459-7755 or 7000, can be contacted from any hotel and will arrange transport. They offer diving and snorkeling trips and sea excursions.

St. Lucia National Trust, Box 595, Castries, St. Lucia, WI, tel 758/453-7656, fax 758/453-2791, email: natrust@candw.lc. This is the best place to start when planning a trip to the island. If they can't help they will point you in the right direction.

Turtle Watch is a program that runs mid-March to the end of July on Grand Anse Beach. Watches are held on Saturday nights from 4:00 p.m. to 6:30 a.m. Contact Jim Sparks at 758/452-8100 or 9951 (before Friday night).

WHERE TO STAY ON ST. LUCIA

Most of the reasonable places to stay are around Castries in the north, but the town of Soufrière, in the south, is another possibility.

Glencastle Resort, Rodney Bay, Box 143, Castries, St. Lucia, WI, tel 758/450-0833, fax 758/450-0837. This 17-room inn offers all the comforts of home and a good restaurant, pool, and bar. Rates $50 to $60.

Still Plantation and Beach Resort, Box 246, Soufrière, St. Lucia, WI, tel 758/459-7224 or 7060, fax 758/459-7301. This property is located on a 166-hectare estate and has fully equipped one- and two-bedroom apartments, a pool, and a good restaurant all under the towering pitons. Rates $60 to $80.

Villa Beach Cottages, Choc Bay, Box 129, Castries, St. Lucia, WI, tel 758/452-2691, fax 758/452-5416. On the coast just north of Castries, with five fully equipped cottages with kitchenettes. Rates $55 to $75.

CAMPING ON ST. LUCIA

There are no organized or secure camping facilities on the island, but you can camp on some beaches. It is best to stay at a hotel.

WHERE TO EAT ON ST. LUCIA

Coal Pot Restaurant, Vigie Marina, Castries, tel 758/452-5566. Reservations are required to sample their New World cuisine.

Hummingbird Beach Resort, Soufrière, tel 758/459-7232 or 7492. The best place to eat in the south of the island, serving great creole and French cuisine.

Rain Restaurant and Cocktail Bar, Brazil Street, Castries, tel 758/452-1515, offers great French creole and Caribbean delicacies.

ST. LUCIA SPECIFICS

Getting There

St. Lucia has two international airports with direct flights from North American cities. Most North American flights arrive at Hewanorra

International Airport in the south, a 45-minute drive from Castries. Flights from neighboring islands land in Castries.

Getting Around

St. Lucia's roads are great and a rental car is best. **Avis, Hertz,** and **Budget** have outlets at both airports and in the capital. Most rental companies will bring the car to your hotel.

Minibuses run up and down the main roads, but on no apparent schedule. Taxis are expensive. If you do the rain forest walk independently, it is a good idea to arrange to have a taxi drop you off at one end of the trail and pick you up at the other. Expect to pay about $50.

The best bet if you plan on spending a fair bit of time in the forest is to use a tour operator who will make most of the arrangements and probably be less expensive.

Tourist Information

St. Lucia Tourist Board, Box 221, Castries, St. Lucia, WI, tel 758/452-4094 or 5968, fax 758/453-1121

St. Lucia Tourist Board, 820 Second Ave., 9th Floor, New York, NY 10017, tel 212/867-2950 or 800/456-3984, fax 212/876-2795

Web site and email: Web site: www.interknowledge.com/st-lucia/; email: slutour@candw.lc

ST. VINCENT AND THE GRENADINES

Located just 150 kilometers west of Barbados, these islands are probably the least visited and best-kept secret in the Caribbean. Stretching south from the main island of St. Vincent is a string of 35 small islands and cays called the Grenadines; only seven are inhabited. On 390-square-kilometer St. Vincent, narrow coastal plains rise steeply to lush tropical ridges that divide the island east and west. The island's rugged landscape is dominated by 1,234-meter La Soufrière, which last erupted in 1979. The majority of the 107,000 inhabitants live along the coastal plains and in the capital, Kingstown. On the main island, biking and hiking are popular activities.

All of the island's beaches are black sand except for two, and the mountainous topography precludes construction of a large international airport. These two factors have given rise to a tourism industry fueled by visitors attracted to the island's natural rugged beauty and off-the-beaten-path appeal. It is ideal for those wanting to truly get away from it all and who don't mind changing planes a few times to get here.

More than 25 percent of St. Vincent is still heavily forested with much of the interior covered in primary rain forest. There are no national parks or official forest reserves; however, 5,000 hectares in the central Morne Garu range are considered a parrot reserve. The government has passed strict logging, hunting, and fishing legislation to preserve the island's flora and fauna. In many places, the terrain is so rugged a single human footstep has yet to disturb them. Like the other Windwards, St. Vincent is signatory to CITIES. The endangered St. Vincent parrot (*amazona guildingii*) has been brought back from the brink of extinction thanks to a concerted effort by local government and the conservation group RARE. Once numbering fewer than 250, the island's national bird now numbers more than 600 and sightings are common.

The less populated and more rugged northern region of St. Vincent features many of the island's major natural attractions, including the most impressive volcanic crater in the Caribbean, La Soufrière. Regular deposits of ash over the last 500 years have provided the nutrients necessary to support an enormously lush forested area covering almost the entire northern third of the island. The steep terrain and 200 centimeters of annual rainfall combine to create spectacular waterfalls.

Primary rain forests cover much of the central and southern ranges while large tracts of northern forests are newer growth, due largely to the two major eruptions of La Soufrière this century. More than 400 species of higher plants and trees, including the endemic 30-meter-high gommier, mahogany, teak, and blue mahoe, as well as introduced varieties like galba, Caribbean pine, and eucalyptus, blanket the island. These great forests teem with more than 200 species of birds, including the rare endemic whistling warbler and St. Vincent parrot, the common cocoa thrush, scaly-breasted thrasher, and purple-throated Carib Hummingbird. A few agouti and large green iguanas can be seen along less-trafficked forest trails.

The Grenadines, a group of 35 islands and islets, stretch south from St. Vincent to Grenada, about 100 kilometers. Surrounded by great reefs and crystal clear waters, these "jewels of the Caribbean" offer some of the best diving and snorkeling in the Caribbean. They can be reached by boat or charter plane and make ideal one- or two-day excursions.

St. Vincent and the Grenadines History

Although Columbus sighted St. Vincent in 1498, the fierce Carib Indians and the rugged topography kept most settlers at bay. No foreigner would set foot on the island until 1675, when a Dutch slave ship floundered off the east coast and the survivors, mostly slaves, were taken in by the Caribs. Over time, slaves and indigenous people (Yellow Caribs) blended into a race known as the Black Caribs.

The Grenadines:
Jewels of the Caribbean

Stretching 120 kilometers south, from St. Vincent to Grenada, are 30-plus islets and islands called the Grenadines. Collectively they offer more than 30 kilometers of spectacular white-sand beaches and more than 100 square kilometers of some of the best coral reefs in the Caribbean. Most divers rate it as the third best diving in the Caribbean. Only seven of the islands are populated.

The largest and most northern of the group, Bequia gets its name from the Carib word becouya ("island in the clouds"). Southeast of Bequia is the jet-set island of Mustique, an exclusive hideaway for the rich and famous such as Princess Margaret, Raquel Welch, and Mick Jagger. Three kilometers southwest of Mustique, hook-shaped Canouan, from the Carib cannoun ("turtle island"), has 900 inhabitants and a spectacular barrier reef along its eastern shore that protects a fabulous two-kilometer-long white-sand beach.

Two kilometers south of Canouan is Mayreau (population 100), which was settled in 1770 by the French St. Heliers family. A kilometer or so off Mayreau's eastern coast are four deserted islets called the Tobago Cays. Surrounding these cays is the magnificent Horseshoe Reef, one of the most popular diving spots in the Caribbean.

Union, the second largest Grenadine, is known locally as the "Gateway to the Grenadines." Most of the charter boats that work the Grenadine waters are based here. A 20-minute ferry ride from Union are tiny Palm Island and Petit St. Vincent, or P.S.V., two exclusive hideaway resort islands.

In 1680 the British claimed St. Vincent. But it was the French that established the first sustained European settlement there, at Barrouallie, in 1719. The island changed hands a dozen times until 1784, when it was officially ceded it to the British. In 1979 St. Vincent won its independence.

KINGSTOWN, ST. VINCENT

Often confused with Kingston, Jamaica, this busy classic Caribbean town of 30,000 lies along the northern rim of a large submerged volcanic crater. Kingstown has many well-preserved historical sites within its 18 square blocks that are worth a quick tour.

The stately Georgian-styled **St. George's Anglican Church**, completed in 1820, is graced by a tall stained-glass window called "the Red Angel." It was originally commissioned by Queen Victoria for St. Paul's Cathedral in London, but when she objected to the angel wearing red instead of white the window was shipped off to the colonies. Adjacent to the Anglican Church is **St. Mary's Catholic Cathedral**, built in 1823. With Gothic spires and Romanesque arches, the church was designed and richly furnished by a famous Belgium Benedictine priest, Dom Charles Verbeke.

Located 200 meters above the town on the western tip of the Kingstown Harbor promontory, stands the impressive **Fort Charlotte** completed in 1806 to defend the capital from the marauding Napoleon. Named after the Inner Consort of George III, today it houses a museum of the Carib Wars and a number of cannons. Just north of town lies the oldest **Botanical Gardens** in the Western Hemisphere (see page 41) containing a small **National Museum**, featuring 3200 B.C. artifacts, the **Calvin Nichols Wildlife Complex** (parrot aviaries), and the last two *spachea Perforata*, "Soufrière trees," in the world.

BUCCAMENT VALLEY AND VERMONT NATURE TRAILS

Situated on the leeward, or west, side of the island about eight kilometers from Kingstown is the fertile Buccament Valley. Nestled in the southern range between Grand Bonhomme and Petit Bonhomme peaks, both about 900 meters, the valley and trails make up most of an estate owned by Sir William Young in 1763. From the coastal town of Layou up into the forested slopes of Grand Bonhomme, the Peace Corps and the Forestry Department have blazed and marked two beautiful trails.

At the lower trailhead just east of the golf course are a number of huge rocks with ancient petroglyphs and a short trail leading to "Table Rock," an enormous slab of flat volcanic rock protruding into the Buccament River. Below the rock is a swimming hole enjoyed by both visitors and locals. The ruins of an old viaduct (circa 1750), which brought water from the river to the old sugar mill, are still visible along the trail and at the golf course.

Carib petroglyphs in the Buccament Valley

The trails get steeper and the canopy gets higher as you progress east up the valley. Tall gommier and mahogany are flanked by 30-meter-high stands of bamboo while the forest floor is carpeted in bromeliads and colorful heliconia. The birdlife along these trails is spectacular. Ruddy quail-doves, black hawks, pearly-eyed thrashers, short-tailed swifts, and tremblers abound. Halfway up the trail is a marked parrot viewing area, where late-afternoon stakeouts will often be rewarded with a sighting of one of the Caribbean's largest and rarest parrots. It is also a good place to catch a glimpse of the even rarer whistling warbler.

For more formation, contact the Department of Tourism, Bay Street, Box, 834, St. Vincent and the Grenadines, WI, tel 784/457-1502, fax 784/456-2610.

LA SOUFRIÈRE VOLCANO

Definitely the most breathtaking view in the Caribbean, St. Vincent's 1,234-meter-high volcano is in a class of its own. Although signs of lava and ash flows are still visible along some of the less-watered slopes, most of the mountain is again wrapped in a cloak of lush rain forest. Most eruptions destroy plants and shrubs covering the forest floor yet leave many of the larger trees denuded but intact. A 200-year-old fig tree near the Bamboo Range, at the start of the trail up the mountain, has survived three eruptions.

There are two trails to the top, one from the east and one from the west. The five-kilometer east trail is shorter but much steeper than the six-kilometer west trail. Most hikers take the east trail for convenience and because it winds up through denser rain forest. The west trail is in a partial rain shadow with less spectacular greenery. The east trail starts about five kilometers north of the small community of **Georgetown** on the northeast coast. The first three kilometers of the trail wind up through verdant rain forest amid bamboo and gommier to 900 meters in elevation. Hummingbird species are readily seen, along with the parrot and solitaire, or Soufrière bird.

Above 900 meters the trail gets much steeper and the vegetation turns to cloud forest. The last two kilometers of the trail are referred to as "three-steps-up-two-back" because the volcanic rock and lack of ground vegetation impairs traction. But the four-hour hike is quickly forgotten at the first glimpse of the smoldering two-kilometer-wide crater with a large lava plug growing in its center some 340 meters below. In the rainy season, runoff forms a ring of water around the plug creating an island-like appearance. This is one of the most beautiful and serene vistas in the Caribbean, but don't get too comfortable. The distinctive, pungent odor of sulfur is an ever-present reminder that, beneath this beautiful and tranquil panorama, the volcano is still active.

For more formation, contact the Department of Tourism, Bay Street, Box 834, St. Vincent and the Grenadines, WI, tel 784/457-1502, fax 784/456-2610.

OTHER THINGS TO SEE AND DO ON ST. VINCENT AND THE GRENADINES

Some of La Soufrière's runoff courses down a series of ancient lava beds to the northern side of the island, where it cascades 25 meters over a great lava ledge to a quiet pool below. The **Falls of Baleine**, the most remote of the island's waterfalls, can be reached only by

The Falls of Baleine

boat on a calm day. On a windy day, large Atlantic swells make going ashore dangerous.

Some of the runoff also finds it way into the Waliiaboo River, which flows west off the volcano. About three kilometers from the coast it splits into three channels and drops 15 meters over a series of rocks to form **Trinity Falls**, another of the island's great waterfalls.

North of Kingstown in the foothills of Mount St. Andrew is the **King's Hill Forest Reserve**, one of the oldest reserves in the Caribbean. It was established in 1991 to protect a unique 25-hectare forest containing white wood, penny piece, and birch gum.

About a kilometer offshore of the island's southernmost point stands a 70-meter-high volcanic plug on top of which are the ruins of **Fort Duvernette**. "Rock Fort," as it is called locally, was built around 1763 to guard the entrance to **Calliaqua Bay**, St. Vincent's first capital. You get to the fort via boat and a steep 219-step climb to the top.

OUTFITTERS AND GUIDES IN ST. VINCENT AND THE GRENADINES

Any of the hotels or the Tourism Board can help you with tours and guides. The Vermont Nature Trails can be hiked independently, but you will need a map from the Tourism Board.

Dive St. Vincent, Box 864, Kingstown, St. Vincent and the Grenadines, WI, tel 784/457-4714 or 4928, fax 784/457-4948, offers diving, snorkeling, and trips to the Grenadines.

Fantasea Tours, Box 639, Kingstown, St. Vincent and the Grenadines, WI, tel 784/457-4714 or 457-4928, fax 784/457-5577, email: fantasea@caribsurf.com, offers diving, snorkeling, and tours to the falls and Grenadines.

HazECO Tours, Box 325, Kingstown, St. Vincent and the Grenadines, WI, tel 784/457-8634, fax 784/457-8105, email: hazeco@caribsurf.com, provides guided tours to all the major attractions.

Sailor's Wilderness Tours, Box 684, Kingstown, St. Vincent and the Grenadines, WI, tel 784/457-1712 or 1274, fax 784/456-2821, email: sailor's@bsi-svg.com or modernp@caribsurf.com, Web site: http://vincy.com/sailor's.htm. Hiking and biking tours to all the major attractions.

SVG Tours, Box 560, Kingstown, St. Vincent and the Grenadines, WI, tel 784/457-4322, fax 784/457-2432, offers nature and water tours.

WHERE TO STAY ON ST. VINCENT AND THE GRENADINES

Beachcombers Hotel, Box 126, Villa Beach, St. Vincent and the Grenadines, WI, tel 784/458-4283, fax 784/458-4385. On one of the only white-sand beaches, five kilometers from town, this 14-room hotel has air conditioning and kitchenettes, a bar, restaurant, and small spa. Rates run from $60 to $80.

Haddon Hotel and Towers, Box 144, Kingstown, St. Vincent and the Grenadines, WI, tel 784/456-1897, fax 784/456-2726, email: dovetail@caribsurf.com, Web site: http://vincy.com/svg. This 15-room hotel is just a few blocks from town and includes air conditioning, shuttle to and from the airport, and a bar and restaurant. Rates $45 to $65.

Umbrella Beach Hotel, Villa Beach, St. Vincent and the Grenadines, WI, tel 784/458-4651, fax 784/457-4930. This is a good place to stay for exploring the Grenadines and leeward coasts. It has nine rooms each with a private entrance, kitchenette, bath, phone, and balcony. Rates $50 to $65.

CAMPING ON ST. VINCENT AND THE GRENADINES

Camping is not permitted on any of the country's islands, but there is one facility offering permanent tented sites.

Petit Byahaut, St. Vincent and the Grenadines, WI, tel and fax 784/457-7008, email: petitbyahaut@caribsurf.com, web site: www .outahere.com/petitbyahaut. Located in a secluded 20-hectare valley just west of Kingstown, this retreat has six self-contained permanent tents with showers and electricity. They offer all sorts of guided tours including kayaking, hiking, snorkeling, and diving. Rates $160 to $190 (includes all meals and transfers to and from airport).

WHERE TO EAT ON ST. VINCENT
AND THE GRENADINES

Most of the good eating spots are found in the more populated southern part of the island. The best places to eat tend to be at the hotels or inns.

Aggie's, Granville Street, Kingstown, tel 784/456-2110, serves great West Indian seafood at reasonable prices.

The Coalpot, near Botanical Gardens, tel 784/457-0197, serves local spicy creole food for lunch.

Lexas Restaurant, Kingstown, tel 784/456-2648. This is a small but convenient place for meals served all day.

ST. VINCENT AND THE GRENADINES SPECIFICS

Getting There

No direct flights land in the islands, but LIAT and American Eagle service the islands through Barbados, Grenada, St. Lucia, and Puerto Rico. Mustique Airways and LIAT provide daily service to the Grenadines.

Getting Around

Minibuses ply the leeward coast between Kingstown and Richmond, as well as the windward coast between Kingstown and Georgetown. They can get you to the beginning points for most of your hiking adventures, but you should use one of the local tour companies that provide transportation. The island is tiny and the two major coastal roads are okay for driving, so a more convenient alternative for independent travels is the rental car. Be warned that the roads are very narrow and extreme care should be used when driving on the island.

Daily ferry service to the Grenadines departs Kingstown's Grenadines Wharf. The schedule is available from the tourist office or the ticket counter at the wharf.

Sam Taxi Tours, Box 92, Kingstown, St. Vincent and the Grenadines, WI, tel 784/456-4338, fax 784/456-4233, has been in the business a long time and can arrange just about any transportation you need, including travel on the Grenadines. They can also arrange drop-offs, pick-ups, and guides for independent explorers.

Kims Rentals, Box 600, Kingstown, St. Vincent and the Grenadines, WI, tel 784/456-1884, fax 784/456-1681, rents dependable vehicles including four-wheel-drives.

Tourist Information

St. Vincent and the Grenadines Department of Tourism, Bay Street, Box 834, St. Vincent and the Grenadines, WI, tel 784/457-1502, fax 784/456-2610

St. Vincent and the Grenadines Department of Tourism, 801 Second Ave., 21st Floor, New York, NY 10017, tel 212/687-4981 or 800/729-1726, fax 212/949-5946, email: svgtony@aol.com

St. Vincent and the Grenadines Department of Tourism, 32 Park Rd., Toronto, Ont. N4W 2N4, tel 416/924-5796, fax 416/924-5844

Web site and email: Web site: http://vincy.com/svg/; email: tourism@caribsurf.com.

Bonaire

6 SCALE 6 KM
6 SCALE 6 MI

Washington-Slagbaai National Park

Spelonk Lighthouse
Punta Blanc
Brandaris Hill
Browenkel Well
Salina Mathijs
Pos Mangel
Salina Slagbaai
Rincón
Fort Oranje
Klein Bonaire
Kralendijk
Bonaire Marine Park (surrounds island)
Flamingo Airport
Lac Bay
Solar Salt Works
Pekel Meer

Curaçao

Boca Tabla
Zorgvlied
Savonet
Westpunt
Mt. Christoffel
Christoffel National Park
Zwehbergen
Santa Maria Bay
Salina St. Marie
Salina St. Marie
Santa Catarina
Hato International Airport
Hato Caves
Otrabanda
Willemstad
Punda
Car Pile
Tug Boat
Curaçao Seaquarium
New Port
Curaçao Underwater Park
Lighthouse (Oostpunt)

10 SCALE 10 MILES
10 SCALE 10 KILOMETERS

Aruba

California Lighthouse
Arashi Beach
Bubali Bird Sanctuary
Noord
Museo Archeologico
Oranjestad
Paadrea
Santa Cruz
Diorite Boulders
Natural Bridge
Boca Daimari
Arikok National Park
Rooi Thomas
Mt. Jamanota
Fontein Cave
Guadiriki Caves
Boca Prins
Boca Prins Sand Dunes
Huliba Cave
Sint Nicolás
Sero Colorado
Colorado Point Lighthouse
Queen Beatrix International Airport

3 SCALE 3 MILES
3 SCALE 3 KILOMETERS
0 SCALE

⬛ NATIONAL PARK   ◆ MOUNTAIN   ☐ POINTS OF INTEREST   — PAVED ROAD   ····· UNPAVED ROAD/TRAIL

NETHERLANDS ANTILLES

14

ARUBA, BONAIRE, AND CURAÇAO

The islands that make up the Netherlands Antilles are the most scattered of all the island groupings in the Caribbean. Aruba, Bonaire, and Curaçao (the ABCs), commonly referred to as the Dutch Leewards, lie 25 kilometers off the northern coast of Venezuela. Almost 900 kilometers northeast lie the second group—Saba, Sint Maarten, and Sint Eustatius (the "3-S's")—called the Dutch Windwards. Sint Maarten (pronounced "saint mar-tan") shares an island with French St. Martin, one of only two shared-island countries in the Caribbean.

This chapter will focus on the ABCs, which offer the most interesting nature and outdoor opportunities for travelers. Curaçao, the largest at 445 square kilometers, dwarfs Saba, which barely covers 13 square kilometers. (Curaçao is pronounced "cure-a-sow.") For the most part, the ABCs are flat coral islands with the highest elevations around 200 meters while the more lush 3-S's have volcanic peaks rising to 853 meters. Geographically the ABCs are far enough south to be out of the hurricane zone, but the 3-S's lie directly in the path of tropical storms. The population of the ABCs is around 263,000 while that of the 3-S's is about 36,000.

ARUBA

The smallest and farthest west of the ABCs, Aruba occupies about 182 square kilometers and is located about 24 kilometers from Venezuela.

The island has a desert-like environment of cacti and other drought-resistant vegetation, including the region's famous divi-divi tree. Aruba's highest point, Mount Jamanota, is less than 200 meters high—not high enough to coax the trades to part with their moisture; less than 500 millimeters of rain falls on the island annually.

The island's multicultural population of 81,000 is made up of more than 35 different nationalities, most of which are a mixture of African, Amerindian, Dutch, and Spanish. All coexist in relative harmony. This congeniality is expressed on every car license plate, which reads "One Happy Island," and the people live by the lyrics to their national anthem: "The greatness of our people is their great cordiality." As a result, visitors are treated well.

Aruba was the first of the group to dive head first into mass tourism. Lacking many of the resources considered necessary for traditional eco-tourism, such as rain forests and hiking opportunities, it instead promoted its many great white-sand beaches and incredible weather. The construction of the world's second largest desalination plant in 1959 took care of the water shortages and paved the way for mass tourism. Aruba quickly became the playground for middle- and upper-class Venezuelans with newly acquired wealth, as well as the vacation capital for Dutch citizens escaping the damp winters in Holland. Once the casinos opened, there was no turning back. Large resorts now occupy most of the prime beach-lined coast.

After the worldwide glut of oil closed the refinery, the government looked into diversifying the tourism industry and began to actively promote the island's unique eco-offerings. The first step was to designate almost 25 percent of the island as nature preserves, the largest of which is the Arikok National Park. At the same time, the government began promoting the clear water and shallow dive sites around the island. Eco-adventures now corner about 27 percent of the tourism industry on Aruba, and they are growing. A new conservation agency called FANAPA (Aruba Foundation for Nature and Parks) keeps tabs on development projects and lobbies for new preserves and parks.

The island's proximity to South America has blessed Aruba with more than 150 species of birds, of which over half are indigenous, including the ruby-topaz hummingbird, belted kingfisher, white-tailed hawk, and rare emerald hummingbird. Almost every variety of cactus and drought-resistant plant has found a home on the island, including the aloe and the divi-divi tree, with its characteristic lopsided forms. Iguanas and a native hare roam the preserves.

Although every outdoor activity is available on the island, diving, snorkeling, deep-sea fishing, and windsurfing are most popular. A number of hiking trails, as well as horseback and mountain biking trails, can be found within the national parks and preserves.

The island's capital city since 1707, **Oranjestad** (population 17,000), was named after the Dutch Royal House of Orange. **Fort Zoutman**, built in 1796, is the oldest building on the island. Just west of the fort is the **Museo Archaeologico** with exhibits of 2,000-year-old artifacts, tools, and skeletons of the island's early inhabitants. On the east side of the harbor is **Harbourtown Market** where you can buy local arts and crafts. In or around the capital is the most convenient place to stay.

Aruba History

Nothing much happened to the island after its discovery in 1499. It was too small and dry to warrant much investment, until the Dutch settled it, in 1634, and began to grow the medicinal plant aloe. The British captured the island in 1805, but returned it to the Dutch in 1816. The discovery of gold in the late 1800s kicked off an era of prosperity that endured through the construction of the Panama Canal, in the early 1900s, and the erection of an oil refinery in the early 1930s. Today tourism is the island's number two industry, after oil. From the time it was first settled until it was granted regional political status in 1987, Aruba was governed from the Dutch *metropol*.

ARIKOK NATIONAL PARK

The 1,000-hectare park lies in a triangle of land between Boca Prins and Boca Daimari (both on the east coast) and Santa Cruz in the center of the island. The focal point of the park is the 176-meter-high **Mount Arikok**, the island's second highest peak. The road from Santa Cruz and Boca Prins passes through the Miralamar Valley between Mount Arikok and the island's highest peak, **Mount Jamanota** (190 meters), on the southern edge of the park. A garden at the foot of Mount Arikok contains a good representation of the island's flora including the divi-divi tree, the slow-growing *kwihi* (a hardwood used for furniture and carvings), the rare Brazilwood, aloe, opuntias, and another famous native, the tall organ-pipe kadushi cactus. At one end of the garden is a restored *kas di pal'l maishi* (house of corn stalks) hut. The hut is typical of slave huts in the ABCs.

The park is home to the brown-throated parakeet, one of the larger species of parakeets in the world. They can often be seen in groups of a dozen or so while feeding on the fruit of the kadushi cactus. The ruby-topaz hummingbird and brown-crested flycatcher are abundant around the *kibrahacha* tree when it explodes in yellow blooms, just after the rainy season. The bright yellow flowers last only a day or two but provide a feast for birds and insects.

Cacti forest in Arikok National Park

The pink flowers of the coralita and the trumpet-like flowers of the purple scopet cover the ground between the taller plants, attracting the very rare rufous-collared sparrow, found only in the ABCs and the Dominican Republic. But the park's real treat is the rarest of Aruba's birds, the burrowing owl.

The park and surrounding countryside, including Mount Jamanota, is also home to the island's two snake species—the harmless *santanero* and the *colebra*, a highly venomous rattlesnake. Mice and small iguanas are staples for the rattlesnakes, which have also been known to take the odd bite out of a hiker straying from the marked trails.

A number of short, dusty, and extremely hot trails crisscross the valley and ascend the two hills. A couple of the trails lead up Mount Arikok to locations with Indian rock markings and petroglyphs.

There is no fee to enter the park. For more information, contact the National Parks Authority of Aruba, Piedra Plat 42, Oranjestad, Neth. Antilles, tel 297/82-8001, fax 297/82-8961.

OTHER THINGS TO SEE AND DO ON ARUBA

At the southeast corner of the park are the 25-meter-high **Boca Prins sand dunes** and a stretch of beautiful white-sand beach. In summer, all four species of sea turtles nest here.

South of the dunes are a series of caves. **Fontein Cave**, the largest on the island, has an immense chamber with side tunnels leading to walls covered with Indian paintings. The validity of these paintings is still in doubt, and rumors abound that the drawings were made by a film crew shooting a cave-man movie here five years ago. Just south of the Fontein Cave are two other cave systems: the **Guadiriki** and **Huliba Caves**. Both have large chambers and side tunnels with stalagmites and stalactites.

On the northern boundary of the park, at Boca Andicuri, is the **Natural Bridge**. At 30 meters long and 8 meters above the water, it is the Caribbean's largest natural arch. Waves break just offshore and flow under the bridge to a small secluded beach ideal for a refreshing dip.

Another good side trip, especially for birders, is **Bubali Pond**, on the west coast just north of the island's capital, Oranjestad. Today this old salt pan, a pond used for making salt by evaporating salt water, is kept wet by the overflow from the water treatment plant. The overflow has already been treated, but still contains enough nutrients to support an extensive food chain including brine shrimp, fish, and a great variety of birds. Black olivaceous cormorants, several species of heron, egrets, sandpipers, glossy and scarlet ibis, and the large woodstork from Venezuela are among the pond's residents.

Aruba's sparkling waters contain about 42 ship wrecks, including the 100-year-old *California*, the ship famous for having received, but failed to respond to, the *Titanic*'s S.O.S. signals. Except for the *California*, which lies off the northeast coast in rough water, most of the island's premier dive sites lie off the calm west coast. In fact, 36 of the wrecks lie along this coast in depths averaging 20 to 30 meters deep. What makes the west coast appealing to divers and snorkelers alike is the long, thin strand of barrier islands that run along it. These barrier islands are no more than the exposed tops of a vast underwater reef system. This barrier proved deadly for the ships that sailed these waters.

One of the best dive sites is the *Antilla*, a German freighter scuttled in 1945 when the Germans invaded Holland. At 130 meters in length, it is the largest wreck in the Caribbean. Another great dive is the **Porto Chiquito Reef** with its giant star coral. The reef is also frequented by huge schools of snapper, giant manta rays, and sea turtles. Snorkelers will be in awe over **Skalahein Reef**, where large coral gardens and the occasional manta can be seen. For stronger swimmers, **Baby Beach Reef** and **Boca Grandi Reef**, along the southeastern tip of the island, are other great spots. The last two offer good snorkeling from shore while most great snorkeling reefs are further offshore along the barrier islands and require a boat to get to them. The entire western coastline is fringed by reefs, but many offer only average snorkeling for those without a boat.

Many operators offering trips to the reefs also rent snorkel gear (see "Outfitters and Guides in Aruba," below).

Aruba has become a favorite stop on the world windsurfing circuit. Each June the waters off **Eagle Beach,** on the west coast, host the annual Aruba HiWinds Pro-Am Windsurfing Tournament. The event attracts more than 200 competitors from all over the world. Along the beach are dozens of water-sport shops where you can rent windsurfing equipment and take lessons. Most of these shops also rent snorkel equipment. Most sport fishing is done outside the barrier islands along the west coast. The 80-meter-deep water outside these islands offers great fishing for white and blue marlin, sailfish, and wahoo. De Palm can make all the arrangements (see below).

OUTFITTERS AND GUIDES ON ARUBA

Aruba is still new to nature tourism and has not yet developed an efficient infrastructure. Nevertheless, it's easy to get to the attractions thanks to accurate, available information, well-marked maps, and good roads. Mix in friendly people, who all seem to know some English, and finding your way around is a snap. FANAPA puts out a small but impressive guide called *Discover Aruba's Wildlife,* sold at most bookstores and many hotel gift shops. It covers the flora and fauna of the island and is worth getting.

Aruba Friendly Tours, Cumana 20, Oranjestad, Aruba, Neth. Antilles, tel 297/82-5800, fax 297/83-3074. This is like De Palm, below, but smaller.

De Palm Tours, L.G. Smith Blvd. 142, Oranjestad, Aruba, Neth. Antilles, tel 297/82-4400/4545, fax 297/82-3012, Web site: www.depalm.com/, offers all sorts of tours and arranges fishing trips, diving, snorkeling, sailing, windsurfing, and horseback riding.

Pelican Tours, Inc., Box 1194, Oranjestad, Aruba, Neth. Antilles, tel 297/82-4739 or 83-1228, fax 297/83-2655, provides all kinds of water-sport equipment rentals.

Red Sail Sports, tel 297/86-1603/82-4500 or 800/255-6425, fax 297/86-6657, Web site: www.redsail.com/, books trips through hotels and offers diving, snorkeling, fishing, and more.

WHERE TO STAY ON ARUBA

Remember that the island is a mass tourism destination and there are few small properties.

Aruba Blue Village Suites, Cunucu Aboa 37, Oranjestad, Aruba, Neth. Antilles, tel 297/87-8618 or 800/338-3108, fax 297/87-0081. This apartment-style complex has 56 fully equipped suites, two pools, and daily shuttle to beach. Rates $85 to $105.

Coconut Inn, Noord 31, Noord, Aruba, Neth. Antilles, tel 297/86-6288, fax 297/86-5433. One of the few small properties, this inn has 24 comfortable rooms with air conditioning, some with microwaves and fridges. Breakfast included and there is a pool. Rates $85 to $100.

Vistalmar, Bucutiweg 28, Noord, Aruba, Neth. Antilles, tel 297/82-8579, fax 297/82-2200, has eight fully furnished one-bedroom apartments with no frills. A rental car is included in the day rate. Rates $125 to $135.

CAMPING ON ARUBA
Camping is not permitted on Aruba.

WHERE TO EAT ON ARUBA
As in the other ABCs, eating is a serious pastime in Aruba. With Dutch, West Indian, and Indonesian influences, the cuisine takes on new meaning. Most restaurants only open for lunch and dinner, but all hotels serve breakfast.

Driftwood, Klipstraat 12, Oranjestad, tel 297/83-2515, serves local Aruban seafood at its best. Dinner only.

The Plaza Cafe, Seaport Marketplace, Oranjestad, tel 297/83-8826, serves delicious Dutch specialties. Dinner only.

Villa Germania, Seaport Marketplace, Oranjestad, tel 297/83-6161. One of the few restaurants that is open at eight in the morning, it is the only German cuisine restaurant on the island.

Warung Djawa, Wilhelmina Straat 2, Oranjestad, tel 297/83-4888, features Indonesian cuisine including *rijsttafel*, or "rice table," an assortment of six to eight dishes served with rice. A must try.

ARUBA SPECIFICS

Getting There
A number of North American carriers, including American Airlines and Air Canada, have daily flights to Aruba. Air Aruba has daily flights from Miami, Baltimore, and Newark; ALM, the official airline of the Dutch Antilles, flies daily from Miami and Ft. Lauderdale. Of special interest to North American visitors is ALM's "Visit Caribbean Pass," which allows very inexpensive interisland travel (in the Dutch Antilles). The pass must be purchased outside the Dutch Antilles.

Getting Around
Taxis don't have meters, but rather set rates from point A to point B. Many, but not all, belong to the Tourism Awareness Program, and possess a Tourism Guide Certification. These taxis abide by the

Papiamentu: The Language of the ABCs

Of the many pidgin tongues and creoles used throughout the Caribbean, the most complex would have to be Papiamentu, the language spoken in the ABCs. Most creoles or patois usually evolve from one or two languages, but not Papiamentu. Curaçao was a trading center for many countries, including Spain, France, Portugal, England, those in South America and Africa, and, of course, Holland. Since the need to communicate was an important aspect of trade, a "middle language" gradually developed. Today Papiamentu shares words and phrases from all of these countries, making it one of the most complex languages in the world.

A unique characteristic of Papiamentu is the way it has taken European phrases and "localized" them. The Papiamentu phrase, "Pampuna no sa pair calbas," which means, "the pumpkin vine does not bear calabash," is probably a corruption of "like father like son." And the Papiamentu version of "once bitten, twice shy," is "Un macacu ta subi palu di sumpinja un biahe so"—"the monkey only climbs the cactus once."

Locals are impressed by any visitor trying to speak a few words in their language, regardless of the way it comes out. The fact that you are willing to try is good enough for them. The following few easy phrases may prove helpful during your adventures in the cunucu, or countryside.

Welcome	*Bon Biní*
Good morning	*Bon dia*
Good night	*Bon nochi*
Goodbye!	*Ayo! (eh-oh)*
Many thanks	*Masha danki*
How are you?	*Kon ta bai? (con-tah-by)*
Stop	*Para*

government's set rates. They have a central dispatch (tel 297/82-2116 or 1604) office at the airport and at Pos Abou z/n, Oranjestad, behind the Eagle Bowling Alley.

Along the main drag and between the towns, there is inexpensive bus service, but it is mostly unscheduled. You can flag them down anywhere, but check at your hotel for information.

Driving on Aruba is easy but not cheap; expect to pay $50 to $65 per day. The roads are good (except for the dirt stretches on the eastern coast) and well signed, making it easy to navigate. **Avis, Budget, Hertz, Dollar**, and the local company **Hedwina Car Rental** all have offices at the airport and in town.

Scooters, mopeds, and mountain bikes are other good options seeing how it seldom rains on the island. **Ron's Motorcycle Rentals**, Gasparito 10A, Oranjestad, tel 297/86-2090, rents motorcycles, mopeds, and scooters for $20 to $40 per day. **Pablito's Bike Rental**, L.G. Smith Blvd. 234, Oranjestad, tel 297/87-8655, rents mountain bikes for $10 per day.

Tourist Information
Aruba Tourism Authority, L.G. Smith Blvd. 172, Oranjestad, Aruba, Neth. Antilles, tel 297/82-3777, fax 297/83-4702, email: ata.aruba@ toaruba.com

U.S.A.: Aruba Tourism Authority, 1000 Harbor Blvd., Ground Floor, Weehawken, NJ 07807, tel 210/330-0800 or 800/TO-ARUBA (U.S.A. only), fax 201/330-8757, email: ata.new.jersey@toaruba.com

Canada: Aruba Tourism Authority, 86 Bloor St. East, Suite 204, Toronto, Ont. M5S 1M5, tel 416/975-1905 or 1951 or 800/268-3042 (Ontario and Quebec), fax 416/975-1947, ata.canada@toaruba.com

Web sites and email: Web site: www.interknowledge.com/Aruba/; email: atanj@ix.netcom.com

BONAIRE

The original Caiquetios Indian inhabitants (an offshoot of the Arawaks) called the boot-shaped island *Bo-nah*, or "low country." The most easterly of the ABCs, Bonaire is the second largest of the group at 288 square kilometers and lies about 80 kilometers off the Venezuelan coast. It is a flat desert island 38 kilometers long by 11 kilometers at its widest point. The landscape is dominated by both **Brandaris Hill**, rising to 240 meters in the northwest, and by large expanses of salt ponds in the south. About 13,000 people share the island with about 35,000 flamingos.

Bonaire was one of the first Caribbean islands to realize the value of its unique natural resources and, as a result, the entire western quarter of the island, as well as a large chunk of offshore waters and reefs, has been designated national parks or sanctuaries.

Bonaire's emphasis on ecotourism started almost 35 years ago with the protection of the coastal waters and flamingo colonies. **Washington-Slagbaai National Park** is the oldest and largest land-based park in the Netherlands Antilles; its marine counterpart is Bonaire Marine Park, which encompasses the entire coastline of Bonaire. Prior to establishing the marine park, the conch and lobster in Bonaire's coastal waters had already been fished out, so the government, with help from private business, established one of the first aqua farms in the Caribbean. Today the farm raises thousands of conchs, lobsters, and giant clams for the local market and reintroduces thousands of young conchs and lobsters to the reefs each year. It also rehabilitates injured baby sea turtles, releasing them when they are healthy.

The marine splendor of Bonaire is so impressive that many divers consider it the top diving spot in the Caribbean and consistently rate it one of the top five diving spots in the world; it attracts around 27,000 divers each year. Unlike its neighbors, Curaçao and Aruba, Bonaire has completely embraced ecotourism to become a Caribbean mecca for eco-adventurers.

Bonaire's unique flora and fauna, especially its marine life and birdlife, are second to none in the Caribbean. Its location close to the Atlantic flyway means its 190 endemic bird species, including the yellow-shouldered parrot (Bonaire parrot) and pink flamingo, share island resources with dozens of migrating species. The island is home to the largest nesting colonies of flamingos in the Caribbean and to a healthy population of peregrine falcons. The dry habitat is ideal for reptiles such as the iguana, which can reach almost two meters in length, and a wide variety of ground lizards.

Land-based adventures such as hiking and bird watching are well established, and mountain biking the 300 kilometers of unpaved roads on the island and trails is becoming very popular. By far the best roads for mountain bikers are those throughout Washington-Slagbaai National Park, where you can bike only on roads, not on trails. The island's small size allows you to easily bike the entire island in a few days. Outfitters on the island offer combination hiking/biking trips that are highly recommended. They can also provide bikes and itineraries for independent adventurers (see "Getting Around," below, for rental information). But the island's true claim to fame is its diving, snorkeling, deep-sea fishing, and sea kayaking.

The small quiet capital of **Kralendijk** (the Dutch word for "coral dike"), is home to 4,000 friendly people who refer to it as "Playa"

(Papiamentu for beach). In the center of town, **Fort Oranje**, which dates back to the early 1800s, has some well-preserved cannons. Two blocks north of the fort, the large pink Greek temple–like structure is the **Fish Market**, which comes alive each afternoon with the catch-of-the-day and fresh vegetables. Most accommodations are found in or around the town, leaving much of the island sparsely populated.

Bonaire History

Bonaire was sighted in 1499, when Amerigo Vespucci's ship was temporarily separated from the four-ship fleet commanded by Alonso de Ojeda. The main De Ojeda fleet missed Bonaire but found Curaçao and Aruba while Vespucci drifted farther east finding Bonaire and the coast of Venezuela. The island remained unsettled until 1639, when the Dutch, having already established settlements on Aruba and Curaçao, realized that Bonaire was suitable for salt production. The island briefly fell into British hands between 1800 and 1816, but was returned to the Dutch in 1816 and has remained under their control ever since. The island's claim to fame came when Trans-World Radio installed the world's most powerful radio transmitter on the island in 1964. Like Aruba and Curaçao, Bonaire was granted regional political status in 1987.

WASHINGTON-SLAGBAAI NATIONAL PARK

Around 1880 the government of Curaçao sold all the land on the western quarter of the island to Dr. Moises Jeserun and the Neuman brothers. In 1892 they sold it to Jean Luis Cadieres, who in turn resold it to the Herrera brothers in 1920. The Herrera brothers sold off a large section to the Beaujon family and established a profitable goat and aloe plantation on their portion. When the last Herrera brother died in 1962, the estate (now called Washington) was turned over to the Netherlands Antilles government under the condition that it remain in its natural state. The government designated it the first sanctuary in the Dutch colonies. Then in 1978, the Beaujon family sold their portion of the original estate (called Slagbaai Estate) back to the government, which combined the two portions into the Washington-Slagbaai National Park.

Occupying almost 5,500 hectares, almost the entire northwestern part of the island, Washington-Slagbaai was the first national park in the Netherlands Antilles. At the visitors center, located at the entrance to the park, you can pick up a free map identifying all the trails or purchase a more detailed guide for about five dollars. Guides are not required in the park, but you might consider hiring one of those hanging around the visitors center to point out the flora and fauna you might otherwise miss.

The island's highest point, **Brandaris Hill** (228 meters), is located in the center of the park, surrounded by a number of salt ponds, freshwater lakes, and secluded beaches. Dry lowland vegetation, including seven varieties of cactus, aloe, and divi-divi, provide ideal habitat for more than 150 species of birds and numerous reptiles. Among the most abundant bird species in the park are the bananaquit, gray kingbird, yellow oriole, hooded warbler, northern water-thrush, endemic Caribbean paroquet, and rare Bonairean lora (Bonaire parrot). The large endemic iguana is endangered and is visible only in the park, where it is protected.

Freshwater **Bronswinkel Well**, near the southern base of Brandaris Hill, is a good spot to view wildlife. Since it is one of only four freshwater sites in the park, it is frequented by feral goats, deer, parrots, iguanas, and the seldom-seen yellow oriole. If you bring along some lettuce, you can usually entice one of the iguanas to come close enough for a good picture. You can drive to within a 45-minute walk of the well.

The flamingos congregate around the five large brackish ponds in the park. The largest of the ponds, **Goto Meer**, is actually a lagoon located on the southwest corner of the park near the entrance. Though the entire park is a sanctuary, this lagoon is the park's official flamingo sanctuary. The other ponds, **Salina Slagbaai** (west side of park), **Pos Mangel**

Wild goats at Bronswinkel Well

(northern tip of park), and **Salina Mathijs** (in the east), are also good birding and flamingo spots.

Two main trails, the 24-kilometer **green trail** and the 35-kilometer **yellow trail,** wind their way through the park. Off these main trails are shorter side trails leading to attractions such as watering holes, bird viewing areas, and beaches. One of the trails, three kilometers west of Goto Meer, leads to a great beach for snorkeling and a few caves with Indian wall paintings and inscriptions. The dirt roads in the park have been left rugged to force visitors to slowly absorb their surroundings rather than zip through them. Some of the other park attractions include the magnificent moonscape-like vistas of **Seru Grandi,** the 1870 ruins of a gold mine near Playa Makoshi, and the sparkling white-sand beach at **Boca Slagbaai.**

The park is open daily from eight to five; admission is five dollars. For more information, contact the Netherlands Antilles National Park Foundation (STINAPA), tel 599/7-8444.

BONAIRE MARINE PARK

Established in 1978, the park surrounds the island, including all coastal waters, from the high-water mark to the 60-meter-deep contour line around the entire island. It also includes the waters around the island of Klein Bonaire, off the main island's central west coast. The International Union for Conservation of Nature and Natural Resources, and the World Wildlife Fund helped finance the park.

Due to the potentially harmful impact of 27,000 divers and countless more snorkelers using the reefs each year, the park authority has implemented very strict rules for visitors. Within the park boundaries, every living and dead thing, including shells on the beach, is protected.

Boats less than four meters long must use a stone anchor while larger boats must use one of the park's 75 permanent mooring buoys. Park rangers make sure all park visitors adhere to the rules, maintain mooring buoys, and upkeep the shore markers used to direct park guests to proper access points along the coast. All diving and snorkeling outfitters operate under a strict set of rules and are held responsible for the actions of their clients. Divers and snorkelers, even those exploring independently, should inquire at the park office about fees and rules. The fee includes a booklet on park and reef safety, and a medallion that must be attached to the snorkel or mask for quick identification by rangers. Medallions are available through all marine outfitters and guides, which also provide snorkeling and diving permits, rental equipment, maps, and itineraries.

The reefs along the coast are famous for their diversity and abundance of marine life. They slope gradually from the beach down to about

10 meters, then in some places drop off over vertical walls that extend down to 60 meters. This is one of the few diving destinations in the world where you can access most diving sites directly from the beach. The diversity of the park's corals support more than 275 species of marine life from the tiny reef shrimp to 40-kilogram groupers.

One kilometer west of the capital is uninhabited 607-hectare **Klein Bonaire**, a popular day trip destination. The island is surrounded with spectacular reefs including "the Forest," which contains large stands of rare black coral and two-meter-long purple tube sponges. The island's several white-sand beaches are also ideal for picnics.

A $10 park fee is usually included in your diving or snorkeling package. For more information, contact Bonaire Marine Park, Box 368, Kralendijk, Bonaire, Neth. Antilles, tel 599/7-8444, fax 599/7-7318.

OTHER THINGS TO SEE AND DO ON BONAIRE

Bonaire's offshore waters teem with fish, making sport fishing another popular activity. Bonaire offers excellent deep-sea fishing for big game like marlin and tuna, as well as coastal light-tackle fishing for tarpon and bonefish. Kayaking and snorkeling in such mangrove-fringed bays as **Lac Bay** is also a popular marine activity.

The **Sea Turtle Club of Bonaire**, fax 599/7-8118, email: tvaneijck@bio.vu.nl, is dedicated to saving endangered sea turtles. The group frequently monitors beaches for nesting activity and conducts regular clean-ups of nesting beaches. Visitors are welcome to help.

On the southern side of the island is **Pekel Meer**, Bonaire's other large flamingo sanctuary. The 55-hectare sanctuary contains the largest breeding colony in the Caribbean, more than 20,000 birds. What makes the sanctuary unique is its location, smack in the middle of the Caribbean's largest salt production facility. The Antilles International Salt Company ensures that its operation is flamingo-friendly and takes great pride in providing ideal salt pond conditions for the breeding birds.

Flamingos feeding at the Pekel Meer Salt Ponds

The mangrove forests of **Lac Bay** and the Gaoen at **Punta**

Blanc are popular kayaking spots where paddlers can get close to more than 80 species of shore and wading birds. A number of eco-operators now offer mountain bike excursions as part of their packages. With more than 300 kilometers of unpaved roads, as well as hundreds of kilometers of hiking and goat trails, Bonaire is quickly becoming popular with mountain bikers.

OUTFITTERS AND GUIDES ON BONAIRE

Bonaire is ideal for the independent explorer. It is small, good information is available, the people are friendly, and a four-wheel-drive vehicle gets you to every possible corner of the island.

All dive operators work in conjunction with hotels or resorts and offer dive/hotel packages.

Cycle Bonaire, Kaya L.D. Gerharts 11D, Kralendijk, Bonaire, Neth. Antilles, tel 599/7-7558, fax 599/7-7690, rents TREK mountain bikes and offers guided tours.

Discover Bonaire, Box 266, Kaya Gobernador N. Debrot 79, Kralendijk, Bonaire, Neth. Antilles, tel 599/7-5252, fax 599/7-7690. This is a good one-stop company offering nature hiking tours, guided mountain-bike trips or rentals, kayak rentals and tours, and guided snorkeling trips.

Great Adventures Bonaire, Kaya Gobernador N. Debrot 71, Kralendijk, Bonaire, Neth. Antilles, tel 599/7-7500, fax 599/7-7507, is a first-class diving operation.

Jibe City Kayaking, Kralendijk, Bonaire, Neth. Antilles, tel 599/7-7363, fax 599/7-5363, rents kayaks and offers guided tours.

Klaas Bakker, Bonaire Nature Tours, Lima 109, Kralendijk, Bonaire, Neth. Antilles, tel 599/7-7714, is a personal guide offering custom tours to all land-based attractions.

Piscatur Fishing, Kaya M.J. Pop 4, Kralendijk, Bonaire, Neth. Antilles, tel 599/7-8774, fax 599/7-4784, offers all types of sport fishing as well as boat charters.

WHERE TO STAY ON BONAIRE

Most accommodations cater to divers so be prepared for diving atmosphere.

Carib Inn, J.A. Abraham Blvd. 46, Kralendijk, Bonaire, Neth. Antilles, tel 599/7-8819, fax 599/7-5295, has 13 comfortable, air-conditioned rooms, a pool, and a restaurant on the beach. Rates $75 to $150.

The Great Escape, E.E.G. Blvd. 97, Kralendijk, Bonaire, Neth. Antilles, tel 599/7-7488, fax 599/7-7480, has 10 basic rooms and a good restaurant, off the beach. Rates $90 to $115.

Hotel Rochaline, Kaya Grandi 7, Kralendijk, Bonaire, Neth. Antilles, tel 599/7-8286, fax 599/7-8258, features 25 very basic but comfortable rooms in town. Rates $55 to $75.

CAMPING ON BONAIRE

Camping is not permitted and there are no facilities, but in some cases it is tolerated on the less-traveled beaches. Inquire at the tourism authority before pitching a tent.

WHERE TO EAT ON BONAIRE

The **Hotel Rochaline**, Kaya Grandi 7, Kralendijk, Bonaire, tel 599/7-8286, has two fine eateries serving breakfast, lunch, and dinner.

Mi Poron, Kaya Caracas, Kralendijk, tel 599/7-5199, serves good local cuisine.

Rendez-Vous, Kaya L.D. Gerharts 3, Kralendijk, tel 599/7-8454, features international cuisine including grilled seafood.

BONAIRE SPECIFICS

Getting There

All flights arrive and depart via Curaçao or Aruba. There are no direct international flights.

Getting Around

Few taxis ply the empty roads of Bonaire since most visitors come for the diving, but fixed government rates are posted at the airport. To truly see the island, rent a four-wheel-drive vehicle. **Avis**, **Budget**, and **A.B. Car Rentals** have booths at the airport. The next best way to see the island is on a scooter or moped. **Hot Shot Rentals**, Kaya Bonaire 4, tel 599/7-7166, fax 599/7-7166, rents scooters, bikes, and mopeds. **Cycle Bonaire** (see "Outfitters and Guides in Bonaire," above) rents mountain bikes.

Tourist Information

Bonaire Tourism Corporation, Kaya Libertador Simon Bolivar 12, Kralendijk, Bonaire, Neth. Antilles, tel 599/7-8322/8649, fax 599/7-8408, email: tcb@bonairenet.org

U.S.A.: Bonaire Tourism Office, 10 Rockefeller Plaza, Suite 900, New York, NY 10020, tel 212/956-5911 or 5900, or 800/U-BONAIR, fax 212/956-5913

Web sites and email: Web sites: www.interknowledge.com and www.bonaire.org; email: 102372.3337@compuserve.com

CURAÇAO

Only 56 kilometers off the Venezuela coast, sandwiched between Aruba and Bonaire, Curaçao is the largest and most populated of the Netherlands Antilles. The island has always been the Dutch administrative center in the Caribbean and its name is believed to have come from the Portuguese word *corazon*, meaning "heart." Occupying 450 square kilometers, the flat, dry island is characterized by 380-meter-high Mount St. Christoffel, in the northwest, and the world's seventh largest natural deep-water harbor. Besides having the world's second busiest port, Curaçao has one of the world's largest oil refineries and the Caribbean's longest airport runway. Some 170,000 people call Curaçao home.

Tourism, Curaçao's number two industry, is quickly becoming number one, with the government doing everything it can to promote it. As in Aruba, the emphasis is on mass tourism with big flashy resorts and casinos. But the island still enjoys large tracts of undeveloped land and coastline unsuitable for mass tourism resorts.

Building on Bonaire's eco-successes, Curaçao decided to diversify its tourism industry and has begun to promote to ecotourism. The first step in the process was to create two large protected areas. In 1978, the Christoffel National Park was established to protect about 1,800 hectares of wilderness in the northern part of the island; the Underwater Park was created in 1983 to protect about 21 kilometers of pristine reefs along the southeast coast. Both protected areas are managed by the Netherlands Antilles National Park Foundation (STINAPA).

The island is rich in plant and animal life, supporting some 170 species of birds, including a few small colonies of flamingos, parakeets, and five species of dove. The Curaçao deer (similar to the American white-tail), feral donkeys, and many species of reptiles like the large iguana make their home on the island. The vegetation is similar to that on the other ABCs, desert-like dry woodland. Hundred-year-old mesquite, divi-divi, thorny acacia, and five-meter-high cactus cover most of the northern half of the island; mangrove forests flourish along the shallow-water coastlines.

Offshore, the reefs and water teem with hundreds of marine species including clumps of brain coral 15 meters in diameter, 25-meter-wide staghorn coral, the rare purple-yellow royal gramma (the world's most expensive tropical aquarium fish), and the majestic angel.

Although there is good hiking, biking and bird watching dominate the island's outdoor activities.

In 1817 Governor-General Vice Admiral Albert Kikkert, bored with predominantly white houses in the capital of **Willemstad**, decreed that every building be painted in bright colors. Today a rainbow of colors greets visitors to this beautiful Dutch island.

Most of the island's inhabitants live in the charming capital, which is divided into **Punda on**, the east side of Santa Anna Bay, and **Otrabanda**, on the west. At the center of town is **Fort Amsterdam**, built by the Dutch in 1634; two blocks north is the **Mikvé Israel–Emanuel Synagogue**, the oldest Jewish synagogue in the Western Hemisphere, built in 1732.

Spanning Santa Anna Bay is the 213-meter-long **Queen Emma** pontoon bridge. Built in 1888, it is the largest floating pedestrian bridge in the world. The bridge, which is swung aside to let ships past, is made up of 15 large boat-shaped pontoons.

Curaçao History

The island was discovered in 1499 during an expedition led by Alonso de Ojeda and Amerigo Vespucci. The Spanish, who first settled the island in 1534, eventually abandoned it to the Dutch West India Company in 1634. Not much happened until the late 1700s, when the island's strategic position became the envy of the British and French. From 1800 to 1803 and again from 1807 to 1815, Curaçao fell under British and French rule. Curaçao returned to Dutch control in 1815 and attained self-rule, as part of the Kingdom of the Netherlands, in 1954.

CHRISTOFFEL NATIONAL PARK

Open to the public in 1978, the park covers about 10 percent of the island's entire land mass and half the northern part of the island. It is dominated by the crest of Mount Christoffel, which rises about 375 meters above the hot, dry plains. A series of caves along the ridges fanning out from Mount Christoffel are thought to be old refuges of the Caiquetio Indians. The walls of these caves are covered with their ancient paintings and petroglyphs.

The park is home to more than 500 species of plants and 170 species of birds, some of which can

Exploring near Boca Tabla in Christoffel National Park

be found only on Curaçao. In this dry, inhospitable terrain, several rare orchid species can be found growing on five-meter-high cactus. The park also supports a herd of about a hundred shy, very rare white-tailed Curaçao deer, which many believe were brought to the island by the Caiquetios Indians from South America in the 1400s. Hummingbirds, parrots, bats, and trupial birds help the park's dynamic ecosystem by pollinating the hundreds of varieties of plants and trees, such as a few rare palms, dyewood, indigo, and mahogany.

Some of the park's feathered residents include the orange-breasted trupial (the national bird), rufous-collared sparrow, white-tipped dove, rare scaly-naped pigeon, and the *warawara* hawk. Where the park boundaries meet the coastline near Boca Tabla, shore birds such as whembrels, grey pelicans, brown boobies, and frigate birds abound.

Four major signed and color-coded dirt roads twist their way through the park. Three are for driving (best with a four-wheel-drive), though you can walk on them, and all are named after the original plantations they pass through. The road to the top of Mount Christoffel must be hiked, not driven. The **Savonet Route**, or blue trail, starts at the park entrance (on the Weg naar Westpunt Highway), just past the old Savonet plantation house (the visitors center), where you will find a small nature conservancy and the Museum of Natural and Cultural History. Visitors can purchase a park guide containing locations and descriptions of the park's geological and zoological features found along trails. Numbered trail markers indicate particular points of interest, which are cross-referenced in the park guide. Shorter feeder trails off the main trails lead to specific points of interest such as caves, archaeological sites, stands of interesting vegetation, bird viewing areas, and panorama lookouts.

The **Zorgvlied Route** (green trail) parallels the northern coast and circles around the eastern flank of Mount Christoffel. The **Zevenbergen Route** (yellow trail) covers the southwest corner of the park and features unique vegetation such as the two rare orchids (*schomburgkia humboldtii* and *Brassavola nodosa*) found only on Curaçao. The **Christoffel Trail** (red trail) leads off from the Zevenbergen Route up to the top of Mount Christoffel, a three-hour climb.

Guided tours are available through the visitors center, and each afternoon between 4:00 and 6:30 park guides take small groups up to an observation tower on the peak for 10-minute deer viewing sessions. Remember to pick up the information park guide at the visitors center; it's worth the $7. The park is open daily from eight to five; admission is nine dollars. For more information, contact Christoffel National Park, Park Entrance, tel 599/9-64-0363, or Netherlands Antilles National Park Foundation (STINAPA), Box 2090, Curaçao, Neth. Antilles.

South of the park and just south of the small town of San Sebastian, along the Weg naar San Willibrordo Highway, are a number of abandoned salt ponds where you can see small flocks of pink flamingos. Near the north-central coast visitors will find the **Hato Caves** (admission four dollars, tel 599/9-68-0379), 4,900 square meters of caverns and pools, with seldom-seen long-nosed bats, dramatic limestone formations, and ancient Indian drawings.

CURAÇAO UNDERWATER PARK

The 607-hectare park stretches 21 kilometers, from Jan Thiel Lagoon (east of Willemstad) to the eastern tip of the island, and covers all the land and water from the high-water mark to a depth of 60 meters. The park was established in 1983 to protect the best sections of reef fringing the island and its almost 500 different fish species, 30 soft corals, and more than 55 species of hard corals. The staghorn and brain coral found here are some of the largest in the Caribbean, as are the enormous beaker sponges, 1.5 meters in diameter. Underwater visibility here is among the best in the Caribbean, most days at least 50 meters.

More than 100 diving sites are found in these waters, and the park authority has planted 16 permanent buoys over areas of exceptional interest such as wrecks, ledges, and special coral formations. The park authority has also constructed a 300-meter-long underwater snorkel and diving trail over some incredible sections of reef.

One of the park's main attractions is the black coral gardens. Here the most magnificent of all Caribbean corals can reach tree sizes of 25 meters in height. Poaching for the jewelry and artist trade has decimated black coral forests all over the Caribbean, but this coral is now protected in all Dutch Antillean waters. Another popular underwater photo spot is **Car Pile**, where old junkers were sunk to form an artificial reef. Nowhere else in the Caribbean can you have your picture taken on the hood of a 1967 Chevy 20 meters under water.

Dozens of ship wrecks, some 100 years old, dot the crystal clear waters around the island's coast. The most popular wreck, called **Tug Boat**, is a sunken tug boat in only five meters of water. The most interesting wreck is the almost-intact **SS *Oranje Nassau***, which hit the reef in 1906. Another interesting wreck is a Navy seaplane, which hit the reef and sank during the last war. It is still nearly intact; scattered around the wreck site is a large quantity of live ammunition that the ship was carrying when it hit the reef.

An excellent 72-page guide titled *Guide to Curaçao Underwater Park* is available at bookstores, dive shops, hotel gift shops, and the tourism office. It contains a map of the park, complete with snorkel trails and dozens of fabulous color photos; it costs about $10. There is no charge for visiting the park. For more information, contact Underwater Park Office, tel 599/9-62-4242.

Just east of the park, at Bapor Kibra, is the **Curaçao Seaquarium** (admission seven dollars, tel 599/9-61-6666), an ideal stop for those who can't make it to the reef. On display are more than 400 species of fish and other marine life common to Curaçao's waters. A glass-bottom boat cruise over the reef is also available at the aquarium.

OUTFITTERS AND GUIDES ON CURAÇAO

Most natural attractions on Curaçao can be seen independently with little more than a compass, map, and a couple of guidebooks, but there are some good operators that can arrange all your adventures. Most hotel tour desks can usually arrange any tour you want. Licensed guides for hikes through the Christoffel National Park are available at the park visitors center for between $14 and $25 per day, depending on length of hike.

If you plan to dive, however, you do need an operator. You can snorkel independently, but an operator can take you to the best spots. There are no less than 30 resorts and 20 dive operators along the coast between the capital and the coastline bordering the marine park. All rent snorkeling and diving equipment. All operators listed below rent snorkel equipment and can provide information to independent snorkelers.

Agua Diving Curaçao, Weg naar Westpunt, Martha Koosje 4, Curaçao, tel 599/9-864-9700, fax 599/9-864-9288, email: dive@ aquadiving.com, Web site; www.aquadiving.com, offers snorkeling and diving trips.

Blenchi Tours, Willemstad, Curaçao, Neth. Antilles, tel 599/9-461-8660, fax 599/9-465-8131, is a smaller operator but offers good tours.

Coral Cliff Diving, Coral Cliff Hotel Santa Marta Bay, Curaçao, Neth. Antilles, tel 599/9-864-2822, fax 599/9-864-2237, is a popular scuba operator in a popular hotel.

Scuba Do Dive Center, Jan Thiel Beach & Sports Resort, tel and fax 599/9-767-9300, rents equipment and offers snorkeling and diving trips.

Taber Tours, P.O. Box 3304, Dokweg z/n, Curaçao, Neth. Antilles, tel 599/9- 737-6637 or 6713, fax 599/9-737-9539, email: tabertours@curacao.com. You name it, they can arrange it.

Top Curaçao, on Seaquarium Beach, tel 599/9-61-7343, rents all sorts of water-sport equipment and can arrange trips to Underwater Park.

Underwater Curaçao, Lions Dive Hotel & Marina, Jan Thiel Bay, tel 599/9-461-8100, fax 599/9-461-8200, rents equipment and offers trips.

WHERE TO STAY ON CURAÇAO

Coral Cliff Resort & Beach Club, Box 3782, Santa Marta Bay, Curaçao, Neth. Antilles, tel 599/9-864-1610, fax 599/9-864-1781, is a bungalow-style beachfront property offering 35 rustic but comfortable rooms with air conditioning; some have hot tubs. Lots of activities on site including pool, restaurant, tennis, mini golf, and dive shop. Rates $68 to $122.

Hotel Pelikaan, Langestraat 78, Willemstad, Curaçao, Neth. Antilles, tel 599/9-462-3555, fax 599/9-462-6063, is another comfortable in-town hotel set back from the beach, with 66 comfortable rooms with air conditioning and private bath. Rates $50 to $75.

Trupial Inn, 5 Groot Davelaarweg, Willemstad, Curaçao, Neth. Antilles, tel 599/9-737-8200, fax 599/9-737-1545. Located away from the beach in a quiet neighborhood, this bungalow-style inn offers 74 comfortable rooms with private baths and air conditioning, pool, restaurant, and tennis court. Rates $80 to $95.

CAMPING ON CURAÇAO

Camping is not permitted on the island.

WHERE TO EAT ON CURAÇAO

Jaanchi's Restaurant, Westpunt 15, Willemstad, Curaçao, Neth. Antilles, tel 599/9-864-0126, is a favorite stop for Curaçaoan seafood dishes.

Rijsttafel, Mercuriusstraat 13, Salina, Curaçao, Neth. Antilles, tel 599/9-461-2606, serves exotic Indonesian delicacies like *rijsttafel* or "rice table," with 16 to 20 different dishes placed on the table around you.

Seaview, Waterfront Arches, Willemstad, Curaçao, Neth. Antilles, tel 599/9-461-6688, serves more traditional-style North American dishes like steak and seafood.

CURAÇAO SPECIFICS

Getting There

Curaçao's international airport receives daily international flights from North American cities such as Miami, New York, Atlanta, Toronto, and Montreal. ALM, American, Air Canada, and Air Aruba all offer daily flights with North American connections.

Getting Around

Many hotels, even the smaller ones, offer shuttle-bus service to beaches, airport, and downtown. Some hotels also rent mountain bikes. Taxis are highly regulated and offer standard fares to various destinations. Official tariff charts are posted at hotels, airports, and at information kiosks downtown.

Curaçao has a great network of roads and a plethora of car rental agencies, all fighting for your business. This translates into competitive rates. All the big guys (**Avis, Budget, National, Hertz,** etc.) have booths at the airport. **Curaçao Car Rental,** tel 599/9-767-1927, and **Jeep Car Rental,** tel 599/9-736-7611, are good local companies.

Easy Going Motorcycles & Scooters, tel 599/9-869-5056 or 560-2621, rents an assortment of two-wheeled transportation.

Tourist Information

Curaçao Tourism & Development Bureau, 19 Pietermaai, Box 3266, Willemstad, Curaçao, Neth. Antilles, tel 599/9-461-6000, fax 599/9-461-2305, email: ctdbcur@ibm.net

U.S.A.: Curaçao Tourist Board, 475 Park Ave., Suite 2000, New York, NY 10016, tel 212/683-7660 or 800/270-3350, fax 212/683-9337, email: curacao@ix.netcom.com

Web sites and email: Web sites: www.interknowledge.com/curacao/ and www.newadventures.com/; http://curacao.com/; email: curacao@ix.netcom.com

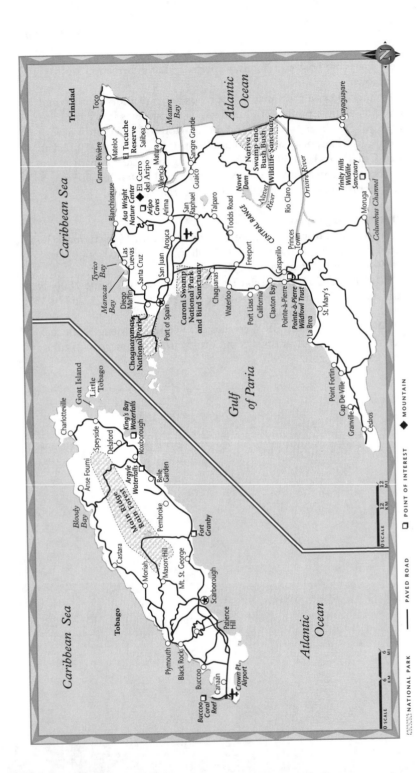

15

TRINIDAD AND TOBAGO

The twin-island nation of Trinidad and Tobago offers some of the most startling contrasts found anywhere in the Caribbean. The southernmost islands of the Caribbean, Trinidad and Tobago are actually an extension of the South American continent. Trinidad is located just off the north coast of Venezuela, separated by the 11-kilometer strait of the Gulf of Trinidad. Trinidad is rectangular in shape, measuring 80 kilometers long by 60 wide; Tobago, its smaller, fish-shaped sibling, is 42 kilometers long by 10 wide. Trinidad is the fifth largest island in the Caribbean (4,828 square kilometers) while Tobago is one of the smallest (330 square kilometers). Trinidadians, mostly of African and East Indian descent, number about 1.3 million. Some 55,000 people live on Tobago.

Although the two islands share similarities in culture, flora, fauna, and topography, the contrasts between them are quite noticeable. Besides the obvious size difference, Trinidad is more South American in character, cosmopolitan, and industrialized while Tobago is more Caribbean and laid-back. The big island has few great white-sand beaches while Tobago is completely fringed with white sand. Most visitors head to Trinidad for business purposes or to participate in Carnival; in contrast, Tobago tends to attract the Robinson Crusoe crowd—those looking for isolation.

The discovery of oil along the southern coast, in the mid-1800s, was a major event in Trinidad's history. The first oil well in the world was drilled in 1857, but the industry did not really take off until the 1930s, when Trinidad became the largest oil producer in the British Empire. Subsequent periods of boom and bust, due mainly to swings in oil prices, prompted the government to find a supplementary source of foreign income. The option it chose was tourism.

The world's obsession with white-sand beaches prompted the government of Tobago to develop mass tourism characterized by lavish beachfront resorts. Trinidad, lacking few white-sand beaches, turned to ecotourism, establishing 13 protected areas in the 1960s, while Tobago had only one protected area, the Main Ridge Forest, established in 1776 to become the first protected area in the New World. Over the last decade other protected sites have been established and strong conservation and ecotourism programs have been developed on both islands.

Trinidad and Tobago are neither volcanic nor coral, like the other Caribbean islands, but rather pieces of Venezuela that broke off from the South American continent about 50,000 years ago. Because of this, the islands' flora and fauna share more similarities with South America's than they do with the rest of the Caribbean's. Trinidad, being larger and closer to the southern continent, has the widest variety, with thousands of species of plants and animals found in South America but on no other island in the Caribbean. The biodiversity includes more than 2,300 varieties of flowering plants, 700 butterfly species, 430 bird species, 32 land mammals, two primates, thousands of insects, and reptiles of all sizes, including the caiman crocodile and 38 species of snakes.

For the nature lover, Trinidad and Tobago are an emerging paradise. Because neither island has yet attracted the eco-traffic common on some of their neighbors, the natural resources are in prime condition. The islands offer some of the best birding and rain forest hiking, as well as some of the best drift diving in the Caribbean. Add in kayaking in river estuaries and swamps, deep-sea fishing, and a taste of South America, and you get one of the Caribbean's best eco-adventure destinations.

Trinidad and Tobago History

History tells us that Columbus sighted Trinidad on July 31, 1498, after being becalmed for more than a week. Grateful for wind at last, he named the island La Trinidad in honor of the Blessed Trinity, and claimed the island for Spain. Over the next 250 years a number of nations attempted settlement, but fierce Indians and dense jungle proved formidable obstacles. In 1783 a Spanish decree called the "Cedula of Population" gave new meaning to the term "land rush." The decree offered free land to Roman Catholic citizens of any country friendly to Spain. Within six years, the island's population shot up to 17,000. Britain did not take kindly to the decree, which effectively ruled out Protestant Englishmen, so in 1797 it attacked and took the island from a makeshift French-Spanish army. The islands remained directly under Britain's control until they gained independent statehood in 1962, followed by full independence in 1976.

TRINIDAD

Trinidad is world-famous for its Carnival and calypso music, but it is quickly becoming a mecca for eco-adventurers as well. Trinidad's large size means that every one of the vegetation zones in the Caribbean are well represented, and there are protected areas within each vegetation zone. Large areas of mangrove swamps, savannahs, and all primary forest zones including dry woodlands, semi-deciduous and tropical rain forest are now protected and being developed for low-impact nature adventures.

Trinidad has three mountain ranges, all east-west, roughly dividing the island into thirds. Between each range are savannas and swamps. The Northern Range is the highest and wettest, and contains most of the island's primary rain forest. The Central Range is a series of lower rolling hills, slightly in the rain shadow of the Northern Range. The Southern Range is the lowest and driest. Rainwater from these mountain ranges runs into the savannahs that divide them, producing lush agricultural areas and large tracts of swamp. The flatter central and southern areas are characterized by extensive agricultural and industrial development (oil fields). Although wildlife is dispersed across the entire island, the heaviest concentrations are found in the less-developed northern third of the island.

The Northern Range extends west to east from Chaguaramas Point, on the northwest tip of the island, to Galera Point, on the northeast tip. Dominating the center of the range is 940-meter-high El Cerro del Aripo peak. The range contains most of the island's tropical rain forest and a number of natural attractions, including the **Asa Wright Nature Centre**, a privately run wildlife preserve and bird sanctuary. It's a great base from which to explore the entire northern half of the island.

The central region, which includes the central lowlands and the Central Range, contains a number of interesting natural sites including the **Caroni, Aripo Savannah**, and **Matura Beach**. The central region can also be explored from the Asa lodge or Port of Spain.

The southern region includes the land south of the Central Range, the Nariva Savannah, and the rolling hills of the Southern Range to the south coast. It includes the **Nariva Swamp and Bush Bush Wildlife**

View from the Northern Range in Trinidad

Sanctuary, Pointe-à-Pierre Wild Fowl Trust, and the **Trinity Hills Wildlife Sanctuary**. The Nariva Swamp is a great kayaking spot for birders and naturalists. The quiet mode of transportation allows paddlers to sneak up on some of the area's diverse wildlife including the rare red-bellied macaw, caiman, and agouti. Wildways (see "Outfitters and Guides in Trinidad," below) offers full-day kayaking trips through the swamp. Kayakers are accompanied by experienced birders and aquatic-life specialists, who share their intimate understanding of this valuable ecosystem. Part of the trip includes a hike through the dense hardwood forest on Bush Bush Island in search of the howlers. The island is in the heart of the swamp and can only be reached by boat or kayak. For information about these and protected areas in general, contact the Forestry Division, Long Circular Road, Port of Spain, Trinidad, WI, tel 868/622-4521, 622-7476, or 622-7256.

The island's busy capital, **Port of Spain,** is not the old Spanish colonial city that the name implies, but rather is unmistakably British with bits of French and Spanish influences scattered about. Established as capital in 1757, Port of Spain has few visitor attractions, but a few 150-year-old buildings, such as Cathedral of the Holy Trinity (1823), the Cathedral of the Immaculate Conception (1832), and Fort George (1804), are worth seeing.

ASA WRIGHT NATURE CENTRE AND BIRD SANCTUARY

Located at an elevation of 400 meters in the Northern Range, 12 kilometers north of the town of Arima, the Asa Wright Nature Centre is a world-class center for those interested in tropical ecosystems and birds.

Established in 1967 on the old Spring Hill Estate (a former cocoa and coffee plantation), the center includes a lodge, wildlife reserve, and bird sanctuary, and attracts amateur and professional naturalists from all over the world. The New York Zoological Society's William Beebe Tropical Research Station, with facilities for scientists and students, is located just south of the center.

Trinidad's proximity to South America, along with its varied vegetation zones and habitats, combine to foster unusually diverse flora and fauna. The species list for Trinidad is impressive, with 108 mammals, 425 birds, 55 reptiles, 28 amphibians, 657 butterflies, and 2,300 flowering plants, including more than 650 orchids. Few areas of comparable size anywhere in the tropical Americas come close to matching this diversity.

Sitting quietly on the veranda of the lodge, which is immersed in the forest, can only be compared to sitting in the center of an aviary: more than 200 bird species have been identified here. On any given morning, it is not difficult to record 40 to 50 species within binocular range. Some of the rarer birds sighted are the bearded bell bird, white-bearded manakin, golden-headed manakin, collared trogon, tufted coquette hummingbird, squirrel cuckoo, toucan, orange-winged parrot, and lilac-tailed parrotlet. Most importantly, the sanctuary is one of only three sites on the island, all in the Northern Range, where visitors can glimpse the only nocturnal fruit-eating bird in the world, the endangered oilbird (*steatornis caripensis*), found only in the northern regions of South America. To protect the oilbird colony, the World Wildlife Fund donated substantial funds towards the center's establishment.

Five trails, ranging in length from one to three hours, wind their way through the preserve under a 30-meter-high canopy of mahogany, Brazil nut, and the beautiful immortelle tree, a favorite nesting site of the crested oropendola. The bird's distinctive hanging nest can be seen throughout the park, but especially in immortelle trees. Off the center's main trail is the Dunston Cave Trail. The trail leads to the Dunston Caves, which are open at certain times of the year so that visitors can see the elusive oilbird.

Brocket deer, white-collared peccary, nine-banded armadillo, red howler and weeping capuchin monkeys, ocelots, and four varieties of poisonous snakes, including the bushmaster, fer-de-lance, and coral, can also be seen along the trails.

Entrance to the nature center and bird sanctuary is free for guests staying in the lodge, six dollars for day trippers. For more information, contact the Asa Wright Nature Centre and Lodge, Box 4710, Arima, Trinidad & Tobago, WI, tel 868/667-4655 or 800/426-7781 (Canada and U.S.A. only), fax 868/667-4540.

OTHER THINGS TO SEE AND DO
NEAR ASA WRIGHT NATURE CENTRE

The **Peak Trail** up El Cerro del Aripo begins in Aripo Village, about 22 kilometers east of the center. The trail also leads to the **Aripo Caves**, another favorite nesting site of the oilbird. The hike is difficult; guides, available at the trailhead in Aripo Village, are highly recommended.

About 20 kilometers west of the Asa Centre is the 936-hectare **El Tucuche Reserve**, named after the island's second highest peak, 936-meter-high El Tucuche. Several hiking trails wind their way around and up the mountain under 30-meter-high canopies of primary rain forest. The starting point for most of the trails is at Ortinola, along the Maracas Royal Road.

The Northern Range ends along a peninsula on the extreme northwest tip of the island. The long, narrow peninsula and a few offshore islets make up **Chaguaramas National Park**. The peninsula's drier habitat supports large groups of howler monkeys. The calm coves and beaches along its south coast are great for snorkeling.

The quiet coves and offshore islands of the **Chaguaramas peninsula** also offer an ideal setting for kayaking. Off the coast are a group of small islands that broke off the main peninsula during the island's formation. **Wildways** (see "Outfitters and Guides on Trinidad," below) offers an exciting full-day kayaking adventure in this region. Starting in Williams Bay, kayakers pass through the narrow channel between Point Gourde and the Diego Islands, riding the tides across Chaguaramas Bay to the north shore of Gaspar Grande Island. Here the kayaks are beached in a quiet bay and paddlers exchange paddles for hiking shoes to explore the island's **Gasparee Caves**. Your guide will take you down into the cave (about 400 meters) to view the limestone formations and a tidal pool where you can take a refreshing dip.

CARONI SWAMP NATIONAL PARK AND
BIRD SANCTUARY

The Caroni River starts high in the Northern Range and snakes its way west towards the coast. Just south of Arima, it hits the Caroni Savannah and slows to a crawl, spreading out on its journey to the coast. About 3 kilometers from the coast it enters a 104-square-kilometer area of tidal flats, mangrove forests, and marshland known as the Caroni Swamp.

Within the swamp is the largest nesting colony of scarlet ibis outside South America. The Caroni Swamp National Park and Bird Sanctuary was created in 1967 to protect the nesting sites of the island's national bird. At certain times of the year flocks numbering 12,000 are not uncommon, but usually flocks of a few thousand frequent the swamp.

Since 1962, ibis have been protected by law, but prior to that they were decimated for food and feathers for the fashion industry. Over the last three decades their numbers have grown. Each evening, just before sunset, the bright red birds begin to arrive in flocks of about 100 and head for their roosting sites in the tall black mangroves. Within an hour the dull green foliage of the mangroves has been transformed into brilliant red.

After the ibis have settled, the herons and egrets start arriving, and soon the mangroves resemble decorated Christmas trees. The ibis get their color from the carotene extracted from the shrimp and other crustaceans that make up their diet. Mixed in with the red adults are pink juveniles. In about three years their carotene levels will be high enough to turn their feathers bright red.

The swamp is one of Trinidad's primary breeding grounds for shrimp and other important food fish. The canals and backwaters nourish 80 species of fish including 30-kilogram tarpon and grouper, snook, mangrove

© Wildways Ltd.

Hiking in Caroni Swamp National Park

snapper, and the rare four-eyed fish. This 30-centimeter-long fish has horizontally segmented eyes, permitting it to feed on the surface for insects while being able to see below for predators. Their two-eyes-followed-by-a-tail form is unmistakable as they swim along the surface.

The swamp contains all four varieties of mangroves; the black, white, red, and the large buttonwood. The swamp and mangroves support 138 varieties of birds, the spectacled caiman, large iguanas, howler monkeys, and the shy 50-centimeter-long nocturnal silky anteater, which spends most of the day curled up in a silver ball around a branch.

There are walking trails through the park, but hiking should be done only with a guide. In some areas the mud is like quicksand, and three poisonous snake species frequent the swamp. The best way to explore the swamp is by boat, which you can take from the side of the road near the park. Most of these tours are provided by local fishermen, who don't really know that much about the swamp. If you really want to explore and learn about the swamp enlist the assistance of one of the nature guides listed under "Outfitters and Guides in Trinidad," below.

There is no entrance fee, but the boat ride to get into the swamp costs about $10. For more information, contact the Trinidad and Tobago Field Naturalists' Club, c/o Secretary Rosemary Hernandez, 1 Errol Park Rd., St. Ann's, Port of Spain, Trinidad, WI, tel 868/625-3386, 645-2132, or 624-3321, fax 868/625-2132.

Other Things to See and Do near Caroni Swamp

Four of the seven sea turtles—the hawksbill, green, leatherback, and olive Ripley—nest on Trinidad's beaches. Most pull up to nest along the 16 kilometers of **Matura Beach**, on Trinidad's eastern coast, between the towns of Matura in the north and Lower Manzanilla in the south. The huge 2-meter, 400-kilogram leatherbacks arrive in large numbers between April and June, and a few outfitters offer trips to see them. A group called Nature Seekers, Inc., monitors the beaches during the nesting months to help curb poaching. If you would like to volunteer your time, call Dennis Sammy (tel 868/668-0171). Permits to view the turtles cost five dollars and you must be accompanied by a licensed guide.

NARIVA SWAMP AND BUSH BUSH WILDLIFE SANCTUARY

The Nariva Swamp, on the eastern side of the island between the Central and Southern Ranges, is the largest and most varied of Trinidad's freshwater swamps. It covers a triangular area bordered by Lower Manzanilla in the north, Pierreville in the south, and Río Clara in the west.

The swamp is bordered on the east by **Cocos Bay**, with its 27-

Carnival

Carnival, also known as mas, *has evolved from a fusion of music and religion to become a showcase for political and cultural expression. For two days each year, starting the first Monday prior to Ash Wednesday, Trinidad and Tobago erupt in a splash of color, pulsating to the rhythms of steelbands and calypso. More than 1 million people come together to enjoy and participate in this yearly multiracial extravaganza, which many now refer to as the "Mother of All Carnivals." It has become an important part of the culture of the islands, producing an almost cleansing effect, which smothers, if only for a few days, the divisions within the islands' body politic.*

The festival originated about 200 years ago as a Catholic custom of the French plantocracy. Each year between Christmas and Lent, people would don costumes and party throughout the countryside. After emancipation the custom was adopted by the slaves as a celebration of liberation, and the rest is history. Today, the noise of thousands of shuffling feet, dancing in unison to the relentless calypso beat, echoes down the main streets of the capital. Elaborate costumed "bands" with thousands of members shake and jump to the beat in front of judges at the Savannah, competing for an array of prizes. This is followed by the King and Queen of Carnival and steelband competitions.

Trinidadian writer Pegi Adams sums it up best in her book, Trinidad's Carnival Celebrates Life: *"Carnival is the ultimate symbol of liberation—the liberation of every man." And when Trinidadians let go, they bring new meaning to Carnival's old phrase, "Live once, die forever."*

kilometer-long strand of deserted golden-brown beach. The picturesque beach is one of the longest in the Caribbean, but its beauty disguises a dangerous undertow that has claimed the lives of many locals and a few visitors. If the urge to bathe is too overpowering, find a place where the Atlantic swells wash far up the beach, then wade in—but always make sure you can stand and walk out if necessary. The Tourism Board manages a safe area for swimming and picnicking at **Manzanilla Bay**. Plans to develop the area, another sea turtle nesting site, have met with much resistance from locals and international conservation groups. It is the least developed beach of its size in the Caribbean and a favorite with locals.

The Nariva Swamp includes mangrove forests (with all four varieties), as well as moriche and cabbage palm forests. Three rivers, the Nariva, Navet, and Ortoire, which originate in the Central and Southern Ranges, constantly supply the swamp with nutrients providing a perfect breeding ground for marine life and the food chain it supports. As these rivers reach the east coast, they widen and slow as they flow through extensive mangrove forests. These calm backwaters are rich in vegetation and provide ideal habitat for a few West Indian manatees. The Ortoire estuary is the best place to view this shy mammal. All too often, the manatees you see are those that have drowned in nets set for the large catfish that live in the streams.

Under pressure to protect the manatee and other endangered wildlife, the government established the Bush Bush Wildlife Sanctuary in 1968 as part of the Manatee Protection Project. The 1,554-hectare sanctuary protects the three forest groups as well as a number of threatened animal species such as the red howler and capuchin monkeys, which locals still hunt for food, and the red-bellied macaw, a favorite in the exotic pet bird trade.

In all, the sanctuary protects more than 70 species of birds and 57 varieties of mammals and reptiles. Other notable species found in the sanctuary are the black-crested antshrike, savannah hawk, red-brested blackbird, moriche oriole, collared peccary, the caiman, and two varieties of water snakes. Unfortunately, the swamp and the sanctuary are still threatened by human encroachment. Squatters and illegal farmers have slashed and burned large sections of the swamp for rice fields and cattle production.

For more information, contact the Trinidad and Tobago Field Naturalists' Club, c/o Secretary Rosemary Hernandez, 1 Errol Park Rd., St. Ann's, Port of Spain, Trinidad, WI, tel 868/625-3386, 645-2132, or 868/624-3321, fax 868/625-2132. Asa Wright Nature Centre also has information (see above), as does **Wildways** (see "Outfitters and Guides," below).

TRINITY HILLS WILDLIFE SANCTUARY

Trinity Hills Wildlife Sanctuary was established in 1934 to protect the watersheds of the Southern Range. Located along the southern coast five kilometers west of Guayaguayare, the 6,483-hectare sanctuary is the largest and oldest protected area on Trinidad proper. The area is largely unexplored and contains large stands of mora trees, 150 species of birds, and 58 mammals. A guide is a must, and you must first get permission from the TRINTOC (Trinidad and Tobago Oil Company), in Pointe-à-Pierre, before setting foot in the sanctuary.

POINTE-À-PIERRE WILD FOWL TRUST

Located on the central western coast, a 45-minute drive south of Port of Spain, this private six-hectare slice of coastal wilderness inside the TRINTOC compound is a haven for 86 bird species, including migratory species such as the wild Muscovy, duck, blue-winged teal, and silver pintail. Numbers of visitors are strictly regulated by TRINTOC. All visitors must contact Ms. Molly Gaskin (tel 868/637-5145) or Mrs. K. Shepard (tel 868/662-4040) to make reservations. A one-dollar entrance fee is charged.

OUTFITTERS AND GUIDES ON TRINIDAD

To get the most out of Trinidad's vast diversity, it is recommended that you hire a naturalist guide. They are knowledgeable about the species on the islands and know their way around. Independent travelers will most likely miss many of the finer details without a guide.

Asa Wright Nature Centre and Lodge, Box 4710, Arima, Trinidad, WI, tel 868/667-4655, fax 868/667-4540. Besides lodging and tours around the nature center, they can arrange trips and guides to other parts of the island.

Avifauna Tours (Roger Neckles), 17 Morne Haven Condominiums, Gilkes Street, Morne Coco Road, Diego Martin, Trinidad, WI, tel 868/633-5614. Neckles is a great guide for both Trinidad and Tobago as well as a wildlife photographer. Camping is part of their trips.

Kayak Centre, Williams Bay, Chaguaramas, Trinidad, WI, tel 868/633-7871, fax 868/628-1404, rents kayaks and offers kayaking instruction and trips.

Ron's Dive Centre, 195D Western Main Rd., Cocorite, Trinidad, WI, tel 868/622-0495, tel and fax 868/673-0549, rents water-sport equipment for windsurfing and snorkeling, and offers dive packages including accommodations. They also arrange deep-sea fishing trips.

T&T Sightseeing Tours, 12 Western Main Rd., St. James, Port of Spain, Trinidad, WI, tel 868/628-1051, fax 868/622-9205, Web site: www.wp.com/trinbago/, email: carvalho@tstt.net.tt. This operator can arrange tours of both Trinidad and Tobago, with or without guides. Tell them what you want and they can usually arrange it.

Wildways Caribbean Adventure Travel, 10 Idlewild Rd., Knightsbridge, Cascade, Port of Spain, Trinidad, WI, tel/fax 868/623-7332, Web site: www.wildways.org, email: wildways@trinidad.net, provides custom tours, hikes, dives, one- and four-day kayak trips, and mountain bike trips on both Trinidad and Tobago. All trips include experienced naturalist and birding guides. One of the few operators to include camping as part of their trips.

WHERE TO STAY ON TRINIDAD

Port of Spain is really too busy. It's best to stay in its northern suburbs or in the Northern Range.

Asa Wright Nature Centre and Lodge, Box 4710, Arima, Trinidad, WI, tel 868/667-4655 or 800/426-7781 (Canada and U.S.A. only), fax 868/667-4540. Stay in the reserve and be close to most north and central island attractions. The lodge, tucked right into the rain forest at an elevation of 400 meters, offers 24 simple but comfortable rooms with ceiling fans. Rates include meals and one free tour each day. Rates $110 to $150.

Normandie Hotel, 10 Nook Ave., St. Ann's, Port of Spain, Trinidad, WI, tel and fax 868/624-1181 or 1184. This is a small northern suburb hotel with 53 well-appointed rooms, each with TV and air conditioning. Pool, restaurant, and great atmosphere. Rates $75 to $95.

Pelican Inn Hotel, 2-4 Coblentz Ave., Cascade, Port of Spain, Trinidad, WI, tel 868/6627-6271, fax 868/623-0978. In a quiet northern suburb of Port of Spain this basic inn has 23 rooms with air conditioning and private baths, a hopping bar and restaurant. Rates $35 to $45.

CAMPING ON TRINIDAD

There are no organized sites, and it is not a good idea to camp unless with a tour group. **Wildways Caribbean Adventure Travel** (see "Outfitters and Guides on Trinidad," above) can arrange camping as part of their eco-packages.

WHERE TO EAT ON TRINIDAD

There are all sorts of places to eat in most towns around the island, especially good East Indian and Caribbean eateries. The hotels listed above all have great restaurants.

Adam's Bagels & Specialty Breads, 15 A Saddle Rd., Maraval, tel 868/62-BAGELS, This not-to-miss place in the northern suburbs of Port of Spain serves breakfast, lunch, and dinner.

Anchorage Restaurant, Pt. Gourde Road, Chaguaramas, tel 868/634-4334, serves surf and turf specialties right on the water. Lunch and dinner.

Mikanne Hotel, Plaisance Village, Pointe-à-Pierre, tel 868/659-2584, serves great local and international cuisine close to the Point-à-Pierre Water Fowl Trust.

TOBAGO

Thought to be the island that inspired *Treasure Island*, tiny Tobago is one of the truly special "islands in the stream." What it lacks in size, it makes up for in atmosphere and some great natural attractions. It is so laid-back and quiet, most visitors usually guess the island's population is around 10,000 (it is actually 55,000). More than 250 species of birds frequent the island, and many of the same mammals and plants found on Trinidad are represented on Tobago.

Tobago's offshore islands, along with their surrounding reefs, are protected. Located off the northeast coast at Speyside, the islands of **Little Tobago** (113 hectares), **Bird Of Paradise** (25 hectares), and **Goat** (30 hectares) are all bird sanctuaries. These islands receive less than 2,000 visitors a year, and are excellent places to view large colonies of red-billed tropicbirds (the largest nesting colonies in the North Atlantic), brown boobies, bridled terns, and 78 other species. Wildways (see "Outfitters and Guides in Trinidad," above) offers one- and four-day kayak trips that include visits to these islands. Trips leave from the tiny fishing village of Speyside and paddle out through Tyrells Bay to nearby Little Tobago and the offshore breeding colonies of the red-billed tropic-birds. Once ashore paddlers can explore the hilly trails, view birds, and have a picnic lunch on a windswept cliff overlooking the wild Atlantic Ocean. From here kayakers head south down the southwest

© Wildways Ltd.

A beach break from kayaking on Tobago's west coast

coast of the island, stopping to explore deserted white-sand beaches, snorkel over pristine fringe reefs, and camp in quiet coves.

Tobago is fast becoming one of the hottest diving spots in the Caribbean. One of its specialties is drift diving, where divers enter the water up-current and drift effortlessly with the current, a few feet above the spectacular reef gardens. Because you don't expend energy swimming, you conserve air and can stay down longer to enjoy the reef and marine life. The heart of Tobago's drift diving is **Speyside**, where the Atlantic surges through the narrow channels between offshore islands—currents between Goat and Little Tobago Islands have been clocked at five knots. The nutrient-rich Atlantic current supports abundant marine life. It is not unusual to see large creatures such as loggerhead turtles, giant manta rays, and large schools of jacks.

Independent explorers who want to visit the offshore islands for hiking, birding, or snorkeling can hire fishing boats in Speyside to take them out to the islands—just don't expect a naturalist type-tour of the islands. The trails are easy and obvious, but beware of the strong currents between these islands. It is best to swim or snorkel on the leeward side of the islands.

MAIN RIDGE RAIN FOREST

The 2,000-hectare reserve was established in 1776 to protect the last remaining stands of primary forest from logging and the island's main watershed. Although legislation did a good job of protecting the forest from the ravages of man, no amount of legislation could protect it from Hurricane Flora in 1963. The 300-kilometer-per-hour winds toppled many old-growth specimens; today only sheltered pockets of primary old growth remain.

The Main Ridge covers almost two-thirds of the island, from its eastern tip to the capital, Scarborough. The forest today, while still magnificent, contains large sections of secondary 35-year-old growth. Most of the reserve is at or above 600 meters in elevation and receives high annual rainfall. Since the hurricane, the combination of abundant rainfall and large openings in the canopy has fostered faster-growing vegetation that has beaten out slower-growing species. The result is a profusion of ferns, cabbage palms, young mahogany, fiddlewood, and gigantic stands of bamboo reaching 15 meters high. The forest is packed with birds of every kind including the collared trogon, cocric (Tobago's national bird), southern lapwing, stripe-breasted spinetail, the very rare white-tailed sabrewing hummingbird, and the rare and beautiful blue-crowned motmot. Noisy orange-winged parrots, armadillos, monkeys, several harmless snakes, and an assortment of reptiles and amphibians round out the fauna in the reserve.

The main focus of the forest is the **Gilpin Trail**, which starts on the Roxborough Parlatuvier Road at mile marker 1.25. The trail, which is named after an old road the locals used to get to Bloody Bay, starts near the Main Ridge Recreation Site, where a small forestry hut displays a large map of the reserve and trail system. From the hut the 3.2-kilometer trail loops around the 600-meter-high ridge and takes about four hours to complete. At the trailhead is a collection of slender walking sticks, placed there by the Naturalist Society, to aid hikers along the sometimes damp and slippery trail. After completing the hike visitors are asked to return the walking sticks.

Off the main trail are shorter side trails to specific points of interest such as scenic lookouts and waterfalls. In all, there are five beautiful waterfalls for you to freshen up in, but remember you are not allowed to bathe in the water, only use it to wet down. Altogether there are a dozen shorter trails worth exploring, some obvious and others requiring a guide.

For more information, contact the Trinidad and Tobago Field Naturalists Club, c/o Secretary Rosemary Hernandez, 1 Errol Park Rd., St. Ann's, Port of Spain, Trinidad, WI, tel 868/625-3386, 645-2132, or 624-3321, fax 868/625-2132.

OUTFITTERS AND GUIDES ON TOBAGO

A guide is not really necessary for exploring the island trails, but there is much that inexperienced hikers will miss without one.

Fishermen in Speyside offer trips out to the islands, but again it's better to hire a guide or amateur naturalist to make the arrangements and accompany you. A number of Trinidad operators (see "Outfitters and Guides in Trinidad," above) can also guide or make arrangements for adventures in Tobago.

David Rooks, Box 348, Scarborough, Tobago, WI, tel and fax 868/639-4276, regularly leads small groups into the Main Ridge Reserve and to the offshore islets. David is an ornithologist and excellent nature guide who also belongs to the T&T Naturalist Club.

Pioneer Journeys, Man-O-War Bay Cottages, Charlotteville, tel 868/660-4327, fax 868/660-4328, can arrange any tour you want.

Tobago Dive Experience, Manta Lodge, Speyside, Tobago, WI, tel 868/660-5268, fax 868/660-5030, is a full-service operator offering total dive packages including accommodations.

Tobago Dive Masters, Box 351, Scarborough, Tobago, WI, tel 868/639-4347, fax 868/639-4180, is a full water-sport provider.

William Trim, tel 868/660-5529, is one of the Forest Service officers based in Tobago who enthusiastically shares his knowledge of the forest.

WHERE TO STAY ON TOBAGO

Blue Waters Inn, Batteaux Bay, Speyside, tel 868/660-4077 or 4341, fax 868/660-5195. This small, 38-room inn sits on its own private bay. All rooms face the beach and some have kitchenettes. A good restaurant, bar, and tennis court round out the amenities. They also rent kayaks and other water-sport gear and arrange diving and hikes. Rates $80 to $120.

Man-O-War Bay Cottages, Charlotteville, Tobago, WI, tel 868/660-4327, fax 868/660-4328. This small, six-cottage complex is popular with the eco-set. Each cottage is fully equipped with from one to four bedrooms. Rates $55 to $95.

Manta Lodge, Windward Road, Speyside, (Box 433, Scarborough), Tobago, WI, tel 868/660-5268, fax 868/660-5030. Primarily a diving lodge, it is in a great location for exploring the offshore islands and reefs and the forest reserve. The 22 comfortable rooms have private bath and air conditioning. Each guest gets one free scuba experience, and you can get your certification right on site. Rates $80 to $105.

CAMPING ON TOBAGO

There is one camping area in Trinidad and Tobago: **Canoe Bay Beach Park**, tel 868/639-3691 or 2631. Not great, but the only one. Rates $5.

WHERE TO EAT ON TOBAGO

The best places to eat are at the many hotels, but a few local spots are worth a try.

Blue Crab, Main Street, Scarborough, tel 868/639-2737, serves good inexpensive local and international cuisine.

Gail's Cafe, Charlotteville. A great spot for breakfast (fabulous omelettes), and they also serve lunch and dinner. Down-home local food.

Jemma's Tree House Restaurant, Speyside, tel 868/660-4066, is built in a large tree over the ocean. Don't expect menus, just delicious home-cooked seafood meals.

TRINIDAD AND TOBAGO SPECIFICS

Getting There

Piarco International Airport is the port of entry for Trinidad and Tobago. American Airlines, BWIA, and Air Canada have daily flights into Piarco from a number of North American cities. There are daily flights into Tobago from Piarco on BWIA or LIAT; the one-way fare runs about $30.

If you want a more local adventure, consider taking the ferry between Port of Spain and Scarborough. The trip takes six hours and the large ferry *Panorama* accommodates cars as well. Cabins cost $14 and a first-class deck seat, $5. Call for reservations and schedules (tel 868/625-3055 or 639-2417).

Getting Around

Buses run only along the main roads between towns and villages in Tobago. They are inexpensive but not that reliable and many times overcrowded.

Shared taxis are the best option if you elect not to rent a car. They are unmarked except for the "H" on the license plate. They run frequently between all points on the island and provide a great opportunity to share a ride with some locals. The atmosphere in these taxis is usually very friendly, so don't be afraid to start the conversation. Flag them down along any main thoroughfare; sometimes you have to use a certain hand signal depending on your destination. Anyone standing waiting for a taxi will help you sort out the signals.

The roads on both islands are pretty good, so a car is your best bet. Expect to pay about $45 a day for a four-wheel-drive and 40 cents per liter for gasoline. Many agencies have outlets at the airport. At Piarco Airport, Trinidad, you'll find **Thrifty,** tel 868/669-0602, fax 868/669-0602; **Econo-Car Rentals,** 868/669-2342, fax 868/622-8074; and **Auto Rentals,** tel 868/623-7368, fax 868/669-2277.

At Crown Point Airport, Tobago, you will find the same car rental agencies as listed above and you can make reservations through them. You can arrange less expensive weekly rental combination packages, which include a car, on both islands.

Tobago is small and quiet, so a small motorcycle or scooter is another good option. Rent one at **Baird's Rentals Ltd.,** Crown Point Airport and Scarborough, tel 868/639-2528 or 4126, fax 868/639-4126. Expect to pay about $25 per day.

Tourist Information

Tourism and Industrial Development Company of Trinidad and Tobago Limited (TIDCO), Box 222, 10-14 Philipps St., Port of Spain, Trinidad, WI, tel 868/623-1932/4 or 623-6022/3, fax 868/623-3848

Tourism and Industrial Development Company of Trinidad and Tobago Limited (TIDCO), Unit 12, IDC Mall, Sangster's Hill, Scarborough, Tobago, WI, tel 868/639-4333, fax 868/639-4514

U.S.A.: Marketing and Reservations Tourism Services (SMARTS), 7000 Blvd. East, Guttenberg, NJ 07093, tel 201/662-3403/3408 or 888/595-4TNT, fax 201/869-7628

Canada: RMR Group Inc., Taurus House, 512 Duplex Ave., Toronto, Ont. M4R 2E3, tel 416/485-8724 or 888/595-4TNT, fax 416/485-8256

Web sites and email: Web sites: www.tidco.co.tt; www.visittnt.com; www.trinibase.com/index.html; www.wp.com/trinbago; www.carib-link.net/discover/; email: tourism-info@tidco.co.tt

APPENDIX
TRAVEL BASICS

PLANNING YOUR TRIP

The following information pertains to the Caribbean in general, but some islands may have specific information that differs from that which is discussed below. Please check the "Island Specifics" section at the end of each island chapter for additional information.

Getting to the Islands

Daily air service links most of the larger islands to major North American cities. Puerto Rico is the most accessible; San Juan is **American Airlines'** Caribbean hub.

Air Canada flies direct from Toronto and Montreal to Antigua, Barbados, Guadeloupe, Haiti, Jamaica, St. Lucia, and Trinidad. **British Airways** flies nonstop to Barbados from London's Heathrow and Gatwick Airports. And **KLM** flies to Aruba from Amsterdam.

In the Caribbean, **American Eagle, BWIA,** and **Leeward Island Air Transport (LIAT)** are the main carriers between the islands. Puerto Rico, St. Thomas, Antigua, and Barbados are good bases from which to island hop.

Naturalist and wildlife cruise packages are offered by **Ocean Society Expeditions,** Fort Mason Center, Bldg. E, San Francisco, CA 94123, tel 415/441-1106 or 800/326-7491, and by **World Explorer Cruises,** 555 Montgomery St., Suite 1400, San Francisco, CA 94111-2544, tel 415/393-1565 or 800/854-3835, fax 415/391-1145, Web site: www.wecruise.com.

Entry and Exit Requirements

For most islands, U.S. and Canadian citizens need only show some proof of identity. The exceptions are Cuba, Haiti, and the Dominican Republic, which require additional tourist visas, available through travel agents (see "Island Specifics" sections for more details). Passports are preferred, but any photo ID card, official birth certificate, driver's license, or voter registration card is acceptable. Passports are a must for St. Lucia, St. Martin/St. Maarten, St. Vincent and the Grenadines, and Trinidad and Tobago. Visitors to any island will be required to have a return ticket (or a ticket for leaving the island and going on to a new destination).

LIAT offers tickets that permit travel between 10 or more islands within a 30-day period (you must buy this ticket outside of the Caribbean).

Each island has an airport departure tax you must pay before leaving the island. Most of these taxes range between $10 and $25.

Most islands also have customs requirements governing the amount of money you can bring into the country and the transportation of items such as cigarettes, alcohol, drugs, fruit, etc. It is always best to check ahead about an island's custom entry requirements. The **Caribbean Tourism Organization**, 20 E. 46th St., New York, NY 10017, tel 212/682-0435, can provide information on entry requirements for any island.

Health

Vaccinations: Vaccinations are not usually required for any of the islands, but if you plan to "rough it" in the wild, check with your doctor about being inoculated against typhoid, poliomyelitis, and tetanus. Infectious hepatitis has been reported on Dominica, Haiti, and Montserrat, so you might want to consider getting a gamma-globulin shot before visiting. Malaria can be a threat on Haiti or the Dominican Republic, so consult your doctor about preventive medication. Good doctors and medical facilities can be found on every island, but certain medications are unavailable, so make sure you stock up on your prescription before leaving. Purchasing travel insurance is always a smart idea.

Note: For the latest information on Caribbean health issues and vaccination requirements or recommendations, contact the **Centers for Disease Control and Prevention (CDC)**, 1600 Clifton Rd. NE, Atlanta, GA 30333, tel 404-332-4559, www.cdc.gov, before departing.

Water: Tap water is safe on most islands but may cause diarrhea on others. It is best to drink bottled, treated, or boiled water. Food is another matter; care should be taken when eating at road stands or in the local markets. Eating at local stalls is safe if you can watch the food being prepared and know it is cooked properly. Seafood lovers should be careful about ciguatera toxin in some fish. Check with local authorities before consuming large seafood meals.

Sun Safety: The biggest safety risk you face in the Caribbean will be heat and sun. Never stay in the sun longer than necessary, wear sunglasses and a head covering, and use lots of good sun block. Drink water often and avoid drinking alcohol when you're engaging in strenuous activity.

Outdoor Hazards: Many islands have poisonous snakes, marine life, and insects, so take care to wear appropriate clothes when hiking and a bodysuit when snorkeling. Make sure you ask about dangers before heading into the forest or sea. Pack plenty of insect repellent and antibacterial cream.

Safety Issues

Crime: Violent crimes against tourists have risen over the last few years, but most islands are much safer than most North American cities. Assault, rape, and murder are very rare, but snatch-and-run crimes are a big problem in some cities. Take the same precautions you would in any large North American city. Don't walk in deserted areas at night and never travel alone. Remember, the islands are all Third World areas with high degrees of poverty, and your valuables will become a target for thieves if you are not careful. Use hotel safes whenever possible for all jewelry, cash, travel documents, etc., and never leave valuables in cars (most rental cars in the Caribbean have the letter "R" in their license plates, so they stick out like a sore thumb). Always take photocopies of identification and carry only as much cash as you require that day; leave originals and everything else back at the hotel.

Hitchhiking: Hitchhiking is okay on most islands and especially popular in Cuba and Trinidad. If you must hitch, take all the same precautions you would back home.

Illegal Drugs: Under no circumstance should you bring, try to purchase, or use illegal drugs while in the islands. They all have been under pressure from North American drug law enforcement agencies to curb drugs and they take the situation seriously. The last thing you want to do is end up in a Caribbean jail.

Hiking Precaution: Don't go hiking without a local guide on islands noted for drug production (Jamaica, Dominican Republic, Trinidad, and some of the Windwards).

What To Bring

Pack comfortable, casual, light-weight clothing, preferably synthetic products and a few cotton pieces. Many people bring only enough clothing for four or five days and opt to launder there rather than cart around heavy bags. Others take as little as possible and buy casual clothes in the islands.

When not on the beach, shorts or long pants are fine during the day. In very informal restaurants, you can also probably wear dress shorts at night (but not cut-offs). Formal attire is hardly ever worn except at the more expensive resorts. Denim, less the holes and tears, is acceptable on all the islands. Sandals, sunglasses, and some sort of head protection are musts.

Pack plenty of sunscreen, repellent, and insect "stop-itch" sticks, and leave the aftershave and perfume at home—it attracts insects.

TRAVEL PRACTICALITIES

Business Hours

Banking and shopping hours vary throughout the islands. Banks typically open Monday through Thursday sometime between 8:00 and 9:00 a.m. and close early in the afternoon, between 1:00 and 2:30. On some islands they shut down after lunch on Fridays to reopen later in the afternoon, at 2:30 or 3:00, then close again at 4:30 or 5:00. In Jamaica most banks are open 9:00 to 5:00 Monday through Friday. Shops are usually open Monday through Saturday from 9:00 or 9:30 to 5:00 or 6:00.

Communications

Telephoning: Each island has its own area code, though some share the old 809 code. The ease with which you can make local and long-distance telephone calls varies from island to island. Phone booths on Puerto Rico and the U.S. Virgin Islands take U.S. coins. You can also access AT&T and other

American operators using your telephone credit card. On all the islands you can buy fixed denomination phone cards ($5, $10, $15, and $25), but the special phones accepting these cards are confined to high tourist areas such as big hotels, shopping malls, and airports.

Mail service: Mail service to and from the Caribbean is slow—letters can take up to three weeks to deliver. Postage rates in Puerto Rico and the U.S. Virgin Islands are the same as in the U.S., but different on the other islands. Most hotel desks will attend to your mailing. *Federal Express* operates on most of the islands, so if speed is a priority, you may want to have your mail or packages delivered via FedEx.

Newspapers and Magazines: In the U.S. Virgin Islands and on the larger islands, newspapers from the U.S. are flown in daily. The best places to get them are at the big hotels or at airport magazine kiosks. Each island has its own local paper (it may be in English, French, Spanish, or Dutch), but don't expect much international news.

Television: Televisions are prevalent in the islands and North American programming is popular.

Electricity
Generally, it is 110 and 120 volts A.C., and the outlets take the same two-prong plugs found in North America, but there are exceptions. You'll need an adapter and a 220 volt transformer for North American–made appliances on most of the Leeward and Windward Islands and in the French and Netherlands Antilles. Ask your hotel for specifics.

Festivals and Holidays
Public holidays vary widely throughout the islands, reflecting independence days and holidays of the parent country (France, England, Spain, the Netherlands, and the United States). Besides the international holidays and festivals like Christmas and New Year's there are jazz, harvest, independence, and cultural festivals, religious and government holidays, and a number of bank holidays throughout the year in the Caribbean. Perhaps the most exciting of them all is Carnival, with its colorful extravaganza of dance, music, and costumed parades. Below are a few events worth catching.

January—Jamaica Maroon Festival (second week), Curacao Carnival (last week)

February—Grenada Independence Day (7th), Havana Jazz Festival (last week)

March—Trinidad's Phagwah Festival (first week), the USVIs Anniversary Day (30th)

April—Jamaica Carnival (second week), Dutch Antilles Queen Beatrix's birthday (30th)

May—French Antilles Abolition Day (27th), Jamaica's Negril Jonkunno (last week)

June—St. Vincent Carnival (last week), Puerto Rico's Bombay Plena Festival (30th)

July—French Antilles Bastille Day (14th), Dominican Republic Merengue Festival (last week)
August—BVIs Summer Festival (first week), Guadeloupe's Fête de Cuisinières (11th)
September—St. Kitts & Nevis Independence Day (19th)
October—Bonaire's Regatta Week (second week)
November—Trinidad's Pan Jazz Festival (30th)
December—St. Kitts Carnival (first week), St. Lucia's National Day (13th)

Language, Culture, and Etiquette

English is widely spoken on most islands. A knowledge of French is useful in the French Antilles, as is Spanish in Cuba, the Dominican Republic, and Puerto Rico. Dutch is the primary local language in the Netherlands Antilles. Most islanders are very religious so watch your language.

While topless sunbathing is common on some beaches in the French Antilles, nudity is an offense punishable by law in the British Virgin Islands and frowned upon on most islands. Swimsuits should not be worn into town or on shopping expeditions.

Ask before pointing a camera at someone, and don't call the locals "natives."

Money and Currency

While the U.S. dollar is widely accepted, there are a dozen currencies in the Caribbean. Most of the British islands in the Lesser Antilles use the eastern Caribbean dollar; the French Antilles use the French franc; the Dutch islands have the florin or gilder; and Barbados, Trinidad, Cuba, and the Dominican Republic all have their own currencies. It is best to change some U.S. dollars for local currency when you arrive at the airport. This will give you tip money and allow you to make purchases at local shops that don't have change in U.S. dollars. About $30U.S. per person per day should cover most of your needs, excluding lodging.

All islands have money changers and most are illegal but tolerated by the local authorities (except in Cuba). They sometimes give better rates than the banks because on most islands locals have to fill out forms to buy U.S. dollars. When exchanging money, change only small amounts—enough for one day—at any time. ATMs and currency exchanges are at the major airports.

Many smaller hotels and inns take U.S. dollars and U.S. traveler's checks, but many do not take plastic. Credit cards can be used only at hotels, larger stores, some large restaurants, and car rental agencies. Most small local businesses do not take credit cards.

Banks open odd hours on different islands, but the best time to visit one is between 10 a.m. and noon.

Tax and Tipping

Every island has an airport departure tax of from $10 to $25 (see "Entry and Exit Requirements," above). A 10- to 15-percent service surcharge is automatically added to your bill in most hotels and restaurants. However, if service is good, it's customary to tip extra. If a service charge is not applied then you should expect to tip. Tip as you would in North America.

Time Zones
The Greater Antilles, except for the Dominican Republic and Puerto Rico, are on Eastern standard time. The Dominican Republic, Puerto Rico, and the rest of the Caribbean are on Atlantic standard time (one hour later). Daylight savings is not observed except in Cuba, Haiti, and Puerto Rico.

Weights and Measures
The British system of weights and measures is observed in the British and American islands (BVIs, USVIs, Puerto Rico, Windwards). Expect pounds, ounces, gallons, feet, and miles. On the French and Dutch Antilles, however, the metric system of liters, metros, and kilometers is used.

ADDITIONAL RESOURCES
Embassies and Consulates

DOMINICAN REPUBLIC
United States: At the corner of Calle Cesar Nicolas Pension and Calle Leopold Navarro, Santo Domingo, tel 809/541-2171
Canada: 30 Avenida Maximo Gomez, Santo Domingo, tel 809/685-1136

JAMAICA
United States: 2 Oxford Rd., Kingston S., tel 876/929-4850
Canada 29 Gloucester Ave., Montego Bay, tel 876/952-6198

TRINIDAD
United States: 15 Queen's Park West, Port of Spain, tel 868/622-6371
Canada: Huggins Building, 72-74 South Quay, Port of Spain, tel 868/623-7254

BARBADOS
United States: Broad Streeet, Bridgetown, St. Michael, tel 246/436-4950, fax 246/431-0249
Canada: High Commission, Bishop's Court Hill, Pines Road, St. Michael, tel 246/429-3550, fax 246/429-3780

Tourist Organizations
CARIBBEAN TOURISM ORGANIZATION
20 E. 46th St.
New York, NY 10017
tel 212/682-0435

Conservation Organizations
Earthwatch Institute
Box 9104
Watertown, MA 02272-9104
tel 617/926-8200, fax 617/926-8532
www.earthwatch.org

Wildlife Conservation Society
New York Zoological Society
185th Street and South Boulevard,
Bronx, NY 10460
tel 212/220-5155
www.wcs.org/

World Wildlife Fund–U.S.
1250 24th St. NW
Washington, DC 20037
tel 202/293-4800 or 800/225-5993
www.worldwildlife.org/

**International Tropical
Conservation Foundation**
c/o Papiliorama, Marin-Centre
Case postale 31, CH 2074
Marin-Neuchatel, Switzerland
tel 032/753-4350.

SUGGESTED READING

HISTORY
The Caribbean, Franklin Knight.
Oxford: Oxford University Press,
1978.

*From Columbus to Castro: The History
of the Caribbean*, Eric Williams. New
York: Random House, 1983.

*Last Resorts: The Cost of Tourism in
the Caribbean*, P. Pattullo. London:
London House, 1996.

GEOGRAPHY
The Caribbean Islands, Helmut
Blume. London: Longman Group
Ltd., 1976.

Isles of the Caribbean, Robert L.
Breeden. Washington, DC: Special
Publications Division, National
Geographic, 1980.

LIFESTYLE AND CULTURE
*Eastern Caribbean: A Guide to the
People, Politics and Culture*, James
Ferguson. New York: Interlink
Books, 1997.

A Continent of Islands, Mark
Kurlansky. New York: Addison-
Wesley, 1992.

Caribbean Ways: A Cultural Guide,
Chelle K. Walton. Westwood,
Mass.: Riverdale Company, 1993.

*Politics and Economics in the
Caribbean*, Thomas G. Matthews and
F. M. Andic, editors. Rio Piedras:
Institute of Caribbean Studies,
University of Puerto Rico, 1971.

*Peoples and Cultures of the Caribbean
Islands*, Michael M. Horowitz.
Garden City, N.Y.: Natural History
Press, 1971.

FLORA AND FAUNA
*A Field Guide to the Coral Reefs of the
Caribbean and Florida*, Eugene
Kaplan. Princeton, N.J.: Peterson's
Guides, 1984.

*Peterson's Guide to Birds of the West
Indies*, James Bond. Boston, Mass.:
Houghton Mifflin, 1995.

Caribbean Wild Plants and Their Uses,
P. Honeychurch. London:
Macmillan Caribbean, 1978.

*Pisces Guide to Caribbean Reef
Ecology*, William S. Alevision.
Houston: Gulf Publications, 1994.

Amphibians and Reptiles of the West Indies, Henderson and Schwartz. Gainesville: University of Florida Press, 1991.

Flora and Fauna of the Caribbean, Peter R. Bacon. Port-of-Spain, Trinidad: Key Caribbean Publications, 1978.

SPECIAL INTERESTS AND ACTIVITIES
Best Dives of the Caribbean, Joyce and Jon Huber. Edison, N.J.: Hunter Publishing, 1998.

The Caribbean: A Walking and Hiking Guide, Leonard M. Adkins. Edison, N.J.: Hunter Publishing, 1996.

Caribbean Afoot! A Walking and Hiking Guide to Twenty-Nine of the Caribbean's Best Islands, M. Timothy O'Keefe. Birmingham, Alabama: Menasha Ridge Press, 1993.

Snorkeling Guide to Marine Life, Paul Humann. Jacksonville, Florida: New World Publications, 1995.

INDEX

ABOUT THE AUTHOR

Michael DeFreitas has the kind
of job many people dream about.
A freelance writer and photographer,
DeFreitas travels extensively around
his native Canada and spends about
three months a year in the Caribbean.
His more than 200 articles and photographs have appeared in publications around the world, including
*Caribbean Travel & Life, Islands,
Explore,* and *Outside.* DeFreitas holds
undergraduate and graduate degrees
from York University in Toronto.
He currently lives with his wife and
two sons just outside of Vancouver,
British Columbia.

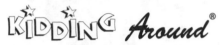